CW00969773

Syria *Revealed*

**a comprehensive guide
to the country**

by

Anthony King

BOXER
Publishing

To my parents

Syria Revealed, First edition 1995

Published by Boxer Publishing,
PO Box 7287, London E16 2QR, UK

Cover photographs by the author:
Front: *Palmyra, view from Qala'at Ibn Maan*
Back: *Water-wheels on the Orontes River in Hama*

Printed at the Guernsey Press, Guernsey,
Channel Islands

British Library Cataloguing in Publication Data.
A catalogue record for this book is available
from the British Library

ISBN 0-9525432-0-6

Contents

List of Plans

List of Information Boxes

INTRODUCTION

TO most people Syria may seem an unlikely country to visit. Many may even find it difficult to place its exact position on a map; few will know of any Syrian city apart from Damascus. They may think of Syria as a ruthless police state, a land bristling with terrorists and a dangerous country to visit. At best they may be told that travelling to Syria is a complex and troublesome procedure, it is difficult to get to and there is not much to see there. The facts are entirely different.

Although the country was to some extent estranged from the West for a considerable time, recent years have seen a rapid opening up. Severed relations with Britain are now back to normal, many European airlines fly into Damascus, and trade and business with Europe and the US is expanding. I do not think Syria is any more a police state than, say, Turkey, Jordan or Egypt (or many other countries for that matter) and you will certainly not feel or notice anything untoward; and the policemen you will encounter are pleasant, polite and, where language difficulties can be overcome, extremely helpful. As for terrorists, well this writer has visited the country many times and the only kidnapping he has been subject to is to be "forced" into the homes of the warm and friendly people for tea, and even a meal! The entry formalities are similar to those of neighbouring countries, it is easy to get to and there is perhaps more to see there than in any other country in the Middle East.

Following the collapse of Communism in Eastern Europe — with whose nations Syria enjoyed its main trade relations — and the subsequent insistence by those countries on hard currency to pay for imports, the Syrian government was compelled to explore new methods of raising that badly needed commodity. One such method was tourism — a resource which until recently had never held a high priority in Syrian policy. Over the past few years many new hotels have been constructed and the general tourist infrastructure improved.

Yet Syria still remains a land to be discovered. You will not be going there to lie on its beaches, even though you can find these north of Latakia; or for the lively nightlife, albeit Damascus and Aleppo have a sprinkling of nightclubs. You will be visiting Syria to see the extraordinary historical sites in which the country is so rich: Roman ruins, Byzantine basilicas, Muslim mosques and Turkish turbas, all and more abound in this ancient land. Yet even at the most renowned site you will not be greeted by swarming crowds. Indeed, if you choose the right time of day you will frequently have the place virtually to yourself! You will find the sites refreshingly uncommercial with an atmosphere of uncluttered authenticity no longer present at more well-trodden historical locations.

With borders set largely by former Mandatory powers, modern Syria has still retained much of its ancient history within its present boundaries. In this land, stretching from the shores of the Mediterranean to beyond the Euphrates, sightseeing opportunities are vast. Who will ever forget their first glimpse of the Krak de Chevaliers, probably the greatest castle in the world, or the magical ruins of Palmyra rising suddenly out of the desert after several hours' drive through a featureless wilderness, or looking down from the top of the Roman theatre at Bosra? Perhaps the eight kilometres of Aleppo's covered souks may not be as grand as the Grand Bazaar of Istanbul, yet they are infinitely more genuine and down to earth.

But as time does not stand still neither will Syria. What is today a tourist's delight in a non-touristic land will change. More people will come and the unspoiled sense of "discovery" will surely alter. Now is unquestionably the time to visit Syria.

For the convenience of the reader this guide is divided into three main parts as follows: Part I deals with the country, its history, geography and culture. Part II is a detailed guide to Syria's sites and sights and Part III covers practical information on how to get there, getting around, accommodation and almost everything else you need to know to make your trip rewarding. In addition, there is a language guide, a helpful glossary which clarifies architectural terms, the different nations, dynasties, and groups mentioned in the histories and, of course, non-English words. There is also an index (see Contents for full list).

PART I

BACKGROUND

1. HISTORY

- Pre 19th century
- Modern history

2. GEOGRAPHY

- The land
- Climate
- People
- Religion

3. SYRIA TODAY

- Government
- Economy
- Education
- Everyday life
- Language

1. HISTORY

This chapter is divided into two sections:

- ♦ **Pre-20th century history**, which provides an outline of the region's history as it relates to Syria and the region as a whole, in a chronological format for easy reference;

- ♦ **The events of the 20th century,** to equip the traveller with an understanding of the development of modern Syria.

The early history of Syria is covered in greater detail in the touring section of this book (Part II) when describing the individual cities, towns and sites, with emphasis on events in the locale visited.

OUTLINE OF SYRIAN HISTORY TO THE END OF THE 19TH CENTURY

Cradle of Civilisation

Pre 10,000 BC

Remains of human habitation discovered in Orontes valley.
Natufian culture supported by hunting, fishing, and gathering of wild grains.

10,000-7000 BC

First signs of settlement at Muraybet where indications of animal husbandry and cultivation of primitive corn found (c.7800 BC).

5000-4000 BC

Sumer, southern Mesopotamia, settled by Ubaidians, a non-Semitic people.

3500-3000 BC

Sumerians, a Semitic people from Anatolia, arrive in southern Mesopotamia.

3000-2500 BC

Sumerians develop an urban society with independent city-states.

Ebla, a powerful city south of Aleppo flourishes (c.2600-2240 BC).

Sumerian language, the oldest written language in history in use.

2500-2000 BC

Sargon I captures southern Mesopotamia (Sumer) and founds dynasty of Akkad.

Sargon controls most of the fertile crescent (Syria and Palestine).

Sargon destroys Ebla (2240 BC).

2000-1200 BC

Akkadians defeated by a dynasty from Ur which had little control over the area of Syria.

The golden age of Ugarit.

Abraham begins his journey to Canaan?

Migration of Semitic Amorites into Syria.

Amorite city of Alalakh founded on the Orontes close to what was to become Antioch.

Damascus mentioned in the Old Testament (Gen 14).

Rivalry for Syria between Hurrians (from their kingdom north east of the Euphrates), Hittites, Egyptians, and the Assyrians.

Damascus mentioned in the Amarna letters.

Arameans migrate into the area and settle in north and central Syria.

Exodus of Hebrews from Egypt?

1200-350 BC

Aramean language (Aramaic or Syriac) and alphabet in common use.

Assyrian capital of Nineveh succumbs to Medes led by Nebuchadnezzar of Babylon.

Jerusalem falls and its people taken into captivity (597 BC).

Rise of the Persians. Babylon defeated by Cyrus, (539 BC).

Persian empire stretches to the Mediterranean and beyond and is the largest the world has known.

Hellenic and Roman Eras

350-323 BC

Alexander of Macedonia invades Asia Minor (334 BC) and defeats Persians at Issus (333 BC).

The destruction of Persepolis, the Persian capital, completes Persian downfall.

Alexander's death (323 BC).

323-200 BC

Division of Alexander's empire.

Seleucus I Nicator rules in north Syria, while Ptolemy I Soter controls the south.

The Seleucids found many more cities including Antioch and Apamea (near Hama).

200-160 BC

Hellenisation of Syria under the Seleucids.

Antiochus III defeats Ptolemy V (199 BC) and gains control over all of Syria.

Seleucids lose territory in Asia Minor after their defeat by the Romans at Magnesia (190 BC).

Antiochus IV Epiphanes spreads Greek culture and political thought.

Increase in urbanization.

160-83 BC

Rival claims to Seleucid throne and civil wars cause fragmentation of Syria.

In the south Itureans, Judeans and Nabateans take their independence.

83-63 BC

Country seized by Tigranes of Armenia (83 BC).

Defeat of Tigranes by Romans under Pompey, and Syria becomes a Roman province (63 BC).

63 BC-33 AD

Romans reorganise the province and Judea, Nabatea, Iturea, and other states in the area made subject to Roman Syria.

Syria becomes one of the most important of the Roman provinces and includes most of eastern Cilicia (today southern Turkey).

Judea becomes a separate province governed by a procurator (6 AD).

Life and death of Jesus.

33-72 AD

Paul's journey to Damascus and his subsequent conversion.
Jews rebel and Romans destroy Jerusalem (70 AD).
Judea joins with Syria to form the province of Syria Palaestina
(the first use of the name Palestine).

72-323 AD

Palmyra comes under Roman control.
Syria splits into two provinces, and later into five.
Diocletian strengthens the frontiers against attacks from Arabia
by horse-mounted Arabs.
Syria enjoys prosperity, and while the upper classes are
Hellenised the lower still speak Aramaic.
Antioch ranked as one of the greatest cities of the Roman
Empire.

323-622 AD

Creation of a second imperial capital at Constantinople (330)
from where Syria is ruled.
Constantine makes Christianity the official religion (392).
Christianity flourishes in Syria.
Sasanian Persians threaten Syria and Byzantium wages war
against them.
The Persians capture Antioch (540) but are rolled back by the
Byzantines.
Constant fighting with Persians and religious persecutions at
home (against those Christians who would not go along with
the Council of Chalcedon) weakens Syria.
Muslim Arabs at the border.

Muslim Conquest

622-640

Muhammad flees Mecca for Medina (the *hijra*) and the
Islamic era commences (622).
Arab forces appear at the Syrian border.
Death of Muhammad (632).
Syria invaded by Muslims under Khalid Ibn al-Walid (633-4).
Damascus falls to invaders (635).
Byzantine Emperor Heraclius tries to counter-attack but is
defeated at the Battle of the Yarmouk (636).
Muslim control of Syria complete (640).

640-680

Muslims divide Syria into four areas, Damascus, Hims, Jordan, and Palestine.

Jews and Christians tolerated.

Mu'awiya from the House of Omayyad governor of Syria (639).

Period of splendour for Syria and, in particular, Damascus.

Mu'awiya becomes Caliph, and Damascus seat of the Caliphate (660).

680-750

Discontent in Syria and Muslim world over succession to Caliphate.

Omayyad Caliphate overthrown by the Abbasid Caliphate in Baghdad (750).

Late 8th-11th C

Centre of power shifts from Damascus to Baghdad, and Syria becomes another province.

Omayyad loyalty still lingers in Syria.

Christian population lose many rights, and conversion to Islam gains momentum.

Arabic begins to replace both Greek and Aramaic, though the latter does survive among some of the Christians (even to this day).

Abbasids begin to disintegrate and Syria annexed by the Tulunids of Egypt (877).

Last Omayyad revolt crushed (907).

Tulunids lose control of north Syria to the Hamdanids of Aleppo (c.950).

Greek recovery of Antioch (969).

Egyptian Ikshidids established in south Syria.

Fatimid Caliphs from Cairo take control of the whole country.

Syria falls to Seljuk Turks from their Sultanate in Asia Minor.

Seljuk Sultan Malik-Shah dies and his empire falls (1092).

12th-14th C

Crusaders occupy Antioch and Jerusalem (1124).

Nur al-Din (Nureddin) becomes ruler of Syria (c.1154).

Nur al-Din dies, Salah al-Din (Saladin) his nephew, first of the Ayyubid rulers, succeeds him.

The Moorish traveller Ibn Jubayr arrives in Damascus (1184).

Salah al-Din defeats the Crusaders in Palestine at the Battle of the Horns of Hittin (1187).

12th-14th C (contd)

Jerusalem recovered.

Ayyubids build palaces and colleges (madrasa) all over the region, and promote Islamic orthodoxy.

Mongols invade Syria and sack Aleppo (1260) but are driven out by Egyptian Mamelukes, a group comprised of slaves and freed slaves of Turkish and Caucasian origin. (They had replaced the Ayyubids as masters of Egypt).

Mamelukes defeat Mongols at Ein Jalut in Palestine (1260).

Mameluke leader, Baibars 1, becomes ruler of a reunited Syria and Egypt.

Acre and other coastal areas taken from the Crusaders.

Qala'at al-Akrad, the castle of the Kurds (Krak des Chevaliers) surrenders (1271).

1290-1400

Syria under Mameluke rule, and relatively prosperous.

Mamelukes, for principally religious reasons, are harsh towards minority Muslim sects such as the Druze, Alawis, and Ismailis who mainly lived in the coastal mountains.

15th C

Mongols under Timur (Tamerlane) invade Syria. Burn Damascus and Aleppo (1401).

Death of Timur and the disintegration of his empire (1405).

Mameluke rule continues, but the country falls into decline.

Ottoman Period

16th C

Rise of the Ottoman Turks in Anatolia.

Mamelukes defeated by Sultan Selim I at Marj Dabiq, north of Aleppo, and Ottoman rule over Syria begins (1516).

Jerusalem captured by Ottoman Turks, making Syria and Palestine all "Syria" for Ottoman purposes.

Aleppo becomes an important Ottoman trading centre, and a crossroads for trade between Far East and Europe.

General prosperity prevails with the rule of Suleiman the Magnificent.

17th C

Syrian fortunes under the Ottomans vary. Ottomans improve agriculture and production and there is much fine architectural activity.

Gradual decline in Ottoman authority with much of the land being administered by pashas, the real power. These come and go as often as bribe money is paid to the Sublime Porte (the Sultan) in Constantinople.

18th-19th C

Constantinople's control over Syria weakens further, and pashas rule with virtual freedom from the Sublime Porte.

Ahmad Jazzar, Pasha of Acre, rules Syria almost as an independent country (1785-1804).

Ottoman Sultan Mahmoud II promises Syria to Egyptian Pasha Muhammad Ali for help during Greek War of Independence (1830).

Mahmoud reneges on his promise and Ibrahim Pasha, Muhammad Ali's son invades and conquers Syria (1831).

Ibrahim centralises government, and a measure of stability and prosperity is restored.

Increase in Christian and Jewish merchants who fare quite well.

European powers oppose Muhammad Ali's rule in Syria as they fear a weak Turkey.

War between Ottomans and Muhammad Ali's Egypt (1839).

Ibrahim (Muhammad's son) defeats Ottoman Turks.

European powers intervene in support of Turkey with Austrian force landing in Syria.

A local revolt against Ibrahim follows and the Egyptians withdraw from Syria (1840).

Syria reverts to Ottoman rule.

Pronounced Western influence on Syria through trade and the presence of missionary activities.

Fighting between government and Maronite Christians in the area of Lebanon sparks a massacre of Christians in Damascus (1860).

France sends in troops; proposes Mount Lebanon to be autonomous.

Syrian Protestant College (later American University of Beirut) established (1866).

French build railway from Beirut to Damascus; extend it to Aleppo.

Upsurge in Arab nationalist sentiment brought on in part by a revival of Arabic literature, and Muslim solidarity.

◆ ◆ ◆

THE MAKING OF MODERN SYRIA

The End of Ottoman Rule

Desire for national identity

The dawn of the twentieth century saw a marked rise in nationalist feeling throughout the Ottoman Empire. The strong pan-Muslim sentiments of Sultan Abdulhamid II (1876-1909) and a desire for a pure Turkish nation (as opposed to an Ottoman one), brought Turkish nationalism to the forefront within Turkey. Seizure of power by the Young Turk nationalists in 1908 heightened this desire for self-identity among the Arab peoples of the Empire.

Although it was initially the educated Muslims who put forward proposals for some form of separate Arab government, many Christian intellectuals soon endorsed their ideas. Syrian nationalist organisations sprang up in Constantinople, Paris and Syria itself.

the wisdom of Lawrence

In 1914 the Turks entered the World War allied to the Axis Powers. During 1915 Sharif Hussein, ruler of the Hejaz, in communications with the British minister McMahon (the McMahon Correspondence), was led to believe that subject to certain reservations the Arabs would get independence in the lands liberated from the Turks. An Arab army was raised to fight alongside the British. T.E. Lawrence ("Lawrence of Arabia"), the British officer sent to command them, firmly believed the ousting of the Ottomans would lead to true Arab independence. In the introduction to his *Seven Pillars of Wisdom* he writes, "I meant to make a new nation".

in the grip of the West

However, in 1916 secret discussions between the British and French resulted in an agreement, the Sykes-Picot Agreement, in which the areas of Syria and Palestine and Mesopotamia were to be divided up: the French and British would control the coastal districts; in the inland region they would set up either a confederation or a single Arab state, with British and French spheres of influence.

In Syria, on the conclusion of the war, an Arab administration under Emir Faisal, Sharif Hussein's son, was set up in Damascus and the interior. A French administration was established in Beirut to control the coastal region which included Latakia and Alexandretta.

The French Mandate

the Cross -v- the Crescent

In March 1920 a Syrian Nationalist Congress meeting in Damascus proclaimed an independent Kingdom of Syria with Faisal as King. A month later at an Allied conference in San Remo it was decided to put both countries under mandate: the French would administer Syria and the British Palestine.

The French Commander General Gouraud occupied Damascus in the summer of 1920. It is said he went straight to the tomb of Salah al-Din, the warrior who had expelled the Crusaders in 1187, and exulted "We are back, Saladin! The Cross defeats the Crescent!"

That same year, France detached the autonomous area of Lebanon from Syria and it became a separate French mandated state. Syria was now more or less confined to the borders which encompass it today.

France proceeded to fractionise the country. The Alawis, a Muslim Shi'ite sect who lived mainly in Jabal Ansariyeh, together with the Druze, another dissident sect inhabiting the Jabal Druze, were each given local authority, while the rest of the country was ruled from Damascus. Much construction work was undertaken and whereas under the terms of the Mandate the country was to be prepared for independence, the French saw this to be a very long way off. France had long posed as the protector of Christians in the Near East, and was therefore reluctant to introduce a system of government in which the Muslims, the vast majority, would be in control.

resentment grows

The Syrians could not come to terms with the fact that "Syria" had been reduced in size, and many among the educated still wanted a "Greater Syria" which would include Palestine, Lebanon and what is now Jordan. The failure of the French to allow any meaningful representative government caused much resentment. In 1925 a rebellion broke out in Damascus which led to a bombardment of the city. The revolt continued in various ways until 1927 with the French raiding Damascus again in 1926. Eventually, the Nationalists were placated by the holding of elections in 1928 for a Constituent Assembly, which would have the task of drafting a new Constitution.

The resulting document was unacceptable to the French High Commissioner, mainly because it did not give him the control he wanted, and because it still aspired to a Greater Syria. In 1930, after fruitless attempts to resolve the issue, the Assembly was dissolved and the French enacted their own version of the Constitution which had suitable clauses safeguarding French control. New elections were held but, predictably, negotiations between the new Government and the French to resolve differences were to no avail.

treaty signed in Paris

The Assembly was again suspended in 1934. Disturbances broke out in 1936 and a Syrian delegation went to Paris to attempt to negotiate with the Government there. The new French Government, the Popular Front, was more understanding of the Syrian position, and a treaty was signed in which Syria would be granted complete independence in three years. The French, however, never ratified the treaty.

A further deterioration of relations between the two countries occurred in 1939 when France ceded the Sanjak of Alexandretta to Turkey. This area included the ancient city of Antioch and the Syrians regarded the ceding as a hostile act. Even today Syria does not recognise the border in that area — on all Syrian maps it is marked as "temporary".

Damascus recognises Vichy France

After the French capitulation to the Germans in 1940 the authorities in Damascus recognised the Vichy Government. In June 1941 Free French and British forces invaded Syria, occupying Damascus a month later. General Catroux, acting for the Free French Government, offered complete independence, an end to the Mandate and declared independence on 28th September 1941.

But true independence was still to prove elusive!

The French remained reluctant to hand over complete power to the new Syrian Government and did this only gradually over the next two years. The final stumbling block was the transfer of the militia made up of part local and part French forces. The French demand for a Franco-Syrian treaty was also rejected. This led to disturbances which culminated in the final French bombardment of Damascus and the final British intervention.

Goodbye to the French and British

1946 saw the French and British troops withdraw completely from Syria after UN Security Council negotiations. The Syrian Republic was proclaimed, with Shukri al-Kouwatli as President and Khalid al-Azem as Premier.

The Syrian Republic

The first 25 years of Syrian independence were years of marked instability. A number of factors contributed to this, the most important being the humiliating defeat of the Arab armies by the new State of Israel. However the problem of ethnic differences also caused difficulties. The minority sects, Alawis, Druze of the mountain districts, together with the large, mainly urban Christian communities, had to be reconciled to majority Sunni Muslim rule. Rivalries between the Arab States themselves only served to compound the predicament.

coups and confusion

Three military coups occurred in Syria during 1949 alone. In March, Colonel Husni az-Zaim ousted the al-Kouwatli Government, in August Colonel Sami al-Hinnawi overthrew az-Zaim, whilst in December another Colonel, Adib ash-Shishakli, supplanted al-Hinnawi. Shishakli permitted civilian government to continue under President Hashim al-Atassi, he himself held all authority. The Chamber of Deputies was opposed to military intervention in politics, and this came to a head in December 1951 when Shishakli removed the Government in a coup d'état and proclaimed himself Head of State. He appointed Fawiz Silu as Premier, but Shishakli wielded absolute power. The Chamber of Deputies was adjourned, and political activity banned.

appearance of the Ba'athists

In 1952 Shishakli founded the Arab Liberation Movement, making it Syria's only political party. A year later a new constitution came into force with Shishakli as President. When political activity was permitted to resume, the Ba'ath Socialist Party was formed. Elections were held in October of that year, Shishakli's Arab Liberation Movement winning by a large majority.

What had characterised the various military coups so far was that the leaders seemed to have no ideology of any significance. Continuing to serve as Army officers they ruled in conjunction with some of the established politicians, who were quite conservative. However, since independence the Ba'ath Party, a group with an ideology that was socialist, secular and strongly nationalistic, had been busy recruiting members from the army and university. They attracted particularly strong support from among the Alawi sect who constituted a sizable proportion of young army officers.

Shishakli flees Syria

In late 1953 demonstrations in Damascus and Aleppo caused Shishakli to flee the country, and in early 1954 his government was overthrown by a coup led by a Ba'athist sympathiser, Colonel Faisal al-Atassi. He formed a new civilian government with Hashim al-Atassi as President. The Chamber of Deputies was restored and in September new elections held under the old Constitution.

alliance with the Eastern Bloc

World and regional events continued to have a bearing on the complicated Syrian political scene. During the 1950s, in answer to Western hegemony in the Middle East, the Soviet Union began to penetrate the area economically. This was especially so in Syria. In the summer of 1955, Shukri al-Kouwatli became President again, and the country took on a profound pro-Egyptian outlook. While the Suez campaign and Israeli occupation of Sinai in 1956 did not involve the Syrians directly, the pipelines which carried oil from Iraq and Saudi Arabia through Syria to the Mediterranean were blown up by the Syrians, who refused to allow repairs until Sinai had been evacuated.

Ba'athist Syria

rapid rise and fall of the United Arab Republic

When elections were held in 1957, the Ba'ath Party won convincingly. In 1958, Gamal Abdul Nasser, President of Egypt and the driving force in Pan Arabism, persuaded Syria to give up her sovereignty and establish a union with Egypt. Thus the United Arab Republic (UAR) came into being with Syria as its Northern Province, and in 1960 a Joint Assembly with an equal number of Deputies from each country was established.

Greeted initially with enthusiasm by many Syrians, events soon converted this into disenchantment. The fact that most of the key positions in the union were held by Egyptians and that Syria's far from thriving economy was linked to Egypt's even more impoverished resources were ample grounds for this discontent. The end of September 1961 saw yet another military coup and the resultant dissolution of the United Arab Republic.

At the beginning of December that year, Syria held elections for a new Assembly. Dr Nazim Kudsi became President, but his regime contained all the old style politicians and was very unsteady. Whilst depending on the (Ba'athist) military for support, it steered away from Ba'athist ideology, in particular socialism, and 1963 saw the government severely weakened by troubles both internal and external. This not uncommon state of affairs culminated in a Ba'athist military coup. A Ba'ath government was set up dominated by Silah al-Bitar. The new leadership purged pro-Nasser elements from the government and the army. A dedicated Ba'athist, Hafez al-Assad was made air force commander. Later that year a pro-Nasserite revolt was put down and a strong Ba'athist, General Amin al-Hafiz became President.

socialism -v- Sunni Islam

There followed a solid socialist agenda, with the nationalisation of banks and industrial concerns. The new regime

17

experimented with agrarian reform, giving land to landless peasants. Yet discontent continued. The Ba'ath party was not purely Syrian in nature, and had branches in the other Arab countries. Many pro-Egyptian and pro-Iraqi Ba'athists were still quite vocal. The Sunni Muslim majority was another thorn to contend with. Most Ba'ath support came from the minority sects, especially the Alawis who the Sunnis opposed. Disturbances broke out and these were particularly violent in Hama, a traditional city.

The government took control of more industries including the generally untapped mineral resources. To repress opposition to these measures a special military court was established which dealt with dissenters. Tightening their grip, extremists seized power in the name of the Syrian Ba'ath in February 1966, with Alawi Colonel Salah al-Jadid in control, and Hafez al-Assad as Minister of Defence.

Syria loses the Golan Heights to Israel

The Six Day War of 1967 between Israel and the Arabs proved disastrous for Syria. In an astonishing assault on the Golan Heights above the Sea of Galilee the Israelis overran Syrian positions and occupied an area up to the town of Quneitra less than 100kms from Damascus. A Security Council-imposed cease fire left Israel in control of all the Golan. A later resolution urging Israel to withdraw in exchange for an ending of the state of war between the countries was to no avail as the Arabs refused to negotiate.

The debacle on the Golan, a feud between the Ba'athists in Syria and Iraq, coupled with Soviet interference all helped to destabilise the regime. The Minister of Defence, General Hafez al-Assad, and a less extreme wing of the Syrian Ba'ath Party seized power in November 1970. The Prime Minister, Dr Atassi, was in hospital at the time. Most members of the Government were either arrested or fled the country.

Assad takes over

By February the following year, after the Constitution was amended, Hafez al-Assad became President. He was elected for a seven year term and has, incredibly, remained President ever since.

General Abd ar-Raham Khlefawi was appointed Premier and in 1972 the People's Council came into being. Assad improved relations with the USSR and in early 1972 the Soviet defence minister visited Syria. Later that year a new government was set up with Mahmoud al-Ayyoubi, the Vice President becoming Prime Minister. Yet another new Constitution came into force which was subsequently approved by the People's Council. It declared the socialist nature of the Republic, the freedom of belief and, whilst not recognising any state religion, it pronounced Islamic law to be an important basis for legislation. During 1972 the Ba'ath Party and its collaborators merged to form the National Progressive Front and in elections held in the spring of 1973 gained 140 of the 180 seats in the People's Council.

war with Israel — Quneitra regained

October 1973 saw the outbreak of the fourth Arab-Israeli war. In the afternoon of October 6th, on Yom Kippur, the most solemn day in the Jewish religious calender, Egypt and Syria launched an attack in the hope of regaining the land they lost in 1967. Much damage was caused to the Syrian economy by Israeli retaliation, and the port at Latakia, the oil terminal at Tartous and the huge oil refinery near Homs were destroyed. Syria's initial advance on the Golan could not be sustained, and the Israeli forces were able to push them back. Mediation by the United States and a disengagement of forces agreement led to Israel withdrawing from part of occupied Egyptian territory and from a very small part of the Golan which included Quneitra.

Subsequent recognition of Israel by Egypt brought about the complete return of Egyptian land. Syria would have no part in this process.

In 1975 diplomatic relations with Britain and the United States which had been severed in 1967 were restored. The following year the then Premier Mahmoud al-Ayyubi resigned and Abd ar-Raham Khlefawi again became Premier.

Syrian troops in Lebanon

Meanwhile, civil war was raging in Lebanon. By 1975 Syria decided the intensity of the conflict warranted her intervention. The Arab League agreed to despatch a force with the task of enforcing a cease fire and maintaining the peace. This force was predominantly Syrian. A strong Syrian presence remains in Lebanon to this day.

Hafez al-Assad was elected to a second 7 year term in 1978, and Muhammad Ali al-Halabi was made Premier. Dissatisfaction with his rule was beginning to show. Most of the important government positions were in Alawi hands, and a number of killings of Alawis occurred. The worst carnage took place in 1979 when some 60 Alawi cadets were slaughtered in Aleppo by the Muslim Brotherhood, an extreme Sunni fundamentalist group active throughout the Arab world.

Iran-Iraq war

In 1980, the Soviet Union and Syria concluded a 20 year treaty of friendship and the Soviets granted huge loans for the purchase of military hardware. The same year saw the outbreak of the Iran-Iraq war. Syria chose to back the fundamentalist Iranians rather than the Ba'athist Iraqis, due to the enmity which existed between the two wings of the Ba'ath Party.

In the 1981 elections to the People's Assembly, Assad's National Front won all of the seats. In spite of this, fundamentalist dissatisfaction with the government continued and in 1982 a revolt by the Muslim Brotherhood broke out in the city of Hama. This proved quite an obstacle for the regime and the Army had to use great force to put it down, destroying much of the old town in the process.

Syrian foreign policy, however, was dominated by the events in Lebanon. With over 30,000 troops there Syria was a major player. Often it appeared that this conflict would escalate into another Syrian-Israeli war. It became clear that Syria regarded Lebanon as its sphere of influence and henceforth any settlement in that country would require Syrian approval.

Soviet influence and demise of Communism

Soviet and East European aid played a vital role in the stabilisation of Assad's regime. It was indispensable to the country's development and included the training of engineers and technicians in addition to cash and hardware. Economic progress was thus maintained despite troubles abroad and at home. The completion of the Euphrates Dam increased arable land, and the rapid development of oil resources helped with revenues. As conditions improved the population became more reconciled to Alawi Ba'ath rule, however unpleasant some of its aspects might be. It should be borne in mind that all Arab States in the Middle East are ruled over more or less by a strongman, and nasty excesses have occurred in all of them. At least Assad has succeeded in bringing about a measure of stability to the country, and without that stability economic progress would have been impossible.

The changes that occurred in Russia and Eastern Europe triggered changes in Syria's attitude to the West. No longer could Assad rely upon economic help and soft trade with those countries. Everything would now require hard currency, even the spare parts that were needed for Russian-made merchandise.

Syria turns to the West

To encourage more Western investment in the country, Assad has relaxed his tight grip, though he remains very much in control. His support and participation in the Gulf War alongside the Americans marked a dramatic change of direction. As the long-drawn-out struggle between the Israelis and the Palestinians appears to be entering its final phase, the greatest obstacle to resolving Syrian-Israeli enmity may also be removed. The peace treaty between Israel and Jordan will, no doubt, give added impetus to Syria to join the process. However, it seems that Syria will not take this step until there is a full Israeli withdrawal from the Golan. Such negotiations may be considerably protracted.

2. GEOGRAPHY

THE LAND

Bounded by Turkey in the north, Iraq in the east, Jordan in the south, Lebanon and the Mediterranean Sea to the west and Israel to the southwest, modern Syria covers an area of some 185,180 square kilometres.

Situated partly in the ancient Fertile Crescent, Syria has throughout history been known as one of the most fertile areas in this part of the world. The modern Syrian republic can be divided into 4 main geographical zones: the coastal region, the mountains, the inland region, and finally, the desert.

The coastal region

The coastal region, stretching from Turkey in the north to Lebanon in the south is a narrow strip some 200 kilometres long. Its maximum width is about 30 kms but almost disappears where the mountains slope down to the sea. There are no river estuaries or natural bays, and the two ports, Latakia and Tartous, are on an almost straight coastline. At the southern end is the Nahr al-Kabir, the Homs Gap. This low-lying valley separates the mountain range of Jabal Ansariye from the Jabal Lubnan (Mount Lebanon) range. It also forms the political boundary between modern Syria and Lebanon.

The earth along the coastal strip is rich, consisting of fertile alluvial plains which can be cultivated all year round. Crops include olives, apricots, grapes, and citrus.

The mountains

Directly east of the coastal region the rugged mountains of the Jabal Ansariye (sometimes called Jabal al-Nusayriye) form a barrier between the sea and the rest of the country. Sloping quite gradually on the western side, they fall suddenly in the east. They are composed mainly of limestone and basalt, and centuries of felling have rendered them virtually treeless.

The Jabal Ansariye terminate somewhat abruptly in the south at the Nahr al-Kabir, or Homs Gap, the fertile valley stretching west of Homs to the coast. To the south of this valley the Jabal Lubnan (Mountains of Lebanon) continue on the west. On the east, the Jabal Lubnan al-Sharqi (Anti-Lebanon) form the frontier between Lebanon and Syria, sloping down to Damascus and al-Ghouta. In Lebanon, al-Biqa (the Beek'a valley) divides the two ranges.

At the southern end of the Jabal Lubnan al-Sharqi is Jabal al-Sheikh, Mount Hermon, Syria's highest peak (2,814 metres). Below Hermon is al-Jawlan, the Golan Heights, and to the east the Hauran Plateau. Both these high plains have rich volcanic soil, and the Hauran was the breadbasket of Syria back in Roman times. Just to the east are the Jabal al-Durruz, known now as the Jabal al-Arab.

The inland region

East of the Jabal Ansariye is the Orontes Valley, or Ghab as it is called in Arabic. This a depression through which the Nahr al-Assi (Orontes) flows. Centuries of neglect turned this into a swamp in which the waters of the river were mostly lost. Now drained, the Ghab is one of the most intensively cultivated parts of Syria. Bordering the Ghab in the north is the Jabal al-Zawiye, a limestone range which climbs to about 1000 metres and merges into the Belus Massif, the heights north and west of Aleppo.

To the south of the river valley the terrain begins to rise until it merges with the lower slopes of the Anti-Lebanon.

Between the Orontes valley and the desert is the steppe, the westerly part cultivated, the east far less so. The yields of the cultivated land are very dependent on rainfall which varies from year to year. As more irrigation becomes available, so the cultivated parts of this area increase. Here live many Bedouin, who roam with their flocks of sheep seeking the available pastures.

The desert

The desert, occupying almost 60 per cent of Syrian territory, is not a sand desert but is made up of rock and gravel. This wilderness is formed mainly of undulating high plains except in the south, al-Hamad, which is mountainous. Here and there this arid land is punctuated by oases, such as that at Tadmor (Palmyra). The desert stretches up to the Euphrates and beyond, the areas along the river banks being green and well cultivated with a variety of agricultural produce, especially cotton. Driving along the road which runs roughly parallel to the river, alternate areas of desert and verdant growth are encountered, depending on how far away the river course is.

But apart from these relatively small pastoral stretches, virtually nothing grows in the rest of this vast desolate region; yet even in a parched land such as this, the nomads and semi-nomads still wander as they have always done, grazing their sheep on every patch of scrub that can be found.

CLIMATE

The Syrian climate can be divided into two seasons: the rainy season — from mid-November to April, and the dry season for the rest of the year. Variations can of course occur, and it is not completely unusual to get the odd downpour in October or May anywhere in the country. Precipitation generally is not uniform over the whole country, the coastal region receiving almost four times as much rainfall as Damascus, decreasing still further as you go east.

Mediterranean clime

The coast and the lower mountain slopes have a Mediterranean climate with average daily summer temperatures of 29°C, not extreme by any means, but which can nevertheless be uncomfortable due to high humidity. Winters are quite mild with temperatures averaging 10°C.

Inland the summer temperature is hotter, the mountains blocking the cool sea breezes. Humidity is low, making it more bearable. In Damascus and Aleppo mean summer daytime temperatures of 33-37°C are the norm. The winters are cold, due to an air flow from Central Asia. with a daily average of between 1° and 4°C.

extremes in the desert

In **the desert** 40°C is normal in summer, while peaks can reach 46°C. Surprisingly, the anti-cyclonic influences from Central Asia often bring frost and snow in the winter.

the hot wind

A few times a year, particularly in the spring and autumn, a strong easterly wind blows across the region laden with fine dust and sand picked up as it crosses the desert. Temperatures soar, often by 10°C or more, the sky turns dark and humidity drops to around 10% causing considerable discomfort. This wind is called *Khamsin* and can last from 1-4 days or more. It is less noticeable along the coast where moderating sea breezes ease the effect.

FLORA AND FAUNA

Wildlife is sparse in Syria today. In the past, wolves, foxes, wild boar and jackals abounded; now they can only be found in remote enclaves. Deer and squirrels are still in the forests, but rarely seen. Desert animals such as gazelles may also be present in small numbers. Eagles nest in the mountains as do other birds of prey. What can be said with certainty is that snakes such as vipers frequent most of the desert!

After a wet winter, spring brings forth a wealth of colour from abundant wildflowers to most areas, making it an ideal time for a visit as the summer heat quickly parches the land.

Tree felling

Lime, fir and poplar are the most common trees found on the mountain slopes. Uncontrolled felling has greatly reduced these forests, especially on the Jabal Ansariye but nowadays many are protected by the government.

In the desert oasis of Tadmor and in the Euphrates valley the date palm flourishes while the hot but humid coastal area is ideal for citrus. Groves of olive, always an important ingredient of the Mediterranean diet, are plentiful.

THE SYRIAN PEOPLE

Population

Syria had a population of 9 million in 1981; the 1993 figure was estimated to be over 13 million — an increase of about 45 per cent. By the year 2000 it could reach close to 20 million! This massive population increase, estimated in 1993 to be 3.8% annually, far outstrips economic growth, making rapid economic progress vital. The statistic for population density of about 73 per square kilometre is deceptive since the majority of the population lives in less than half the land area. Fastest growth is in the urban areas of Damascus and Aleppo, with the natural increase compounded by the movement from the land into the major cities. The birth rate is higher among Muslims than Christians.

As would be expected in a country with such a high birth rate the population is young. Roughly half are under the age of 14 with less than 3 per cent over 65. In 1986 life expectance was 65 for men, and 67 for women.

diverse ethnic groups

Ethnicity must not be confused with religion. Over 90% of Syrians are ethnically Arabs. These include, besides mainstream Muslims, Christians, Ismailis, Alawis, Bedouin and Druze.

DIVISIONS OF ISLAM

Islam is divided into two main branches, Sunni and Shi'ite. The orthodox Sunnis comprise the vast majority of Muslims worldwide. Most ethnic Arabs are Sunnis, and they control Mecca and Medina, the major holy places of Islam. The minority Shi'ites are further divided into numerous sects.

After the death of Muhammad in 632 disagreement arose as to his successor. Abu Bakr, Muhammad's father-in-law (father of his favourite wife, Aisha), became *Khalifa* (caliph) or successor. There was opposition to his appointment from rivals who asserted that only members of the Prophet's family, and more specifically the branch of his daughter Fatima and her husband Ali, could hold this position. Adherents to this opinion were called *shiat Ali*, the party or faction of Ali, and from this term the name Shi'ite is derived.

Fatima's husband, Ali, eventually become the fourth Caliph in 655 but was murdered in 661 and Mu'awiya, founder of the Omayyads, replaced him. Many followers, however, supported the claims of Ali's sons, Hassan and Hussein, and a struggle began. Hassan died under mysterious circumstances in 669, and Hussein was murdered by soldiers loyal to the Omayyads at Kerbala in 680. Now in Iraq, Kerbala is the major shrine of pilgrimage for Shi'ites.

The Shi'ites are divided into many groups. The majority are known as the *Itna Ashariyya*, meaning "Twelvers". Their leaders are *Imams*, and they believe in the first 12 Imams, the 12th having disappeared in 873. According to Twelver doctrine he will return someday as the *Mahdi* or messiah. The Shi'ism of the Twelvers is the official religion of Iran. They also constitute the majority in Pakistan, and have sizable minorities in Iraq, Bahrain, and Lebanon.

The Shi'ism of the Ismailis originated in 765. After the death of Jafar ibn Muhammad, the 6th Shi'ite Imam, the majority accepted his younger son, Musa al-Kazim as the 7th Imam. Others supported the pretensions of the older son, Ismail, and he became their 7th Imam (Ismailis are sometimes called "seveners"). The Ismailis attained significance under another Shi'ite sect, the Fatimids, who claimed descent from Fatima (the Prophet's daughter).

In the late 11th C the Ismailis themselves split, with one faction, the Nizaris, moving to the mountains of Iran and Syria. Bent on murdering their opponents, they earned the title *Hashasheen* or hashish eaters: it was said they fortified themselves with hashish before setting out on killing missions. From hashasheen our word "assassin" is derived. Much calmer today, the Ismailis survive in Pakistan and India as well as Syria, with the Aga Khan as their spiritual leader.

Other Shi'ite sects include the Alawis (see box on page 29), the Druze (see box on page 186) and the Zaidis of northern Yemen.

Kurds, many of who came in the 1920s as refugees from nationalist Turkey account for about 11 per cent. Most are now assimilated into the general Arab milieu, having largely abandoned their language and traditional dress. There are also groups of Turkomans and Circassians who as Sunni Muslim are also absorbed into the Arab populace.

Other non-Arabs include the Armenians, the majority of whom arrived as refugees from Turkish massacres. They number between 150-200,000 and are concentrated in and around Aleppo. There are also some thousands of Assyrians from Iraq who live in Syria and, being Nestorian Christians, live a more separate life.

Jews, once an important and prosperous community in Syria have mostly left. Those who remain live either in Damascus or Aleppo. It can be expected that this community will eventually dwindle away.

Officially the Syrian government does not recognise ethnic groups — all are Syrians!

RELIGION

Unlike many other Arab states, Syria does not have a state religion. The constitution originally made no mention of Islam. Public dissatisfaction with this resulted in the insertion of a clause which specified that the Head of State must be a Muslim. Assad is very firm about keeping religion out of politics and any sign of religious fundamentalism is quickly put down.

Muslims

Islam is the religion that burst out of Arabia in 630AD, preached by Muhammad, who according to Muslims was the last of God's prophets, a list which includes Abraham, Moses and Jesus. Islam means submission (to the will of God) and is, like biblical Judaism, a total way of life, encompassing a social system and code of values. Islam's holy book, the Koran, was not actually written down by Muhammad, but some time after his death. It is a collection of his teachings and revelations as told to his followers and remembered by them. The Muslim era, and the year from which its calendar is counted, started with the flight of Muhammad from Mecca to Medina, the *hijra*.

There are basically two streams in Islam. The orthodox, who are called Sunni and the breakaway Shi'ites. This can be likened to Catholics and Protestants within Christianity. Like the Christian Protestants, the Shi'ites have split into a multitude of other groups, but all believe that Ali, the prophet's son-in-law (who was murdered), was his true successor. (See information box on the divisions of Islam, page 26.)

Muslims make up 90 per cent of the Syrian population and

due to their higher birth rate this percentage is increasing. 78% are Sunni, or traditional Muslims; the remainder being made up of the different Shi'ites, Alawis, Ismailis, and Druze.

call to prayer

The orthodox Muslim is called to prayer five times a day:

fajr	-	dawn;
dhuhr	-	hour before sunrise;
'asr	-	noon;
maghreb	-	sunset;
isha	-	hour and a half after sunset.

There is no God but God

The call is made from the minaret of the mosque. In days gone by the call was by voice with the caller, the muezzin, walking around the minaret parapet so that he could be heard in different parts of the city. In today's technological world it is done via tape, amplifier and many speakers. The call starts with the words "*Allah Akbar!*", "God is great!" and finishes, "*La allah illa Allah*", "There is no god but God".

Jesus the Prophet

Allah is Arabic for God, and He is the God of Judaism and Christianity. Jesus figures prominently in Islam, but as an important prophet, not the Son of God. Indeed, one of the minarets over the Great Mosque of Damascus is called the Minaret of Jesus. All the prophets of the Old Testament are revered by Muslims, and Muhammad is revered as the last of the prophets in that he received the revelation of the Koran from the Archangel Gabriel.

The Five Pillars of Islam

Islam rests on five fundamental pillars:

shahada	-	this is the profession of faith: "There is no God but God (Allah) and Muhammad is his prophet";
salat	-	prayer five times a day;
zakat	-	the giving of alms;
sawn	-	sunrise to sunset fasting during the month of Ramadan;
haj	-	the pilgrimage to Mecca, at least once in a lifetime.

The day of rest for Muslims is Friday, and the main service in the mosque is at noon. Non Muslims are not allowed into the prayer hall at that time, although some mosques do allow them to

THE ALAWIS

THE basis for Alawi belief was laid down in the teachings of Muhammad ibn Nusayr an-Namiri who lived in the 9th century at the time of Ali al-Hadi, the 10th Imam, but the sect's actual founder was probably Hussein ibn Hamdan al-Khasbi who died around 960.

The 9th and 10th centuries saw the Shi'ites splitting into a number of factions (see box on the *Divisions of Islam* on page ...). One group, known under various names, and following the teachings of Muhammad an-Namiri, believed in the divinity of Ali, the Prophet's brother-in-law, in a manner not dissimilar to Christian interpretation of Jesus. The followers of this teaching were the Nusayri, Namiri and the Ansari who eventually adopted the collective title Alawi though they were not officially called by that title until much later.

The Nusayri lived in Syria and tended to dwell in the mountains west of Hims (Homs), hence the name of the mountains, Jabal al-Nusayriye. Considered heretics by most Muslims, they were despised by Mamelukes, Crusaders and Ottomans alike. The medieval Arab traveller Ibn Jubayr refers in his journal in 1184 during his sojourn in Syria, to *"...the Nusayrites who are infidels for they attribute divinity to Ali..."*.

Alawis do not have houses of prayer, and only very few learn the fundamentals of their faith.

The collective term Alawi for the "Alis" came into official use in Syria in 1920. The French then allowed the Nusayri to use the title and it nowadays generally refers to those of the sect who live in Syria. The French recognised them as a separate ethnic group, at one time making their region autonomous, which promoted fears among the nationalists that it would be detached from Syria.

Although a small minority in Syria, accounting for about 14-15% of the population, Alawis are the dominant political force, especially since Hafez al-Assad, himself an Alawi, came to power.

remain in the courtyard. Business is permitted after the noontime prayer, and this is the custom in many Arab countries. In Syria virtually all businesses remain closed all day.

Christians

Christians of various denominations make up 8-10 per cent of Syrians. They can be divided up into three main traditions: Eastern Orthodox (more commonly called Greek Orthodox), Oriental Orthodox (Syrian and Armenian), and Catholics and Uniates. A few thousand Assyrian or Nestorian faithful also exist as do some thousands of various Protestant groups. These last are in the main those who have been drawn out of the Orthodox rites by missionary activity.

Orthodox rite

Half of the Christians belong to the Eastern Orthodox rite which follows the Byzantine rite and is essentially the same as Greek Orthodox but has a liturgy in Arabic and is subject to the Patriarchate of Antioch.

The first to be called Christians

The Syrian Orthodox Church claims to be the original Church of Antioch and Syria. (Antioch was where, according to the New Testament, followers of Jesus were first called Christians.) Together with the Armenians and the Egyptian Copts the Syrians broke away from the Orthodox family after the 4th Ecumenical Council which met in Chalcedon in the year 451. At the Council the natures of Christ were at issue and in a controversy that defies the comprehension of a layman, East and West went in their own direction. These Eastern Oriental Churches are since referred to as "Monophysite".

The great champion of the Syrian Orthodox Church was a Jacob Baradeus (Yacoub Bourd'ono) who lived around 543. Due to his zeal, adherents to this communion are often (erroneously) referred to as "Jacobites". The Patriarch's title is the Patriarch of Antioch and all the East, his residence, today, being Damascus.

allegiance to Rome

The Catholics and Uniates together form the second most numerous Christian group in Syria. Of these the Melkites and Maronites together account for well over half.

The Armenians

The Armenian Orthodox Church came into being following the conversion of the Armenian King Tirdate in the year 301, making Armenia the first Christian nation in the world. For Armenians, their faith and race are inseparable, the church an integral part of their culture; where one goes so does the other. They have lived in Syria for centuries, but with many fleeing Turkish persecutions of the First World War, when over one and a half million were slaughtered, their numbers greatly increased.

The Druze

The Druze live mainly on the Jabal al-Durruz (now called Jabal al-Arab), the Hauran and the Golan Heights (Al Jawlan). They number about 100,000. (For further details see information box on Druze, page 186).

3. SYRIA TODAY

GOVERNMENT

The official name for modern Syria is al-Jumhuriyah al-'Arabiyah al-Suriyah, the Syrian Arab Republic. Its capital is Damascus, Dimashq in Arabic. The Head of State, Lt-General Hafez al-Assad is also Commander-in-Chief of the armed forces, Secretary General of the Ba'ath Socialist Party, and President of the National Progressive Front.

There is a legislative assembly, the People's Assembly, with 250 members, the majority from the NPF. In practice, all power is in the hands of Assad who has been Head of State since 1971.

Thirteen provinces

Syria is divided into 13 provinces, or *muhaafazat*. These are *Dimashq, Halab, Hamah, al-Ladhiqiyah, Tartous, Daraa, Hims, Idlib, al-Qunaytirah, al-Suwayda, al-Raqqah, al-Hasakah, Dayr al-Zawr.* Each province is ruled by a governor or *muhaafez.*

ECONOMY

Apart from the period 1961-63, Syria's economy has, since 1958, been socialist in character — if not always in deed. After the Ba'ath led coup in 1963 the banks were nationalised, and in 1965 most major industry was brought under state control. The retail side of the economy remained in private hands except for official participation in consumer cooperatives. (An Arab country without a souk and its accompanying bargaining ritual would be unthinkable!)

economic woes

After the 1973 war with Israel which badly damaged the Syrian economy, the Government launched a massive reconstruction program. Some controls were eased in an effort to encourage investment. A five year Development Plan was introduced, and by its end in 1975 the economy had experienced a measure of growth. This growth, however, was not sustained. Successive five year plans were set, but none achieved their targets.

The second half of the 1980s saw the Syrian economy in crisis. Foreign currency was scarce, causing a lack of raw materials and spares. Combined with general mismanagement and corruption, industrial and agricultural output fell drastically.

Petroleum, first discovered in commercial quantities in the mid 1950s, has now become the leading foreign currency earner and as such the mainstay of the Syrian economy.

towards reconciliation with the West

Syrian participation in the Gulf War against Iraq has proved to be a catalyst. Aid from the USA and the EEC has increased and the easing of controls is stimulating some western investment. More foreign companies are being encouraged to perform in the economy, particularly in the sphere of upgrading the generally out-of-date infrastructure. This has helped cushion the effects of the collapse of the Soviet Union and the changes in Eastern Europe, till then Syria's principal trading partners.

Agriculture, always a backbone of the Syrian economy, has retained its position but its share of the overall GNP has declined. It is now 22% of the GNP. This is in spite of the population move from rural to urban areas. Textiles, both raw and manufactured play a significant role, supplying the bulk of domestic needs as well as being exported.

unpredictable services

Electricity supply has failed to keep pace with demand. The hope that the Euphrates Dam would rectify this was not fulfilled. The erratic water flow along the river, due in the main to Turkish restrictions as they draw off immense amounts for their own purposes, plus poor maintenance of the generating station have contributed. In 1993, to alleviate this power shortage, the Government approved 3 new generating stations.

The telephone system is also in a poor state and it is easier to phone Damascus from London than it is from Tartous!

fledgling tourist industry

In the late 1970s to help the country's foreign exchange shortage, the Government decided to develop the tourist industry, a much neglected resource. It was hoped that by the mid 1980s it would become a major hard currency earner. Expectations were not fulfilled. In 1986 the number of visitors was less than 600,000, most of these from other Arab countries, particularly

Lebanon and Iran. Those who came from western countries amounted to no more than 50,000. Clearly, the general unsettled conditions of the region combined with a bad public image in the West, must have acted as a deterrent. But in any event the tourist infrastructure was so poor and the level of investment in it so minimal that it could not have supported many more. Syrian restrictions on visitors, especially as regards exchange rates, were also very unfavourable for tourism to flourish.

a boost for tourism

Conditions in the area are now more stable and, as mentioned, Syria has regained favour with western governments. Combined with improvements to amenities and the relaxing of regulations, tourism has begun to grow rapidly. In 1993 Syria was host to over 200,000 western visitors.

But the constraints on overseas trade are only very gradually being relaxed. Most date back to the early 1950s and are the cause of widespread smuggling and a black market. This, as in any third world country which imposes restrictions on imports, constitutes a constant drain on the economy.

The future depends on the willingness of the authorities to give way to the private sector. There was recently some talk of permitting foreign banks to operate, but whether this and other non state-controlled operations will reach the ordinary citizen, only time will tell.

EDUCATION

school till age 12 (sometimes!)

Six years of schooling is compulsory for all children from the age of six. Secondary school education is free at state schools for those who wish to continue but in practice many children drop out of school after only a couple of years as the pressure on parents to get a child out to work — especially a boy — is immense. All across Syria you see school-age boys hawking in the streets, helping out in eating places or doing a thousand and one jobs. No one, it seems, enforces the law! This state of affairs leaves many young people more or less illiterate. The adult literacy rate in 1990 was only 65%, but this is high by (Arab) Middle Eastern standards.

Soviet training

Secondary schools prepare the young person either for vocational or university studies. There are universities in Damascus, Aleppo and Latakia, whilst vocational training establishments exist all over the country.

In the recent past many Syrians, especially budding technicians and engineers, were sent at state expense to the former

Soviet Union for studies. Those Syrians who continue to study abroad do so, generally, at their own expense.

EVERYDAY LIFE

Compared to many third world countries, including others in the region, the average standard of living in Syria is not too bad. The extreme poverty, so prevalent in Egypt for example, is not present at all in Syria and there are very few street beggars.

the new rich

Yet even so, life is still hard for most of the population. The lifting of many economic restrictions has enabled a small middle class or even affluent group to develop. In the better areas of Damascus, new Mercedes or BMW cars are parked outside fancy homes, and the expensive restaurants of the Meridien and Sheraton hotels have plenty of Syrian diners. The ordinary Syrian, though, may be able to see the "goodies" of the better life displayed in shop windows, but few are able to purchase them: a normal monthly salary will rarely exceed US$100.

Corruption, endemic in most Middle Eastern countries, is found at every level. To get most permits (and in Syria they are required for practically everything), "baksheesh" (bribe or backhander) has to be paid. I have heard that government salaries are so low that without baksheesh a civil servant could never manage — it is considered part of his pay!

the peasant poor

The official literacy rate of 65 per cent quoted above is deceptive. It is actually much higher amongst city dwellers, perhaps reaching 90 per cent. This leaves a mass of uneducated, and therefore indigent, rural peasantry, which is very noticeable as you travel around.

lack of extremism

One refreshing difference in Syria (in comparison with some other Muslim countries) is the lack of excessive Muslim fundamentalism. The Ikhwan al-Muslimin (Muslim Brotherhood), the extreme fundamentalist group, was once quite active in Syria. They did, in fact, stage a major revolt in Hama as recently as 1982 (see chapter on Hama). Many Syrians at first believed the group would succeed in bringing about a change for the better, but their extreme sectarianism and brutal methods only succeeded in alienating them from the general populace, and they are no longer a serious force in the country. It would be true to say that of the numerous Arab countries I have visited, the Syria of today seems to practice and preach its religion the most placidly.

pin-ups of the President

Almost everywhere you go there are huge portraits and statues of President Hafez al-Assad. Al-Azmeh square in Damascus, for example, has three gigantic portraits of the President each one vying with the other for size! (The largest covers the entire side of a six-storey building!) This phenomenon is repeated in virtually every town. Many shops, homes and taxi cabs also display his picture — whether as a genuine sign of affection or as a prudent sign of loyalty will have to be left for you to decide!

The press, radio and TV are all strictly controlled, and they will never criticise the government. Everything that Assad does will be soundly approved of and looked upon as part of the leader's grand foresight. This, though, should not diminish his political ability and stature. Hafez al-Assad is a shrewd politician, and an undoubted Syrian patriot.

LANGUAGE

Modern Standard Arabic (MSA), derived from the Classical Arabic of the Koran is Syria's official language. This is the language that is spoken from the Persian Gulf to the Atlantic, including Yemen and Sudan. MSA is used in this area for all literary purposes including journalism.

Additionally, every region has its own colloquial Arabic which is used for verbal communication only. In Syria this is known as Syrian Arabic which is also spoken in Lebanon and to some extent in Jordan. The colloquial dialect of Egypt is different, and if you are familiar with that you will notice a difference in Syria. (Refer to the Language chapter for more information.)

variety of ancient tongues

In addition to Arabic most ethnic groups have their own traditional tongue: Kurdish, Armenian and Turkic. One or two small Christian communities even use Syriac (or Aramaic).

Most educated Syrians speak a European language, and even those without a formal education have managed to pick up a smattering of French and English from the cinema or on the streets. Until recently French was the most commonly spoken second language because of the Mandate influence, but English is gradually catching up.

PART II
TOURING SYRIA

4. PLANNING YOUR ITINERARY

ITINERARY POSSIBILITIES

> ► **Full tour - 15-20 days**

To give the reader a sense of reality while studying this book, the chapters follow an actual itinerary which circles the country in an anti-clockwise manner. This tour encompasses almost every site which the inquisitive traveller will want to see. All the locations visited in this route are shown in the sketch map of Syria above. This itinerary will take (by car) **15-16 days** so it can be done within your visa time. However, if you want to do it more leisurely, extending your visa will only take about an hour, so don't be put off by this consideration. By public transport it will, of course, take longer and some sites may be too difficult to reach (see text).

If you have less time available, some examples of reduced itineraries are given below. These are all based on arrival in Damascus but are easy to adjust for those entering by land borders.

As nearly all flights into Damascus arrive in the late afternoon or evening, the first day will be the one after arrival.

> ► **10 Days - Tour 1**

This route omits the Euphrates valley, and makes the itinerary in a clockwise direction, as follows:

Days 1 & 2:
Two full days (3 nights) in Damascus, of which one half day could be spent visiting the Christian villages.
Day 3:
Travel via Homs (day 3) to the Krak des Chevaliers, spending the night in Tartous.
Day 4:
After a quick tour of Tartous if you didn't have time on day 3, continue to Latakia visiting the castles of Marqab and Saône on the way.

Days 5 & 6:

On day 5 make a brief visit to Ugarit before driving to Aleppo, stopping at Bara if you feel you have the time. Days 5 and 6 can be spent exploring Aleppo, with the afternoon of the 6th day reserved for visiting St Simeon.

Day 7:

Travel to Hama, where you will spend the night. This drive will take you no more than 90 minutes so you should have plenty of time to visit Apamea (2-3 hours) on the way and then tour Hama in the late afternoon. If not, you can do so the following morning.

Days 8 & 9:

Drive from Hama to Palmyra (via Homs). The journey to Palmyra should not take you more than 3 hours. You will have time that evening to visit Qala'at Ibn Maan (see text) and perhaps some of the ruins. Spend the night in Palmyra. Get up early on the 9th day so you will have enough time to complete your tour of the ruins before returning to Damascus late in the day. It's a 3 hour drive.

Day 10:

The last full day should be used to visit Bosra etc. Any extra time can be used for shopping.

▶ 10 Days - Tour 2

For those who would prefer to visit the stark splendours of the Euphrates valley, a 10-day itinerary missing out the coastal region could be as follows:

Days 1 & 2:

Spend one and a half days in Damascus. In the afternoon of day 2 travel to Palmyra (2-3 hours) arriving in time to visit Qala'at Ibn Maan in the late afternoon.

Day 3:

Visit the ruins of Palmyra. Spend a second night in Palmyra. (Alternatively, you could leave Palmyra late on day 3 and spend the night in Deir al-Zor. This would shorten the amount of driving the following day but would also shorten your time in Palmyra — see text in relevant chapter.)

Day 4:

This will be a long day. Start early and drive from Palmyra via Deir al-Zor to visit Doura Europos and Mari returning to Deir al-Zor for the night.

Day 5:

Drive north along the Euphrates to Aleppo, visiting the sites of Halebiye and Resafa and Lake Assad en route.

Days 6 & 7:

In Aleppo, using half of one of these days to visit St Simeon.

Day 8:

Drive to Hama, branching off to visit Apamea on the way (see Day 7, Tour 1 above).

Day 9:

On the 9th day, assuming you had time to explore Hama (if not do so before leaving, 3 hours will be plenty), drive via Homs to the Krak des Chevaliers (1 hour). Return to Damascus for the night (2½-3 hours).

Day 10:

Visit Bosra and the south.

► 7 Days

Day 1:

Spend the first full day visiting Damascus. Night in Damascus.

Day 2:

Drive to the Krak des Chevaliers, continuing to Hama where you can spend the night.

Days 3 & 4:

Tour Hama (if you didn't have time on day 2) and go on to Aleppo and spend the night there. Use the whole of day 4 visiting the city spending a second night there. (You may wish to use half of day 4 visiting St Simeon.)

Days 5 & 6:

Drive to Palmyra via Homs, and use the 6th day to sightsee, returning to Damascus in the evening.

Day 7:

Visit Bosra and the south.

► 5 Days

This is a very brief amount of time to spend in such an interesting country. However if this is all you have available I suggest as follows:

Day 1:

Spend the first full day in Damascus, following the Limited Time Tour on page 76.

Day 2:

Travel to the Krak des Chevaliers early in the morning. After visiting the castle, reverse your direction and drive, via Homs, to Palmyra. It's just over 200 kilometres and will take 3 hours at the most.

Day 3:

Explore Palmyra, returning to Damascus in the late afternoon.

Day 4:

Visit Bosra and the south. Night in Damascus.

Day 5:

Can be used to visit parts of Damascus you did not have time for at the beginning or the Christian villages, shopping etc.

There are also organised coach tours available from Damascus which squeeze in the main places in a matter of days.

General

♦ With all these itineraries you may find it more convenient to visit Bosra during the initial stay in Damascus.

♦ There are 5 places which every traveller should try to see: **Damascus, Palmyra, (Aleppo), Krak des Chevaliers, and Bosra.** I have put Aleppo in brackets only because of the distance from Damascus which may make it inconvenient for those with very limited time. (You can of course plan your own route with the help of a good road map.)

♦ A note on the plans in this book. These are for following the described walks and to help in locating the points of interest. They have not been drawn to scale, and are not intended as substitute for a city map which can be obtained from the Syrian consulate in your country before you leave or in Syria from the tourist offices listed in the Amenities chapter.

♦ **To get the most from this guide a pocket compass is essential and the guide has been written with this in mind.**

There are also organised coach tours available from Damascus which squeeze in the main places in a matter of days.

General

♦ With all these itineraries you may find it more convenient to visit Bosra during the initial stay in Damascus.

♦ There are 5 places which every traveller should try to see: **Damascus, Palmyra, (Aleppo), Krak des Chevaliers, and Bosra.** I have put Aleppo in brackets only because of the distance from Damascus which may make it inconvenient for those with very limited time. (You can of course plan your own route with the help of a good road map.)

♦ A note on the plans in this book. These are for following the described walks and to help in locating the points of interest. They have not been drawn to scale, and are not intended as substitute for a city map which can be obtained from the Syrian consulate in your country before you leave or in Syria from the tourist offices listed in the Amenities chapter.

♦ **To get the most from this guide a pocket compass is essential and the guide has been written with this in mind.**

5. DAMASCUS

"Damascus is a faire city and full of good merchandise... There is nowhere such another city of gardens and of fruit..."

The Book of John Mandeville, c1360

Introduction

William Biddulph, writing in the 17th century, recounts the legendary story that when the Prophet Muhammad looked down upon Damascus from Mount Qassioun for the first time, it seemed to him so glorious that he dared not enter it *"lest the pleasantness thereof should ravish him and move him there to settle an Earthly Paradise and hinder his desire of the Heavenly Paradise"* ("Purchase His Pilgrimes" 1625).

paradise lost?

Countless other words of praise extolling her beauty and pleasant aspect have before and since been showered upon this most ancient of cities, but it is doubtful whether today's visitor will experience the same sentiments. War, modern urban sprawl and neglect have all taken their toll.

Situated below the Anti-Lebanon, Damascus is dominated to the north by Jabal Qassioun, part of that range. Here lies the Ghouta, an elevated (730 metres) depression and oasis nourished by the River Barada which rises in those lofty heights. Damascus's position on the well-watered banks of the river ensured not only its prosperity but also its fabled fertility in which all manner of fruits grew in abundance.

extending boundaries

The walled Old City lies just to the south of the Barada while the Salihiye area, which was founded in Ayyubid times, is to the north on the lower slopes of Jabal Qassioun. The Midan quarter to the south of the old city, settled from the 13th and 14th C, was expanded by the Ottomans to cope with the flow of people on the *haj* to Mecca.

The newest districts lie to the northwest and northeast of the river, the directions of greatest modern development. In recent years haphazard residential areas have spread up the sides of Jabal Qassioun where the houses climb ever higher towards the summit. It is from up here that the best views of the city are to be had.

ten-fold population increase

With a population in excess of 2.5 million compared to 0.3 million in 1946, modern Damascus is a crowded metropolis. At the time of independence in 1946 Aleppo was the largest city in Syria and its chief manufacturing and trading centre. Today Damascus has replaced Aleppo in all these. Despite this rapid growth, however, Damascus manages to convey the impression of being compact. Indeed, as most of the main spots of interest are found in or near the Old City, one can easily get around on foot.

on the banks of the Golden River

The Barada river (in appearance hardly more than a stream) which flows through Damascus — and without which the city would never have been founded — was called Chrysorroas or Golden River by the Greeks. Damascus flourished around its gushing waters which irrigated gardens and orchards, creating a rich oasis on the edge of the desert which enchanted travellers, even as recently as the early 20th century:

" Lovely with almond-blossom and flooded water
With wind-flushed sheen of swaying orchard-meadows;
With azure starred of infrequent grape hyacinth
Meshed blue with the fig-groves' wintry haze;
Ruddy with budded apricot; snowy with apple -
Damascus now into April glory awakening."

Edward Thompson, "Damascus Orchards" 1930

afflicted by pollution

Sadly, as the population increased the Barada became nothing more than a sewer, while random buildings overran parks and supplanted groves of fruit trees. The political turmoil of the first years of independence served to compound the neglect. It took the strong-arm regime of Hafez al-Assad to arrest this decline, and by the early 1980s much cleaning up and renovating was under way. The part of the Barada that passes through the centre of the city is now covered over, and other efforts to eradicate the pollution have met with a fair measure of success. Much, however, remains to be tackled.

unspoiled on outskirts

The river flows down from the mountains almost parallel to

the old Beirut road. Along this road are many pleasantly sited restaurants and their delightful setting in the Barada valley is only 20 minutes or less from Damascus's busy centre. Before entering the city the river divides into two main channels, with the Tora going off to the north. This part of the river is still quite clean as it passes through the ever-shrinking orchard area on the city periphery.

As the river makes its way around the city walls the waters lap the old dwellings — in some instances running right under the front doors so footbridges are built to give access. It is this part of the watercourse that is the most polluted, which is doubly unfortunate as it could also be the most picturesque.

vibrant Old City

It is of course the Old City of Damascus which is the focal point of every visit. Unlike many ancient walled cities in the region, here you will find the crenellated ramparts almost intact along their entire circumference, pierced by eight gates through which to enter. Traffic is allowed inside the walls even though the streets are so narrow that overhanging balconies almost touch across the alleyways. Many vehicles squeeze down with only millimetres to spare!

Though most of the main sights are concentrated within these ramparts, the old city is not simply a tourist attraction. Almost half the area consists of dwellings, new and old; many of the older buildings have been renovated (but by no means all!) and some still have secluded, shady courtyards.

gold and silver and damask silks

Traditional handicrafts also continue to be made in the workshops of the old city: carpets, leatherwork, inlaid woodwork on trinket boxes and furniture, gold and silver filigree, and the varied Damascene brocades.

discovering the orchards

Despite the rapid urbanisation, Damascus is more than the hustle and bustle of the crowded, centre.

Although many of the orchards and gardens that made the city famous are now built upon, some still remain. If you have a car you should drive around the city suburbs to glimpse these vestiges of the poets' Damascus. It is unexpected to encounter groves of apricot, walnut, almond and quince growing in abundance so close to the noisy, traffic-infested heart of the city — and easy to understand how the flowing river and greenery presented an even more precious sight to travellers of an earlier era, who arrived suddenly upon Damascus, weary from a hot, thirsty journey through the vast and arid desert to the east.

apricot delicacy

Apricots in particular grow profusely in the Damascus region but the crop has shrunk in recent years due to urbanisation. J A Tower, in his book *"The Oasis of Damascus"* (1905), gives the output at 14,000 tons per year. The apricot has a very brief season and as all cannot be consumed fresh in so short a time, much of the harvest is dried. An even tastier delicacy than the excellent dried fruit sold in abundance in the city's souks are the crystallised or candied apricots — a speciality of Damascus and a treat not to be missed!

an old-new world

All over the city Damascus's past mingles with its present. This is especially so in the old city, the two blurring at times indiscernibly into one. And like most things in this part of the world tradition plays a very important role. If, therefore, more than a little imagination is required to identify the Bab Sharqi Street with the Street Called Straight of the Bible, then it is this extra imagination you will have to summon. Perhaps the sight of a donkey and Arab rider in flowing robes and headgear may help!

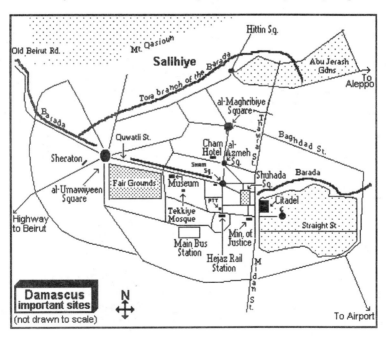

History

> *"Damascus ... the pride of Syria ... the oldest metropolis on earth, the only city in all the world that has kept its name and held its place and looked serenely on while the Kingdoms and Empires of four thousand years have risen to life, enjoyed their little season of pride and pomp, and then vanished..."* (from the last sentences of "The Innocents Abroad" by Mark Twain, 1867)

In a region where a few cities claim the title of the world's oldest city, Damascus's credentials are formidable.

Josephus attributes Damascus to Uz, the grandson of Noah, from whose father, Aram, the Arameans are descended.

Archaeological excavations have shown that a settlement existed at Tell al-Salihiye in the fourth millennium BC, and pottery from the third was unearthed in the old city. In the Ghouta a system of irrigation canals was dug prior to the second millennium and this was expanded by successive rulers.

Abraham's heir

Perhaps the first record of Damascus as an established city comes from the Bible. Genesis Chapter 14 relates that when Abraham's nephew Lot was kidnapped, Abraham chased the kidnappers "as far as Hobah, that is north of Damascus" (v.15); and in Chapter 15:2 we are told that Abraham's heir (prior to the birth of Isaac) was Eliezer of Damascus.

Whether or not that account pre-dates the first historical written record of the city, which comes from the tablets discovered at Tell al-Amarna in Egypt, is a matter for conjecture. In this record *Dimashqa* is mentioned as being among lands conquered in the 15th C BC by Tuthmosis III.

biblical wars

By the end of the second millennium the Arameans had made Damascus the capital of a prosperous and powerful kingdom. The clashes between this kingdom and ancient Israel fill pages of the Old Testament.

Invaded by the Assyrian Shalmaneser III in the mid 9th C BC, the king, Ben-Hadad I, was able to prevent the capture of the city with the help of other local rulers. The city eventually fell to the Assyrians under Tiglath-Pilesner in 732 BC thus ending centuries of Aramean rule.

The Assyrians were themselves defeated by the Babylonian King Nebuchadnezzar in 572 BC, who conquered all of Syria and

Palestine. His control did not last long and in 539 BC the whole region fell to the Achaemenian Persians under Cyrus.

Alexander takes Damascus

After the Persian defeat by Alexander at the Battle of Issus in 332 BC Damascus was taken by one of his generals, Parmenion. After the death of Alexander and the division of the empire, Damascus became a point of contention between the Seleucids and the Ptolomies with control fluctuating between the two. In this period parts of the city took on a Hellenised character, existing side by side with the old Aramean quarters.

conquerors from Petra

As the power of the Seleucids declined, peripheral nations began to seize the advantages that lay open. Among them, the Nabateans from their capital at Petra were making advances northward. In 85 BC the Nabatean King Harithath III became master of Damascus, and the city remained under Nabatean control until all of Syria became Roman in 64 BC. So began 700 years of Roman and Byzantine rule in Damascus.

Paul in Damascus

Pompey allowed the Nabateans to keep some degree of control over the city in return for an annual tribute. This lasted until 54 AD. It was during this period that the New Testament saga of Paul as related in Acts Chapter 9 took place.

The Roman and Aramean influences continued to live side by side. The temple to the Semitic god, Hadad, (who was adopted by the Romans as Jupiter) was redeveloped in lavish style and likewise the Romans enhanced the entire city with their architecture. A forum was constructed, and the city walls were furnished with great columned gates dedicated to Mars, Venus, Mercury etc. The streets were lined with columns, and although these are long gone, there are some recently discovered remains on the Street Called Straight. The citadel is a predominantly Arab structure, but it rests upon foundations built by the Romans.

era of prosperity

Damascus was prosperous. The great caravan route from the Far East which passed through Palmyra traversed Damascus on its way to the coast. Similarly, the caravans which journeyed up from Arabia via Arabia Felix (Yemen) stopped to rest in this city of plentiful water.

In 117 the Emperor Hadrian, while on a visit, gave Damascus the title of metropolis and in 222 it was raised to the status of colonia by Severus. But with the demise of Palmyra during the latter part of the third century and the rise of the Sasanians in Persia, the fortunes of Damascus took a downward turn.

FABLES AND LEGENDS ABOUT DAMASCUS

There are numerous Muslim legends surrounding the area of Damascus. Most are not orthodox tradition, but they are still frequently encountered:

Garden of Eden: The fruitfulness of the land on the edge of the wilderness and the splitting of the Barada into two rivers has caused speculation for centuries (even among serious researchers) that Damascus was the site of Eden.

Tomb of Abel: Near Souk Wadi Barada, about 25 kms west of the city in the Barada valley, is a place the Romans called Abila (Abel?). Muslim stories about this place say it was where Qabil (Cain) slew Habil (Abel) (Genesis chap 9). The rock is red here and this is supposedly the staining by Abel's blood. The medieval traveller Ibn Jubayr in 1184 records visiting "the cave of blood" on the site:

"... above it on the mountain is the blood of Habil who was killed by his brother Qabil...The blood reaches from about halfway up the mountain, and god has preserved red traces of it on stones...".

Birthplace of Abraham: Ibn Jubayr writes, *"The birthplace of Abraham...our venerated Prophet - is on the slopes of Mount Qassioun near a village called Burzeh..."* A mosque built over a cave marks Abraham's house. Biblical and historical sources put his birthplace to be in Mesopotamia.

Jesus and his mother: Another legend which is based upon the Koran. Again Ibn Jubayr:

"Damascus was honoured when God Most High gave asylum there to the Messiah and his mother...on a hill having meadows and springs". (Koran 23:50)

Moses: In the village of Kadem, south of the Midan quarter is the Mosque of al-Qaddam, the Mosque of the Footprints. Here, according to Ibn Batutta, an Arab traveller who arrived in Damascus in 1348, are preserved the footprints of Moses.

earliest Christians

Christianity began in Damascus almost from the foundation of the faith, as attested by the book of Acts. It can thus be assumed that when Constantine issued his edict in 313 making Christianity the Empire's official religion, it was already well established in the city.

In 379 Emperor Theodosius ordered the destruction of the Temple of Jupiter and the erection instead of the Cathedral of John the Baptist, in which his head was to be interred.

Because of its location close to the desert, the Byzantines used Damascus as a base to keep watch for the ever-present danger from the Sasanian Persians. The Persian threat seemed to be removed when in 532 Justinian made peace with them. But it did not last and in 612 Chosroes II took Damascus which he occupied until it was regained by the Emperor Heraclius in 628.

In the meantime events were taking place in Arabia which were to shape the face of the region and bestow on Damascus her most glorious years.

the triumph of Islam

Damascus was captured by the invading Islamic forces in September of 635 but Heraclius, with a relieving army, forced the conquerors to withdraw. But not for long!

On 20th August 636 the fate of Syria and Damascus was sealed. In the battle of the Yarmouk the Byzantines were totally routed by the Arabs, and shortly after the victors entered Damascus, apparently to the acclaim of the populace. Apart from the short period of the French Mandate, Damascus has been under Muslim rule ever since.

Umar, the Caliph, appointed Yazid as governor of Damascus, and on his death in 640 his brother Mu'awiya took the title. In 661, after the murder of Ali (the 4th Caliph), Mu'awiya ascended to the Caliphate, quickly making Damascus his capital. For nearly 100 years Damascus was not only the seat of this, the powerful Omayyad Caliphate, but was also the political and cultural centre of the expanding Islamic world.

construction of the Great Mosque

The Omayyad Caliphate became an hereditary affair, and several caliphs later Walid I succeeded to this position. In 708 Walid, aspiring to build the greatest mosque of all Islam, expropriated the Cathedral of St John the Baptist and erected in its stead Damascus's most splendid and impressive building, the Great Omayyad Mosque, acclaimed as the most opulent ever constructed.

In 750 the Abbasids from Mesopotamia destroyed the Omayyad Caliphate and the centre of power was moved to Baghdad. Damascus was greatly reduced in importance; local rulers came and went. From the mid 9th C it was in the hands of the rulers from Egypt. Then Seljuk Turks took the city in 1076 and it remained under their control until the middle of the 12th C.

failures for Crusaders

In the first years of the 12th C the Crusaders twice attacked Damascus but were unable to take it. A more determined effort was made in 1148 when Conrad, the German king invaded the city. However, he too proved unsuccessful, and Damascus never succumbed to the Europeans.

successes for Salah al-Din

Nur al-Din captured Damascus from its Turkoman rulers in

1154 and under him and his successor, the celebrated Salah al-Din, Damascus entered an illustrious era in which many fine monuments were built. Ibn Jubayr, writing about his visit there in 1184, records the large number of colleges, hospitals and caravanserais that were in the city. He recounts that Damascus was populous and wealthy, and enjoined young men seeking prosperity to move there.

Mongols -v- Mamelukes

All this came to an abrupt end. In 1260 the Mongols under Hulagu invaded Syria and put an end to Salah al-Din's Ayyubid dynasty. This invasion (which threatened the whole Middle East) was quickly checked the same year by the Mamelukes, the ruling dynasty in Egypt. At the battle of Ein Jalut (Goliath's Spring) in north Palestine, the Mameluke Sultan Baibars defeated Hulagu and the Mongol menace receded temporarily.

Under the Mamelukes Damascus entered another splendid era, particularly during the Sultanate of Baibars (to 1277). Many of the city's grandest buildings were constructed during this time, and the city reached out beyond the walls.

In 1280 the Mongol hordes struck again. They were met by the then Mameluke Sultan Qalaun (sultan until 1290), who defeated them before they reached Damascus. Another invasion by the Mongols in 1300 resulted in Damascus being occupied with parts of the city destroyed. Mameluke rule of the city returned in 1303 with the defeat of the Mongols outside Damascus.

Tamerlane's reign of terror

The invasion in 1400 by Timur (Tamerlane) wreaked the harshest devastation of all on a people by now accustomed to chaos: the city was looted and burned and the best of its craftsmen were taken as captives to Samarkand, Timur's capital. Only his death in 1404 and the subsequent bickering of his generals prevented a disaster of monumental proportions. The Mameluke sultans who followed were unable to restore Damascus to its former standing, though Qait Bey, sultan from 1468 to 1495, did succeed in rekindling a measure of prosperity.

within the Ottoman Empire

In 1516 the Ottoman sultan, Selim l, captured Damascus and for the next 400 years the city was to be part of the Ottoman Empire.

Selim divided Syria into three *vilayets* (provinces) with Turkish pashas (governors). Damascus was the capital of one province and a certain al-Ghazali was its first pasha. He, however, was an ambitious man and of doubtful loyalty to the

Sultan. When Selim died in 1520, al-Ghazali declared Damascus independent of Ottoman rule and himself ruler. Selim's successor, his son Suleiman, who is known in history as the Magnificent, sent an army against al-Ghazali and in January 1521 destroyed his forces and killed him. As a punishment to the inhabitants for supporting al-Ghazali (if they did), Suleiman reduced a third of the city to ruins. In spite of this, Suleiman is remembered in Damascus by the lovely Tekkiye Mosque, which was built in his honour in 1555.

the dutiful pashas

During Ottoman times the fortunes of Damascus varied according to the control the sultans were able to exercise in the large empire. The governors also had a profound effect on the well-being of the city. Men such as Dawish Pasha, Murad Pasha and especially Assad Pasha al-Azem were able to do much for the city and its population. However, because of its commercial importance, Damascus was gradually eclipsed by Aleppo as Syria's principal city.

Damascus's main claim to status at that time was its location as the last major city on the route between Turkey and Mecca, and as such was a gathering place for those performing the *haj*, the obligatory pilgrimage to the holiest shrine of Islam.

role of the Executioner

In 1780 Ahmad Pasha al-Jazzar, the ruthless Pasha of Acre, became Governor of Damascus. He governed as a virtual viceroy and his despotic rule earned him the title of "the Executioner".

Meanwhile, in 1805 in Egypt, the Pasha Muhammad Ali had established himself as ruler defying the Sultan's authority. In 1831 he invaded Syria, and his son Ibrahim Pasha took Damascus in 1832. His jurisdiction lasted only until 1840 but during that time some improvements were made to the city which had been stagnating for some time.

massacre of Christians

In the middle of the 19th C trouble between Druse and Christians in Lebanon spread to Damascus and in 1860 three days of strife resulted in the massacre of thousands of Christians, and severe damage to the Christian quarter.

into the 20th century

By the time the 20th century dawned Damascus had a population of 150,000, increasing steadily. In 1908 the Hejaz railway which linked Damascus with Mecca was opened. In the First World War Damascus became the headquarters of the Turkish and German forces in the Middle East, and as such was an important goal for the Arab forces under T.E. Lawrence.

the French replace the Ottomans

On 1st October 1918 the city was entered by troops under General Allenby which included Arab soldiers commanded by Faisal, son of Hussein. Four hundred years of Turkish domination had come to a close, but Damascus was yet to be free.

Before the French, who were given the UN Mandate over Syria, finally withdrew in 1946 they were to bomb Damascus twice. The French withdrew from Damascus in the spring of 1946, and it became the capital of the Syrian Republic.

Visiting the city

Two full days are the minimum required to see Damascus, three would be better. You will also need half a day to visit villages in the Anti-Lebanon range (a full day if you want to visit a few) and another full day to visit the south of the country (Bosra, etc). All-told, therefore, you will ideally require a 5 night stay in the city. (The visit to Bosra and the south could be saved until the end of your tour of the country.) The lengthy stay makes it important to find as comfortable a hotel as your budget allows and, if you have a car, you should ensure that the hotel has parking either attached or nearby.

The walks I have described, while not exhaustive, will enable you to see the most important of Damascus's many sites. You can do them either as described, shorten them or join them together. It all depends on the time available and your staying power in a very busy and crowded part of the city.

limited time tour

For those who cannot spend more than one day in Damascus I have given at the end of the walks a **limited time tour** which picks out the essentials from the routes described. The three marginal asterisks (***) on some walks are reference marks for this quick tour and are explained below.

NOTE

On the sketch plans of the walks, the street route to follow is traced with a thick line.

► Walk No 1

START: **Entrance to Souk Hamidiye** MAIN FEATURES: **Souk Hamidiye — Nur al-Din Hospital and Museum — Madrasas Zahiriye and Adiliye — Tomb of Salah al-Din**
TIME: **1½-2 hours**

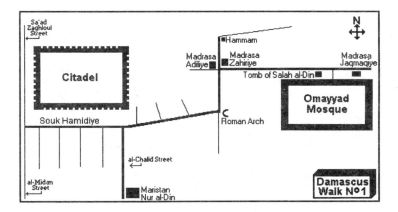

This first tour introduces you to the old city of Damascus and visits the important buildings in the north west area of the city. It should be followed immediately by Walk No 2 to the Omayyad Mosque.

Most visitors first enter the old city through Souk Hamidiye, situated at the junction of Nasser and Sa'ad Zaghloul streets just south of the Barada.

busy bazaar

This corrugated-roofed street looks very dreary from the outside. The usually harsh Damascus sunlight is in sharp contrast to the lamp-lit interior of the covered souk. Once inside, however, the bright lights of the shops and adjustment of the eyes soon dispel the gloom — and it is often a relief to dodge in there out of the sun.

Built in the last years of the 19th C on the site of an existing market, the then governor, Rashid Nasha Pasha constructed the street in honour of the Ottoman Sultan Abdel Hamid II. This broad, formerly elegant, cobbled street is lined with shops which today sell everything from mundane household goods to damascened brocades, inlaid wooden articles, carpets and kilim and all manner of handicrafts. Here is where you are most likely to be mildly accosted by shopkeepers anxious to relieve the tourist of his dollars. The street is almost straight, c500 metres long and, as we shall see later, leads to the Great Omayyad Mosque.

forerunners of modern medicine

Walk down the souk and turn right at the 5th street, the point just where there is a break in the roof. About 70 metres on the left is a gateway with a white arch. This is the **Maristan (Hospital) Nur al-Din**. This institution, opened in 1154, was a medical school as well as a hospital. Hospitals existed in most great Arab cities and were open to all regardless of financial ability (first National Health Service?). As strange as it may seem today, the Arabs, and others who lived in Arab lands (principally Jews) were the most advanced surgeons and physicians in the world. They had made discoveries in the use of drugs, herbs and chemicals for medication that were unheard of in Europe, and many an Arab and Jewish doctor attended the courts of Europe. Only when Arabic texts began to be translated into Latin did Europeans begin to progress in medical (and other scientific) knowledge. The hospital was in use as a medical centre until the 19th C.

Since 1978 it has housed the **Arab Science and Medical Museum**. The courtyard is particularly fine, with iwans at each end that were used for study. Whether or not you find the exhibits interesting is a matter of taste. The room on the right as you enter is the Salle de Science. The display here includes Arab astronomical instruments and Turkish weights — *okes, ratls,* and *dirams* — still in use not so long ago. (I encountered them in Cyprus as late as 1985).

cure for toothache?

The Salle de Medecin across the courtyard has some frightening surgical and dentistry tools from the middle ages. There are also inhalation jars — the Arabs were the first to use alcohol in conjunction with belladonna as an anaesthetic.

Back in the Souk Hamidiye continue until you come to the Roman arch (described in Walk No 2) at the end. Turn left into Bab al-Barid street, quite a picturesque alleyway. After c100 metres, over a cross street, you come to **Madrasa Zahiriye** on the right, and facing it **Madrasa Adiliye**, both with fine entrances.

tomb of the Mameluke Baibars

Madrasa Zahiriye also houses the **Mausoleum of Baibars**, and here the most renowned of the Mameluke sultans is interred. It was built in 1277 by the Sultan's son. Previously the building was the rather modest home of Ayyub, Salah al-Din's father and founder of the dynasty which bears his name. Note the monumental entrance, in black and yellow stone with insets of marble. The room where the tomb lies has marble panelling and is topped by a dome and at the time of writing was undergoing renovation. Today the madrasa is part of the National Library. The Madrasa Adiliye, opposite, is where Salah al-Din's brother, al-Adil Saif al-Din, who died in 1218, is buried. He had been Sultan of Egypt, and to protect Damascus from the Crusaders reconstructed the citadel in 1217.

The building was begun by Nur al-Din in 1171, but was only completed in 1222 by al-Adil's son. The entrance is an example of Ayyubid architecture. The domed tomb chamber, on the left of the entrance, and the tomb itself are quite austere. Like the tomb of Baibars in the madrasa opposite, this chamber is currently being restored. The madrasa is today the library of the Arab Academy.

restored baths

Just past the Madrasa Zahiriye are some excellent baths, the **Hammam al-Malik al-Zaher**. These date from the 11th or 12th C. The bath rooms are in their original style, but they have been completely restored and modernised.

modest tomb for the great Saladin

Return now to the crossroad at the edge of the Madrasa Zahiriye, turn left and continue past the northeast corner of the Omayyad Mosque. Not too far along you will see on your right a courtyard full of trees and a central fountain. This is the **Tomb of Salah al-Din.**

The small building with the red cupola which houses the tomb is at the end of the courtyard, often partially obscured by the foliage on the trees. It is not perhaps the palatial tomb one might expect for the greatest warrior the Arabs have ever produced, but nonetheless may be more in keeping with what Salah al-Din himself would have desired. In his lifetime never seeking after material possessions, he died without any personal wealth.

gift from the Kaiser

Salah al-Din died in 1193, and was first interred in the Citadel. His remains were transferred here in 1196. Over the years the tomb became very neglected and during a visit to Damascus in 1898 the German Kaiser, Wilhelm ll, donated a new cenotaph. The old wooden one still lies alongside, with funerary turbans wound around the head of each.

"We are back, Saladin"

An oft-repeated tale from Damascus's modern history relates how the French General Gouraud, on entering Damascus in 1920 to take up the French Mandate, is reputed to have gone straight to

Salah al-Din's tomb and gloated, "Nous sommes revenu, Saladin".

A short way past Salah al-Din's tomb, on the right is the **Madrasa Jaqmaqiye**, dating from 1418. It is now the Museum of Epigraphy.

The present tourist entrance to the Omayyad Mosque is between Salah al-Din's tomb and the Madrasa Jaqmaqiye, but it's worthwhile back-tracking a little in order to get a proper perspective of the Great Mosque. Therefore return to where you turned off at the end of the Souk Hamidiye, by the Roman columns. However, if time is important or if you want to cut your walking to a minimum, by all means start the next walk by entering the mosque directly.

> ▸ **Walk No 2 —**
> **The Omayyad Mosque**

START: **End of Souk Hamidiye**   MAIN FEATURES: **Remnants of Temple of Jupiter (Roman arch etc) — Omayyad Mosque** TIME: **1-1½ hours**

History

The Omayyad Mosque of Damascus is considered to be the fourth holiest shrine in Islam.

At least three houses of worship have stood on the site of this Great Mosque.

We know that the Arameans had a temple to the Semitic god Hadad here. The Romans identified Hadad as the god Jupiter and expanded the temple, Emperor Septimius Severus redeveloping it in the late 1st century AD.

When Christianity became the official religion of the Roman Empire, the Emperor Theodosius I, in 375, rebuilt the temple, naming it the Cathedral of St John the Baptist. The head of the Precursor was, supposedly, buried in the crypt of the building.

After the capture of Damascus by the Muslim Arabs in 635 the cathedral continued to exist as a place of Christian worship under the tolerant Caliph, Umar. Part of the compound was used by the Muslims but this did not cause friction between the two faiths. In 708 the less open-minded Caliph al-Walid decided to build a magnificent mosque instead of the church. Most of the Cathedral was destroyed but much material was recycled into the mosque building which also retained the basilica design.

Islam's most beautiful building

Construction lasted over 7 years, and when it was finished it was the most magnificent building in all Islam. Covered in the choicest mosaics, marble, marquetry, gold and other decoration, visitors marvelled at its beauty. The medieval Arab traveller, Ibn Jubayr writes in his journal of 1184, *"For beauty and perfection of construction, marvellous and sumptuous embellishments and decoration, it is one of the most celebrated mosques of the world"*. His description of the mosque covers almost 8 pages!

The building was damaged by the rampaging Mongols under Hulagu in 1260 and again in 1400 by Timur (Tamerlane). But an even worse catastrophe struck the building in 1893 when it was almost entirely consumed by fire. The subsequent reconstruction by the Ottomans did not restore the glory of the past, but the mosque is still an outstanding structure.

Visit

The Great Omayyad Mosque is open every day between 9am and 5pm. Tourists are not allowed in during Friday prayers, 12.30pm-2.00pm

temple remnants

The Souk Hamidiye ends with the **triumphal arch** of the **Roman Temple of Jupiter**. The temple had an interior court (approximating the area of the mosque today) where the sanctuary and other religious offices were located, and an outer court which was surrounded by a portico under which were bazaars. The whole was enclosed by an outer wall, and the triumphal arch (or propyleum) was the western entrance to the temple through this wall.

Passing through the arch you are now facing the western wall of the mosque, which in ancient times was also the west wall of the Roman inner court. In the centre of the wall is the main entrance gate to the mosque, the **Bab al-Barid**, the Western Gate. Between the arch and the mosque walls an open square is under construction.

tourists' entrance

Tourists are not allowed to enter by the main gate. Until recently the tourist entrance was c50 metres to the north (left), through a special door. However, this is not presently in use due to works inside the mosque. (In future this will possibly revert to being the visitors' entrance.) In the meantime the entrance is through the **Bab al-Amara** on the north side. To get there, walk to the north west corner of the walls and turn right. The entrance is c150 metres along, past the tomb of Salah al-Din (if you just completed the first walk you will know where to go.) Turn right

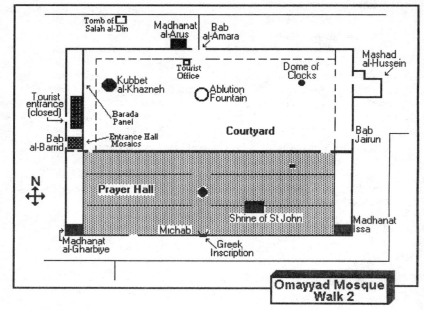

Omayyad Mosque Walk 2

when you reach the entrance (signed) and the approach is past some Byzantine columns. Just inside the gate on the right is the booth where tourists pay a small entrance fee and women are provided with a black hooded coverall.

vast courtyard

Before you is the immense courtyard and the prayer hall. The splendour of centuries past may have gone, but there is still a dignified magnificence to the place, and much of this has to do with the size. Measuring 50 by 120 metres, the dazzling white marble paving increases the initial impact of first sight. On three sides the court is arcaded at ground level with smaller arcading on the upper level. At the present time these arcades are undergoing renovation, section by section.

the mosque's treasury

Moving to the west side (on your right as you enter) you will see a small structure resting on 8 columns, all recycled from ancient times. Perhaps the loveliest part of the complex, this little domed building dates from the Abbasid era. The beautiful mosaics covering the sides date from the 13th or 14th C, replacing the originals. This building is the **Treasury** (Kubbet al-Khazneh), where the mosque's funds were kept, and is almost identical to the one in the Omayyad Mosque of Hama (see that chapter).

mosaics of paradise

On the arcade wall behind the treasury are the mosaics known as **the Barada panel**, depicting scenes along the river. These are Omayyad and Mameluke (13th C) and were uncovered in the late 1920s. They were restored about 30 years ago. A particularly good view of the mosque is obtained by standing under the colonnade here and looking through the treasury pillars towards the centre of the prayer hall.

In the entrance hall of the Bab al-Barid, the west or main gate, are some remnants of the mosque's original building. The roof dates from the 15th C. The mosaics, restored in the 1960s, are representative of the mosque's original grandeur. Executed by Byzantine craftsmen, they convey a world of luscious groves, bubbling streams and fancifully located palaces all pointing to visions of Paradise — some say of Damascus!

In the centre of the courtyard is an ablution fountain, built in quite modern times, and to the east a small 18th C domed structure with Byzantine columns, once used to house the mosque's clocks.

On the east side is a doorway leading to an important Shi'ite shrine and place of pilgrimage. There are a number of Shi'ite shrines in Damascus, and if you see lots of Iranians around, the women dressed in the black *choudah,* the shrines are the reason.

revered head of Ali's son

This shrine, **Mashad al-Hussein**, is associated with the martyrdom of Hussein, one of Ali's sons who was killed in Kerbala. According to legend his head was brought to Damascus. Inside the chamber is a silver-covered niche where his head was put on public display. The Shi'ite faithful queue to kiss all sides of this niche.

weeping women

Off the chamber is a small prayer room where black-clad women sit on the floor, facing the mirhab, weeping and wailing at the fate that befell Hussein. It is all quite strange with the atmosphere more in keeping with the mourning of a recently departed close relative. A cenotaph (of Hussein's son) by the prayer room entrance is also the object of veneration. No historical evidence exists for this story.

Further down the east side, near the prayer hall, is **Bab Jairun**, the eastern entrance to the mosque.

The Omayyad Mosque has three minarets. The one to the south of the main (west) entrance is the **Madhanat al-Gharbiye**, the Western Tower. It was built in 1488, in keeping with the Egyptian style, by the Mameluke Sultan Qait Bey.

minaret of Jesus' return

The tower in the south east corner, the tallest, is the **Madhanat Issa**, the Tower of Jesus. According to Muslim tradition Jesus will descend to earth via this tower to fight the Antichrist before the Day of Judgment. There was an earlier tower on this spot built by the Omayyads, but this one dates from 1247, with the upper part being Ottoman. The third tower by the north gate is **Madhanat al-Arus**, the Tower of the Bride, and dates from late Omayyad times with the upper part from the 12th C.

If you stand near the fountain in the centre of the courtyard facing the prayer hall you'll notice some superb mosaic work in the centre of the building. This is the façade of the central transept. This work, like most of the mosque's mosaics, was most likely executed by Byzantine craftsmen and was restored in the 1960s. There are entrances to the prayer hall at each end of the courtyard.

plaster and paint replace the gold

As noted in the history of the mosque, the prayer hall was consumed by fire in 1893, and although rebuilt along the original plan much of the decoration is modern and does not approach the former splendour. Ibn Jubayr, writing in 1184, notes how the walls were inlaid with gold mosaics and that the mirhab, the most wonderful in Islam, gleamed with gold. Nothing like this is to be seen today.

The hall is basically a three-aisle basilica with the aisles broken by the **central transept**. In the centre of this transept is a dome. Ibn Jubayr called this dome the mosque's "most impressive thing". The dome today is of Turkish design.

another revered head

To the east of the transept is the **shrine to John the Baptist**. Many Christians may find it odd seeing Muslims venerating this spot. In the Koran, Jesus is the number two prophet, and Yahir ben Zakharia, John son of Zacharia, as His herald, is likewise a prophet.

Further east on the courtyard side of the hall are two large, stone jar-like structures. This was originally the cathedral's infant **baptismal font** and was at one time used in the mosque for ceremonial washing purposes.

leaving the mosque

You may exit the mosque by any gate unless, if a woman, you have a black coverall which will have to be returned at the north gate, where you came in.

At the time of writing the south wall of the mosque is being extensively renovated. The door just along from the south west corner is the **Bab al-Ziadeh** and goes straight into the prayer hall. Halfway along, just past the façade of the transept, is the outline of a doorway. This was an entrance to the Cathedral of St John. Above it is a Greek inscription which reads: *"Thy Kingdom O Christ, is an everlasting Kingdom; and Thy dominion is from generation to generation."* (An adaption of Psalm 145.)

Continue to the east side, where just as you turn the corner is a Roman gate. This was part of the **monumental entrance** to the Temple of Jupiter from the east. Down the steps on your right is a pleasant spot to have a rest and some tea. Walk back to the south west corner of the mosque for the start of the next route.

▸ Walk No 3

START: **SW corner of Great Mosque** MAIN FEATURES: **This walk takes you to some of the khans of the old city, the Azem Palace museum and other points of interest along the way.** TIME: **1½-2 hours**

Damascus's old city is full of khans. These were the city's hotels or inns for travelling merchants. Generally comprising a courtyard surrounded by rooms on two floors, the merchants could bring their goods here, store them safely and enjoy lodgings while they conducted their business. Some khans were large, lavish affairs while others were small and simple. Often called caravanserais, there is a slight difference: a khan is the term for a hostelry inside a town and a caravanserai was either along an open route or just outside town.

pass through the gold market

A few metres east of the Omayyad Mosque's southwest corner turn right (S) into Souk Assagha. There are many gold shops along this street.

About 80 metres along on the left is the **Khan al-Safarjalani**, dating from the mid 18th C. A passageway leads to a courtyard 15m long and 5m wide, and covered by three partially open domes. Further along on the right is the slightly larger **Khan al-Tutan**. This dates from the 18th C and also has three domes, the two outer ones open and the central one partly closed. Used nowadays largely as a storeroom for spice merchants, the aromas fill the air of the khan. Unlike most khans, neither of these two have verandas and are simple affairs.

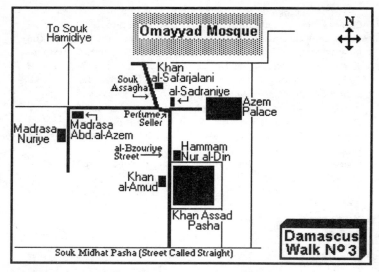

To Souk
Hamidiye

Omayyad Mosque

N

Khan
Souk al-Safarjalani
Assagha al-Sadraniye
Azem
Palace

Perfume
Seller

Madrasa Madrasa
Nuriye Abd. al-Azem

al-Bzouriye
Street

Hammam
Nur al-Din

Khan
al-Amud

Khan Assad
Pasha

Damascus
Walk Nº 3

Souk Midhat Pasha (Street Called Straight)

all the perfumes of Arabia — and of Paris, too!

At the top of the souk turn left into Osman Aidi St. A few
metres along, on the corner of the street going right, al-Bzouriye
St, is a perfume seller who will make up any of the well-known
fragrances for an extremely modest sum. You will see a large
number of these perfume vendors in Damascus's souks, but this
particular gentleman is always the busiest; I have found his
products for both men and women amazingly authentic, and
surprisingly long lasting!

On the left facing the end of Souk al-Bzouriye is the mid
18th C **Khan al-Sadraniye**. You enter through a 15 metre long
domed passageway leading into the courtyard.

the Azem family mansions

Exiting from the passage turn left into a small square. Facing
you is one of the most splendid Ottoman mansions in Damascus,
perhaps in Syria, the Dar al-Azem, **Azem Palace**, built in 1750 by
the Ottoman governor of Damascus, Assad Pasha Azem, from
1743 to 1757. Previously governor of Hama, he had earlier
erected there another exquisite (but smaller) dwelling (see chapter
on Hama). This wonderful residence remained in the Azem
family until the 1950s when it was purchased by the Syrian
Government and turned into a museum.

After buying your entry ticket, follow the red arrows which
guide you round. Turn left through an archway into a leafy
courtyard with chequered tile flooring. From there you enter the
main courtyard, the *haremlek*, which is flanked by the palace
rooms, all with beautifully decorated façades.

how the rich lived

These rooms are the museum exhibit rooms which aim to depict the life of the wealthy in Ottoman times. Following the red arrows the first room is a schoolroom elegantly panelled in wood. The arched portico on the north side, in front of the music and reception rooms, has three pretty inlaid marble fountains. Also along the north side is the marriage room which has an indoor fountain of inlaid marble. Note the particularly detailed lacquered decoration on the ceiling. Along the eastern side is a room that bears the title of "mother-in-law's room". Maybe not so grand as the bridal chamber, but not too bad for a mother-in-law!

On the south side is a huge diwan, and next to that the most ornate part of the palace containing the large reception hall.

To the right of the ticket office is the *selamlek*, the private quarters of the palace. This area was badly gutted in a 1925 fire, but has been restored.

Return to the fragrance seller on the corner of Osman Aidi St and Souk al-Bzouriye and turn left up the latter. This souk is full of nut, spice and sweet vendors.

hot baths — but for men only

About 40m along on the left side are the **Hammam Nur al-Din**. These baths built in the latter half of the 12th C are the oldest in the city. Over the centuries they have been restored many times and they continue to provide a real Arab (or Turkish) bath in authentic surroundings. Full treatment, including scrub, massage, coffee and narghile (hubble-bubble pipe) costs around $5.00, but a bath only is less than $2.00. They only cater to men and are open 8am to midnight; recommended, if it's your sort of thing. Even if you don't want a bath it's worthwhile to visit them.

grandest of all the khans

Another c50m and on the left is the **Khan Assad Pasha**. At the time of writing this huge khan, the largest in Damascus, was being completely renovated for use as some tourist project. Built by the same governor who constructed the Dar al-Azem, the khan dates from the mid 18th C and is exceptionally large for an in-town khan. The central dome, which collapsed, has now been rebuilt. There are eight other domes surrounding the main one which has a fountain beneath it. The original khan must have been a marvellous structure, spacious and beautiful with its walls of charcoal and white stone. The khan facing the Khan Assad Pasha is of no special interest.

***

tempting handicrafts

Return again to the perfume seller, turn left and walk down

Osman Aidi St and c100 metres along on the left, almost on the corner of Nur al-Din al-Chahid St, is the **Madrasa Abdullah al-Azem Pasha** built by another Azem Governor of Damascus in 1779. This building is no longer a madrasa but is a fine antique and handicrafts bazaar.

Step inside just to browse around, no one will pounce on you! However, if you are in buying mood and can bargain you should be able to find what you want at a fair price. The ground level courtyard is tastefully laid out with oriental carpets, kilim, copper and brassware. More carpets are draped all around from the veranda balustrade.

silk worms and an ancient loom

In a tiny room in one corner of the courtyard a weaver works on a 150 year-old punch-card loom making damask brocade, a basket of silk worms to hand.

From the balcony, some very rickety wooden stairs lead onto the roof where you get an excellent view across the domes of the souks to the Omayyad Mosque.

Nur al-Din's tomb

From here turn left into Nur al-Din al-Chahid St. Just down on the right is the **Madrasa Nuriye**, which houses the tomb of Nur al-Din. Of the original structure only the part fronting on the street survives and it is here where the tomb of the leader rests. You can peep into the tomb room from the grilled window behind the drinking fountain to the left of the entrance (in the souk alleyway).

To return to Souk Hamidiye turn right outside the madrasa and crossing over the cross street, keep straight all the way until you reach the Roman arch by the Omayyad Mosque.

> **Walk No 4**

START: **The Citadel**   MAIN FEATURES: **This route takes you past the citadel and along the city's north wall, to its north gates and along some of the picturesque residential streets, finishing at the Bab Tuma in the Christian quarter.**   TIME: **1½-2 hours**

The **citadel** stands between Souk Hamidiye and the Barada river. In front of its crenellated walls, on Sa'ad Zaghoul St, is a recent statue of a victorious Salah al-Din mounted on horseback with the

Carlton

Damascus

فنـدق كارلتـــون دمشـق

Syria - Damascus - Mezzeh - P.O. Box 35005-35006
Tel: 2122000/1/2/3/4/5/6 - Fax: 2122007 - Tlx: 413457 CABLE CARLTN

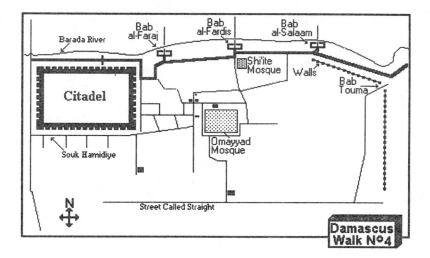

leaders of his vanquished nations at his feet.

At the present time the citadel is being completely renovated and excavated and is closed to the public. The site dates back to Roman times when the area was a castrum, (barracks). In its present form it dates from the Ayyubid and Mameluke periods, and all the successive rulers have made use of it. Until 1985 it was a prison.

Turn right (E) at the citadel's corner. It is here the Barada emerges from underground, having been covered over west of Port Said Street to try to prevent it being used as a sewer.

ironmongers' market

Walk along the lane between the citadel's northern wall and the river, through an arch, until you reach the end of the north wall. At the corner turn right, then almost immediately left and left again. You are now in a covered souk with chandeliers hanging from the roof! This is a street of ironmongers and blacksmiths, and the noise of their hammering can be quite deafening. Near the beginning you'll see **Bab al-Faraj**, Gate of Deliverance. This gate is in two parts, the inner portion dating from the Ayyubid era, c1240, and the outer section (around a bend) from the mid 12th C, but was rebuilt in the 15th C.

attractive alleyway

Return to where you made the last left turn and continue east along Bein Assorian St. This mainly residential alley is very picturesque. The upper storeys of the quaint houses are supported by wooden beams and lean over the alley, almost blotting out the sky — at one point two houses actually touch overhead, and occasionally the buildings on each side join to form an arch across the lane.

Continue to the end where there is a modern Shi'ite mosque, decorated in colourful tiles. Turn left into a covered souk, Amara Jaranieh St. In the middle of this street is the **Bab al-Faradis** also know as Bab al-Amara. Of Ayyubid construction (c1140) this was once a double gate, of which the outer door remains. The inner door was rebuilt in the 15 C but only its arch is standing today. The Roman gate of Mercury stood near this site.

the Gate of Peace

Return to the Shi'ite mosque and turn left (E) along Narkib St. Despite (or perhaps because of) the peeling state of many houses along here, the route captures the flavour of old Damascus. A 250 metre walk brings you to the **Bab al-Salaam**, the Gate of Peace. This, I think, is the most handsome of Damascus's gates, enhanced by its setting alongside a bridge over the Barada. Formerly the Roman Gate of the Moon, it was rebuilt by the Ayyubids in 1243. Above the arch on the lintel the praises of the Ayyubid Sultan are preserved in Kufic script:

> *"In the name of Allah the Merciful this gate has been rebuilt in the reign of Sultan al-Salih, the learned, the pious, the victorious etc, etc..."* (a rough, shortened translation!)

crumbling houses

Outside the gate you have a good view of the river from both sides of the bridge. Some of the falling-down wooden houses lapped by the waters are, incredibly, as the washing lines testify, still lived-in despite their advanced state of dilapidation.

Continue east, parallel to the city walls. The river here breaks into 3 channels, one passing under the road and emerging a little later. On this stretch you have a chance to view the walls of which you have seen very little until now. Eventually, on the left is a small channel of the river that passes right by the front doors of a row of houses which are in (somewhat) better condition than those by Bab al-Salaam. Notice also on your right dwellings built into the top of the old city walls.

potentially picturesque

This area is, sadly, particularly run down, and there is much debris dumped into the watercourse. It's a great shame — you don't require a vast amount of imagination to see how attractive the entire scene could be after a good clean up!

former cardo

The street ends at **Bab Tuma**, St Thomas's Gate, which is in the heart of the old city's Christian quarter. It's a busy traffic intersection, and the gate is now on an island in the centre of the roadway. This early 13th C gate is the Ayyubid remodelling of the Roman Gate of Venus. In Roman times it marked the end of the cardo maximus which ran to the Bab Kaysan, Gate of Saturn. (The Roman gate no longer exists, but an arch which was part of it can be seen by St Paul's Chapel (see the end of the next walk).

► **Walk No 5 —**
The Street Called Straight

START: **Outside Souk Hamidiye** MAIN FEATURES: **Dawish Pasha Mosque — Madrasa Sibaiye — Sinaniye Mosque — Street Called Straight — House of Ananias — St Paul's Chapel.** TIME **2½-3 hours**

This walk takes in the southern part of Damascus's old city, especially the thoroughfare known as the Street Called Straight, which earned its place in history from the New Testament narrative as the street where Paul was taken after his conversion on the road to Damascus: *"Arise [Ananias] and go to the street called Straight and inquire at the house of Judas for a man named Saul [Paul]..."* (Acts 9:11).

when is a street straight?

Called in Roman times the Via Recta, it was a main east-west route (decumanus maximus) across the city, a broad road lined with columns. It was (and is) not *completely* straight, having two barely discernible deflections on its approximately 1.4 km length.

Perhaps these slight deviations were what caused Mark Twain to write in his 1869 travelogue, "The Innocents Abroad", a typically humorous paragraph on the street, in which he reminds us that "he (the writer of Acts) does not say it is the street which *is* straight, but the street which is *called* straight". That notwithstanding, most of the route is certainly straight enough to warrant the name!

tiled mosques

To reach the western end of the Street Called Straight walk south from Souk Hamidiye along Zaghloul Street. After about 70 metres on your right is the **Mosque of Dawish Pasha**, who as governor of Damascus from 1571 to 1574 built it for his funerary

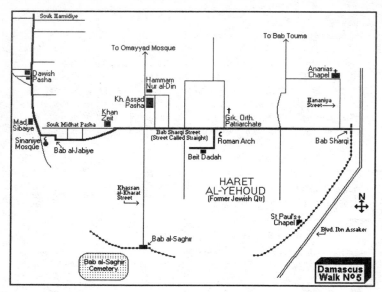

mosque. This mosque has a particularly attractive courtyard with the entrance tiled in traditional Damascus tiling. This glazing, together with what you will see at the **Sinaniye Mosque** further on, may be some of the best in the city. The Pasha's tomb is in the domed octagonal building linked to the main mosque by an arch.

Continue along the main road, which is now called Midan Street, past the **Madrasa Sibaiye** on the right, with tiny arched cubbyholes in the lower wall where all manner of merchants have their premises.

the louse market

Almost facing, on the left is the **Street Called Straight**, here called **Souk Midhat Pasha**. Instead of entering the street here continue another 25 metres or so to the Sinaniye Mosque. This stretch of the road is a second-hand clothes market and is usually very crowded. It is jokingly termed "Souk al-Kumeileh", "the louse market" by the locals. The market can become very animated as buyers struggle to find bargains among the sacks and mounds of garments. Many not-so-well-off citizens buy here, and come not only from the city, but from the villages nearby — you will see a large number of Bedouin among both the buyers and sellers.

The Sinaniye Mosque was built by Sinan Pasha who was, like Dawish, a governor of the city in the 16th C (late). As mentioned above, this mosque is also endowed with delicate Damascus tiling in the arcade. The minaret is covered in tiles of blue and green. The mosque, like the Dawish, has a restful courtyard which seems miles away from the hustle and bustle of the souks around.

the original gate

Take the lane, left, just before and at the side of the mosque, and then immediately turn left again. Here you will see the vestiges of **Bab al-Jabiye**, Gate of the Water Trough. A plaque marks the spot. In Roman times this was the site of the Gate of Jupiter and marked the western end of the Via Recta or Straight Street.

Continue through the gate and along the alley which is parallel to the Via Recta or (as this end is called today) Souk Midhat Pasha. Now a bit of imagination is required. As already mentioned, the Via Recta was a very wide thoroughfare, over 20 metres across and the alley you are now passing through was part of this great street. Over the centuries, as shops and other buildings were constructed, alleys were formed creating the situation that exists today.

Any turning to the left will bring you to Souk Midhat Pasha (the first section of the actual Straight Street of today) which, depending how soon you turn, becomes covered.

olive oil khan

Along the covered section are a number of khans but only one is worth visiting, the **Khan al-Zait**, the Khan of (olive) Oil. It lies about half way down the covered part, on the left. As its name implies, this khan, dating from the late 16th C, was a centre for trading olive oil. It is quite attractive, with trees and vaulted arcades.

***

At the next crossroads a right turn into Hassan al-Kharat Street will take you to **Bab al-Saghir**, the Little Gate. The Romans called it the Gate of Mars, and together with Hassan al-Kharat Street and its continuation to the left, Bzouriye Street, it would have formed a decumanus that led to the Temple of Jupiter.

There is nothing more of special interest along Straight Street until you reach the reconstructed **Roman arch**, about 400 metres further east. This 3rd C edifice was part of a tetrapylon that stood over an important intersection. It was uncovered by workmen digging foundations. After being excavated it was reconstructed on the surface.

To the south of the arch is the quarter called traditionally Haret al-Yahud, and here most of the Jews lived *(see information box on the Jews of Damascus, page 71)*.

A LEGENDARY DETOUR

For those with an interest in folk-tales, outside the Bab al-Saghir is the Cemetery of Bab al-Saghir, one of the most ancient Muslim burial locations in Damascus, in use since the days of the first Caliphs. Among the hundreds of tombs are two that have become places of pilgrimage to many Shi'ites. The first, a double-domed structure, is supposedly the tomb of Sukeina, daughter of Hussein (whose head is in the Omayyad Mosque), and great-granddaughter of Muhammad. The shrine is much visited but it is unlikely to be the tomb pilgrims believe it to be. The coffin is not old enough and Sukeina died in Medina. Nearby, another mausoleum is said to be that of Fatima, daughter of the Prophet, and wife of Ali who is venerated by the Shi'ites. There is no factual basis for this to be her grave either.

Notwithstanding, both these tombs are much visited by large numbers of devoted Shi'ites, especially women from Iran.

---

antiques and lemon trees

An interesting house which you can visit near here is **Dahdah Palace** and you will notice a number of signs pointing to it (some say simply "Arab palace"). To find it turn right along the alley just before the arch, and follow the signs. Ring the doorbell and George Dahdah, the present family elder, will probably open it himself and will be pleased to show you around. He speaks several languages and is an antiquarian.

The house is an outstanding example of an Ottoman residence. The lovely shady courtyard, fragrant with lemon trees, has a large summer iwan at the end, and adjacent to it the winter salon. The very big reception room is used by Mr Dahdah as his antique showroom and is tastefully adorned with copperware, jewellery, carpets and many archaeological finds.

arriving at the Eastern Gate

Return to Straight Street, where it is now called Bab al-Sharqi St (Eastern Gate St). This is the Christian Quarter of the city, and the modern building you can see on the left past the arch is the Greek Orthodox Patriarchate and **Church of al-Mariam**, the Virgin Mary. Continuing east Straight Street ends at **Bab al-Sharqi**, the Eastern Gate, which the Romans called the Gate of the Sun. Here the street is at its original, full width. Bab al-Sharqi is the oldest monument in Damascus, being the only survivor of the original 7 Roman gates. Of the three entrances, the central one was for carriages and the outer openings led directly into the colonnaded arcades. It was via this gate that Khalid Ibn al-Walid, the conqueror of Damascus, triumphantly entered the city in 636.

THE JEWS OF DAMASCUS

Jews have lived in Damascus since at least Roman times and the south-east section of the walled city is still known as the Jewish Quarter. Ananias who sheltered Paul was a Jew, and the fact that there were many Jews in the city is confirmed in the New Testament by Acts 9:20: *"He [Paul] began to proclaim Jesus in the synagogues..."*; and in verse 23: *"...the Jews plotted together to do away with him [Paul]..."*.

In Talmudic literature the waters of Damascus's rivers are mentioned as being suitable for ritual use (Encyclopedia Judaica).

Jews were mentioned in the terms of capitulation when the Muslims took the city in 635, the Muslim rulers allowing them to continue to live in the south-east of the city. Though generally treated then with a measure of tolerance, as non-Muslims they were taxed more heavily.

The Jewish traveller from Moorish Spain, Rabbi Benjamin of Tudela passed through Damascus around 1270 and records in his itinerary "Massa'ot" that he found many Jewish families. 15th C documents exist which recount that at least 500 Jewish families lived in Damascus at that time, and many others fleeing the Spanish Inquisition arrived later.

In the mid 19th C an estimate put the number at 4000 and in 1900 it was 10,000.

The establishment of the State of Israel changed the position of the community to a disadvantage. After 1948, the number declined and by 1968 only 1,000-1,500 remained (Encyclopedia Judaica.) Now there can only be a few hundred and most of these live outside the walls.

the house of Ananias

Immediately preceding the gate on the left is an attractive lane, Hananiya (Ananias) Street. At the top is the Chapel of Ananias. To reach Ananias' house you enter the church and go down some stairs into a stone cellar. This is supposed to be *the* house where Paul (or Saul as he was known till then) sheltered after being blinded on the road to Damascus. Age-wise, the house is certainly old enough. A Byzantine church once stood on this spot. It has been made into a modest chapel and an adjacent room is decorated with simple pictures presenting the whole story as recorded in the Book of Acts.

escape of Paul

Not too far away there is also a **Chapel to St Paul**, erected on the spot which some believe was the place where Paul's disciples *"took him by night, and let him down through an opening in the wall, lowering him in a large basket"* (Acts 9:25). The chapel is very modern and run by Greek Catholics. To get there, exit the old city through Bab al-Sharqi and turn right. Follow the road around till just before you reach the roundabout. You'll see the chapel inset into the walls. As noted at the end of Walk 4, this is the site of **Bab Kaysan**, the Roman Gate of Saturn. Whether this was the spot from which Paul escaped is pure conjecture. From my experiences in this part of the world, the positions of biblical happenings have been identified either through archaeological facts or through tradition/fable going back 1500 or more years. Pretensions to this site's place in history are far more recent than that!

You have walked a long way; I suggest you return by taxi.

► **Walk No 6 —
Mount Qassioun**

START: **Hittin Square** MAIN FEATURES: **Salihiye Quarter and Jabal Qassioun** TIME: **As long as you like!**

The very best view of the city is obtained from Mount Qassioun. The higher you go the better the view, but go up in the late afternoon when the sun is in the west. Take a taxi (see below).

refugees from Crusaders

On the very lowest slopes of Jabal Qassioun is the **Salihiye Quarter**. First developed in the early 12th C by those fleeing the Crusaders, especially after the fall of Jerusalem, it expanded more rapidly in Ayyubid times when many turbas (tombs) of devout men were erected there. Some of these became madrasas and mosques, and at one time almost 70 such establishments were situated in Salihiye. Most were built closely together and you can find them along and just off Abdul Ghani al-Nabelsi Street. To get to this street take a taxi to the junction of Sharia Roken al-Din and Sharia Ibn al-Naffees, just north of Midan Hittin (Hittin Square).

affluent neighbourhood

Because of its evolution and less crowded conditions, Salihiye was an area of escape or retreat for the wealthy, and over the centuries many opulent residences where built there.

In the 19th C the quarter began to expand further up the slopes and pushed westwards to form another area, Mohajirine, where Muslim immigrants from Crete settled, and eastwards where the area came to be known as Akrad because of the numerous Kurds who made their home there. Until the 19th C Salihiye was more or less separated from the old city by fields and orchards. During the last years of Ottoman rule and under French occupation the area between the quarter and the city became more built up. Some greenery is still left in these French-planned tree-lined streets and boulevards but in recent years the appearance of the quarter has changed, especially in the southern parts where new apartment buildings have been constructed in place of the old, but the tree-lined streets and spacious fountained squares still elicit a more refreshing atmosphere than the downtown districts.

the rivers of Damascus

Salihiye was always well watered. The Tora and Yazid (which is more of a canal) arms of the Barada run through the quarter, making some of the avenues especially delightful. The Abu Jarash Gardens which lie to the east of Sharia Roken al-Din and through which the Tora flows may give you an idea of how most of the area once looked.

Further north on the slopes of the mountain some of the character of the old district remains. Here you can still find pretty courtyards shaded by orange and lime trees. A walk around here, among the rough lanes, often quite steep, will show a different Damascus to that you have seen either in the walled city or the smart areas of the "new".

parks and palaces

West of Mohajirine is the **Tishreen Park** and nearby the **Tishreen Palace**, the Syrian Government Guest House. A little further northwest and across the old Beirut road in splendid isolation is the **Presidential Palace**. (I doubt whether you'll get very near it.)

Recent rapid expansion of the city has pushed the houses higher and higher up the mount. So dense is the building now that you have to climb quite a long way up to gain an unobstructed view of the city. Still, the ascent is very worthwhile as the panorama is quite fantastic.

family-built dwellings

The best way to get there is to take a taxi and get off when you feel like it. Go in the late afternoon so the sun will be from the west. The higher you rise the steeper it gets, and the layers of houses seem almost endless, each row looking down on the roofs of the lower. Most of the building is done by the family. They move in as soon as sufficient of the outer structure is standing, and continue the work as and when money and time are available. The overall effect is one of a permanent building site! Steps often link each layer with only a narrow street at the end.

view from the summit

The gradient is so steep that many of the microbuses do not go into the highest areas, but if you want to get to the very summit a taxi will take you by the road leading to the communications antenna where there is an observation platform — you can imagine the view from there on a clear day!

▶ **Walk No 7 —
West of the Old City**

There are a number of localities to visit in the "new" city, including the National Museum. They can be seen together in ½-¾ day (depending on how long you wish to spend at the National Museum).

▶ Qanawat Area

Qanawat means aqueduct, and this area was where the Romans' water system entered the city and is located to the west of the Dawish Pasha Mosque (see Walk No 5). Go down the alley, through the arch between the mosque and the octagonal tomb. Continue for about 100 metres and turn left into a twisting lane. Near the steps you can see some remains of the **aqueduct** which transferred water into the city. Parts of this quarter are picturesque with old wooden houses dating from the 18th and 19th C.

▶ Hejaz Railway Station

Situated on al-Nasser Street about 400 metres west of the Souk Hamidiye, this Ottoman station was the start of the German-built **Hejaz Railway** which linked Damascus with Medina, thus making the Muslim holy places easily accessible for the first time.

Built in 1908 it is a handsome building that incorporates both Turkish and local design. The ticket hall has an ornate ceiling. Unfortunately the terminal is very dilapidated despite its central location and is virtually unused nowadays. Except for a summer excursion train that winds its way up into the Anti-Lebanon mountains, trains use the new Khaddam Station, south west of the city.

▶ Tekkiye Mosque

Located west of the main Post Office, and just before the National Museum.

Perhaps one of the loveliest buildings in Damascus, the **Tekkiye Mosque** is beautifully situated in a flowered courtyard with a central fountain. Designed by the great Ottoman architect Sinan, it was erected during his reign to honour the greatest of the Ottoman sultans, Suleiman the Magnificent, who ruled until 1566. (Sinan also designed the fabulous Suleimaniye Mosque in Istanbul.) The graceful, slim minarets, together with the alternating layers of black and white stone, give the mosque an almost mystical appearance.

from handicrafts to aircraft

Next to the mosque (E) is a large khan with an open courtyard, once used to shelter pilgrims. Today it houses an attractive handicrafts centre where all kinds of locally made items can be purchased.

The buildings on the west side and the yard on the north house the **Army Museum**. The relics of fighter aircraft are dotted in the grounds, semi-camouflaged by trees and jasmine vines — strangely out of place in such a peaceful setting.

▶ National Museum

Located on al-Kouwatli Street west of the Tekkiye Mosque.

This is one of the world's greatest archaeological museums, founded in 1919. It is not within the scope of this book to describe the vast collections housed here, but the Concise Guide on sale at the entrance can do that for you.

transposed gateway

The museum building is approached along a short avenue from the main gate and ticket office. The entrance to the building proper is through a magnificent stone façade, a tremendous gateway which was transferred from the Omayyad desert retreat of Qasr al-Heir al-Gharb, a fortress in the wilderness west of Palmyra. As grand as it is, it must surely have looked far grander in its original desert locale, appearing somewhat incongruous in this urban setting! However, as the fortress itself is barely accessible, the re-siting of the gate does at least allow visitors the opportunity to see it. The entrance hall is also embellished with bits and pieces from the same location.

The museum is divided into five sections (which are further split down to specifics): Oriental, Greco-Roman and Byzantine, Prehistoric, Arab-Islamic and an art gallery. In the Prehistoric, such finds as statues from Mari, inscribed writing cylinders from Ugarit and artefacts from Ebla can be seen. The Arab-Islamic section has a selection of Korans from medieval times, old Arab weapons and many coins.

transposed synagogue

For many, the leading exhibit is the synagogue found at Doura Europos in the 1920s and transferred to the museum in the 30s (see chapter on Euphrates Valley). Consisting of beautiful frescoes which survived almost 1800 years buried under sand, the synagogue is normally kept locked but an attendant with key can usually be found. Being frescoed, the synagogue is very unusual as Jewish prayer houses do not have decoration depicting human or animal likeness.

The synagogue is unlit and there are no windows in the room, in order to protect the paintings from the effect of light. The attendant will leave the door ajar to allow some light to filter in, but you may need a few minutes to adjust to the dark in order to appreciate the frescoes properly.

stories from the Bible

In the centre of the far wall is the niche for the Torah scroll (the Pentateuch).

The frescoes on the left of the niche depict the story of Esther, Solomon on the throne and Moses striking the rock that gave water. Above the niche is a portrayal of Abraham about to sacrifice Isaac. To the right you will find Samuel anointing David, Pharoah's daughter finding Moses in the bulrushes, the Temple and the Exodus.

► Midan Shouhada or Midan Merjeh (Martyrs' Square)

The Martyrs are those killed by French bombardment in 1945.

Just north west of Souk Hamidiye, Martyrs' Square is one of the busiest areas in Damascus. The centre of the square has a monument, a miniature mosque atop a high pillar. This commemorates the opening of a telegraph between Damascus and Mecca.

In and around the square are many mid-price hotels and restaurants. Also some of the best baklawa (oriental pastry) patisseries are located here as are stores selling the preserved Damascus apricots. Both these items are suitable to take home with you. Buy them as close to departure as you can.

► Limited Time Tour

I do recommend you see as much of Damascus as possible, but for those who have a very limited time the following itinerary (which can be covered in one full day) will, at least, introduce you to the essential city.

▸ Walk down **Souk Hamidiye** to the remains of the **Roman Temple**.
Visit the **Tomb of Salah-al-Din**. (Details in **Walk No 1**)

▸ Visit the **Omayyad Mosque**. (**Walk No 2**)

▸ Follow **Walk No 3** until you come to the point marked ***; then instead of returning to the perfume seller continue straight on (S). At the cross street, which is the **Street Called Straight** turn left (E) and follow **Walk No 5** from the point marked ***.

▸ Visit the **National Museum**.

▸ Take a taxi up **Mount Qassioun** in the late afternoon to see the view.

AROUND DAMASCUS

▸ THE BARADA VALLEY

Rising high in the Anti-Lebanon mountains (as does the River Jordan), the Barada, though a very small river, has always been the lifeblood of Damascus, watering the renowned orchards of the Ghouta about which poets have sung for centuries.

better than the Jordan?

To the Greeks the Golden River, the biblical name for the Barada was Abana: *"Are not Abana and Pharpar, the rivers of Damascus better than all the waters of Israel?"* demanded the leper Na'aman of Elisha, who had told him he should wash in the Jordan to be cured (II Kings 5:12).

As the river flows down from the mountains, collecting more water at the spring of Fijeh, from where the French built a direct water pipeline into the city, it parallels the old Beirut highway, now superseded by a fast motor road.

If you have a spare couple of hours, a drive along this (ie the old) road, or a bus ride (take a microbus to Doummar) is very enjoyable.

Location

Leave the city, westwards, on Shoukry Kouwatli Boulevard. At Umayiyeen Square (near the Sheraton Hotel) keep straight on (NW) in the direction of Doummar. As you leave the city limits you will see the vestiges of the orchards and fields that once covered the entire region but which now, regrettably, are fast receding in the wake of urban expansion.

riverside restaurants

The road runs along the river and close to a narrow gauge railway track, operational only in summer when it chugs up into the mountains with Damascenes bent on a day out in the cool heights. Along the road are delightfully situated restaurants, some spanning the river like a bridge. It's surprising how quickly the congestion of the city is left behind for the hilly expanses.

a breath of fresh air

Take some extra time and continue right up into the mountains to the resort town of Zabadini. Here, many better-off Damascenes have summer retreats, in the cool mountain air. As mentioned, a narrow gauge railway comes up here in the summer, leaving from the Hejaz Terminal (see above). The trains are crowded with whole families enjoying a day out. If you want to meet the ordinary Syrian in a relaxed atmosphere you are sure to do so on this ride which, however, is slow — taking about 3 hours.

Microbuses do the trip in about an hour, leaving from the main bus station.

► THE CHRISTIAN VILLAGES of the Anti-Lebanon

Location

Two mainly Christian villages lie at differing altitudes high in the Anti-Lebanon range, Maaloula and Seydnaya. You can visit them by car or by bus. The microbuses leave from a bus station just south of Al-Abbasiyeen Square. It's best to take a taxi there. Ask for Midan Bilal.

Drivers should leave Damascus by the Aleppo highway and after about 12kms take the left turn signposted al-Tal. Seydnaya, the first stop, is reached after about 15kms.

birthplace of Abraham?

The route to Seydnaya is very scenic. The road passes through the village of Barzeh, where some Muslims believe Abraham was born: *"The birthplace of Abraham...near the village of Barzeh, which is one of the most beautiful of villages..."* (Ibn Jubayr 1184).

The road then ascends through a gorge to a bare plateau with promontories on each side. Seydnaya is built on one of these promontories.

► SEYDNAYA

At the very summit is the monastery said have been erected by Justinian in the 6th C after the Virgin appeared to him. A steep climb takes you there.

remove your shoes in the church

The **Chapel of the Virgin** is the focal point of this monastery. You should remove your shoes before entering. Among the array of icons near the altar is one that has, supposedly, a concealed image of the Virgin and, according to tradition, was painted by the Evangelist Luke.

In Crusader times the chapel was a major place of pilgrimage, rivalled only by Jerusalem. The Crusaders called it Notre Dame de Seydnaya.

The monastery is occupied by the Eastern (Greek) Orthodox, the Greek Catholics having held it until a couple of centuries ago. Christians of the both rites still venerate the church, and it is quite often very crowded.

► MAALOULA

Maaloula is 35kms further on past Seydnaya, at an altitude of over 1700 metres.

speakers of Aramaic

This beautifully situated village is much visited by tourists, and deservedly so. It's chief curiosity is in the fact that many Christians here still speak Aramaic (Syriac), once the lingua franca of Syria and Palestine. It is widely assumed that Jesus spoke Aramaic. Aramaic remained the vernacular of Syria until replaced by Arabic after the 7th C conquest. It was only perpetuated among some Christians who lived in isolated villages in the mountains. Here as elsewhere traditions that have been safeguarded for centuries in the face of adversity are being swept away in a few tens of years by the tide of the modern world. I have my doubts as to how widespread the everyday use of the ancient tongue is today — or will be in another generation.

delightfully different

Maaloula lies at the end of a canyon at the end of the road. The colourful houses, limewashed in pastel shades, seem to be piled one on top of the other as they cling to the side of the escarpment.

The approach, particularly in spring, when I was last there, is enchanting. The road runs round a ridge and on the right side green fields and orchards in the valley below stand out in contrast to the bare mountains behind. At the side of the road colourful spring flowers push their way through the sandy earth.

The best view of the village is from a distance as you round one of the many bends on the road. After you reach Maaloula you have to crane your neck to see it all. It is unlike anywhere else in Syria, and the inhabitants are justly proud of their village.

Paul's disciple

High up in the village is the **Convent and Church of St Thecla**, or Mar Taqla in Greek. Taqla is supposed to have been a disciple of Paul, and is buried in a cave above the convent.

through a narrow canyon to 4th C church

Around the side of the (modern) building is a path leading to a passage through the rock, very reminiscent of the Siq gorge at Petra in Jordan. This narrow passage, with sheer rock sides and through which a rivulet flows, twists and turns as it gently ascends, finally emerging on the plateau of the rock. Here you will find the Byzantine **Chapel of Mar Sarkis**, (St Sergius) with its cupola. Belonging today to the Greek Catholics it purports to be among the oldest of churches. Scientific testing of the altar dates it at c300 AD. Note the wonderful icons by the altar.

The general view from the plateau is breathtaking.

Back in the village take a little time just to stroll about. There is nothing particular to see, but the very charm of the village is most agreeable — especially if you've just spent a couple of days sightseeing in the hurly-burly of Damascus!

If you came by car you can return to Damascus by the Damascus-Homs motor road.

6. PALMYRA

Location

From Damascus Palmyra is reached by a fairly monotonous desert road. Take the Aleppo autostrada (north) for c25 kms and you will see the signpost pointing east to Palmyra. The whole journey is quite well signposted and if you keep watching for the signs you should not go wrong.

For those without a car, Karnak offer a daily service (c3 hours). Book a day in advance. Other luxury buses leave Damascus from the bus station near the Tekiyye Mosque or behind the Karnak bus station.

Introduction

Queen of the Desert

Sometimes called the Queen of the Desert, Palmyra is one of the great sites of Syria — indeed one of the great sites of antiquity.

Situated in the Syrian desert about midway between the Mediterranean and the Euphrates, this oasis city was an essential stopping and watering place for all the many caravans which formerly traversed the route from the coast to the Arabian Gulf and beyond.

unknown in the west

Palmyra was virtually unknown to Europeans until it was rediscovered in 1678 by two English merchants from Aleppo. In 1752 the historian Robert Woods visited the site and made drawings of it which fascinated Europe. But until this century very few travellers visited Palmyra due to the hazardous nature of the journey as a result of the threat from Bedouin tribes. Even 80 years ago it was still a very arduous trek, taking 4 or 5 days each way by camel. It was only during the French occupation that Palmyra became anything like accessible, and even then it was only for the experienced and hardy traveller.

A DETOUR IN THE DESERT - THE OMAYYAD DESERT PALACES

Two desert palaces, one west and one east of Palmyra, were built by the pleasure-seeking Omayyad Caliph Hisham. (Other desert retreats constructed by Hisham can be found in Jordan and near Palestinian Jericho.) The Omayyads' roots were in the deserts of Arabia, and by retiring to these refuges felt that they were keeping closer to their ancestry. The eastern one is certainly worth a visit if you have the time, a vehicle, and there has been no recent rain. Bear in mind though that if you visit on your way to Deir al-Zor it will add at least 3.5 hours to your journey time. Also make sure you have sufficient fuel and drinking water!

▸ **Qasr al-Heir al-Gharbi (Walled Palace of the West)** lies c90 kms west of Palmyra or c180 kms from Damascus. Take the road that branches off the Damascus/Palmyra highway signposted to Homs. After about 30 kms the palace can be seen to the east, about 2kms from the road. About 15kms to the south is the Harbaqa dam, first built by the Palmyrenes. A canal brought water from the dam to the palace, which was first settled by the Palmyrenes. After the Roman destruction of Palmyra the site was forsaken. Reoccupied by the Byzantines and their allies, the Arab Christian Ghassanid tribe, a monastery was built there. In c727 Caliph Hisham constructed this retreat.

There is little to see now as the palace's finest surviving piece, the great central gateway was taken down, piece by piece, and re-erected to form the colossal entrance to the National Museum in Damascus (see Damascus chapter).

▸ **Qasr al-Heir al-Sharqi (Walled Palace of the East)** is off the Deir al-Zor road. About 35 kms past Sikne (75 kms from Palmyra), a signposted track on the left (north) points towards the Qasr. (Keep a look out as you can easily miss it!) There are plans to asphalt it but the track is passable by ordinary vehicle if taken slowly provided there has not been rain for some time. The distance is about 30kms and will take about 75 minutes each way.

Like its western companion, Qasr al-Heir al-Sharqi was dependent on a water supply some distance away. In this case it came from al-Qawn to the north west. Although Palmyrene and Byzantine remains have been discovered on the site, it was only properly developed by Hisham. After the fall of the Omayyad dynasty, Qasr al-Heir continued to be inhabited, probably as a small desert town, until abandoned at the time of the Mongol invasions.

The Qasr consisted of a vast walled enclosure about 16 kms in circumference inside of which were gardens, buildings and two castles, each with separate enclosures. The eastern and smaller one is quite well preserved. About 75m square, the entrance side has two semi-cylindrical towers. It was most likely used as a khan, but does appear to have some military aspects. The larger western castle is less well preserved. Over double the size, some 170m square, it contained 6 residences all of similar design, a mosque in the SE corner, and services such as an olive oil press. With streets between the buildings it was in all respects a desert settlement. The minaret between the castles may have been part of a mosque built when the Qasr was first constructed. If so, this would make it one of the earliest of minarets.

Now, thanks to the modern asphalted road, Palmyra is but 3 hours away from Damascus, and although I would not recommend it, you could visit briefly and be back in the capital by nightfall.

mirage in the desert?

For all who journey there, the appearance of the ruined city emerging from the barren landscape is almost as dramatic today as it was years ago. The dark green foliage of the dense palm groves suddenly interrupts the monotones of the dull desert drive while Palmyra's strange ancient tower tombs loom up alongside the road. A little further on you are greeted by the graceful columns and arches of the ancient Palmyrene city rising from the desert sand. It is indeed a sight you will never forget.

▶ TADMOR

Bedouin settlement — now a town

The adjacent, mainly Bedouin, settlement of Tadmor (the ancient Semitic name for Palmyra), which 20 years ago was a tiny rural village with but a handful of people, has, in the past ten years, grown into a small town. Building activity is seen everywhere — a sure sign that Tadmor's position on the tourist map is established.

There is nothing to see of the original old village, though there is a special Bedouin atmosphere. If you want to buy kilim rugs or camel saddlebags of the cheaper, but still colourful, Bedouin-style weave you will find plenty of sellers. But your bargaining skills had better be up to scratch!

tattooed women

If you have half an hour or so to spare, a visit to the local souk will introduce you to the Bedouin, particularly the women with their tattooed faces and hands.

Most of Tadmor's residents wear traditional dress. The women wear either satiny robes in vivid hues of emerald, gold, magenta and the like or the more customary black dresses embroidered with regional designs in multi-coloured thread. The latter can be very attractive when well made (and you will find them temptingly displayed for sale in Tadmor's tourist shops). The men sensibly wear mostly loose, white galabiyas, much lighter and cooler than the ladies' ensembles!

Everyone seems to have a bicycle (identical!), and three-wheel, brightly painted open-backed vehicles are the most popular form of motorised transport — people stand up in the back holding on to bars. You can hire one to take you round the site.

palmy oasis

South of the main street and east of the ruins, mud walls enclose the orchards and olive groves of the oasis. No-one will mind if you wander in through an open gate to be instantly transported from the heat of the plantless desert to the cool of a verdant leafy garden. You will find yourself amidst mixed orchards of date palms, olive trees and pomegranates. In spring the pomegranates blossom with beautiful scarlet flowers, but if you come in the autumn, like the palms and olives they will be heavy with ripe fruit. You will more than likely meet up with the grove owner who will offer you hospitality — water to drink and fruit from his trees.

delicious dates

Very colourful in autumn are the date vendors who line the main road to the site. Their stalls, decorated with hanging clusters of golden, semi-dried dates and huge, circular mounds of ripe amber ones, are a clear indication of how the oasis got its name: Tadmor, Semitic for city of dates, and Palmyra meaning city of palms. By the way, you are strongly advised to thoroughly wash any dates before eating!

I am, however, digressing! No matter how enjoyable these distractions may be, you came here to see the ruins.

▸ PALMYRA

History

The fact that there is an oasis here has made settlement from earliest times very likely. Known since antiquity as Tadmor, Palmyra is the Hellenisation of that Semitic name, which appears in texts dating from the 2nd millennium BC. A 19th C BC tablet found in Cappadocia (Turkey) mentions Tadmor, as do 18th C BC documents discovered in Syria at Mari (on the Euphrates). In the Old Testament Tadmor is listed as one of the cities built by Solomon in the wilderness *(II Chronicles 8:4)*.

caravan route

In succeeding centuries the town must have become an important settlement on the caravan route to the east, hosting travellers on their way to India and China. The Seleucids used this route but they made no attempt to occupy the city. In 41 BC Antony (Cleopatra's one) tried to plunder it, but was unsuccessful: the inhabitants deserted the city, taking their treasure with them.

Some ties to Rome were established during the reign of Tiberius in the early 1st C. By the end of the century the city had become part of the Roman Empire, and its name was now Palmyra. Around 130 AD Hadrian visited Palmyra and gave it the status of a "free city" and renamed it Palmyra Hadriana. This was an era of great prosperity for the desert oasis. As part of the Roman Empire, the caravan trade with the east increased still further, and in economic importance the city rivalled even Antioch.

During the first years of the 3rd C, the Emperor Caracalla granted Palmyra the title *colonia,* thereby exempting it from taxes. Palmyra now reached the zenith of its affluence and most of the colonnaded streets and the Temple of Bel were constructed at this time.

threat from Persia

With the rise of the Sasanians in Persia and southern Mesopotamia, the trade route through to the Persian Gulf became difficult — a catastrophe for Palmyra whose lifeblood depended on their passage. The Sasanians had taken Doura Europos in 256 and in 260 they defeated the Romans at Edessa (Homs) and captured the Emperor Valerian (he eventually died in captivity).

This setback for the Romans enabled a local leader to rise to power. Valerian had earlier appointed this leader, Septimius Odenathus, to be in charge of the legions in Syria and in 262 he became governor of the whole province. This was a time of reverses for the Romans in the east. Odenathus, seizing the opportunity, campaigned for the Romans and his efforts helped bolster Rome's fortunes as well as his own.

Queen Zenobia takes control

In 266, while fighting for the Romans in Asia Minor, Odenathus and his elder son (and heir) Herodianus were assassinated — most likely on the orders of his ambitious wife Zenobia (Znwbya bat Zabbai in Aramaic). Zenobia became ruler on behalf of her second son Vabalathus (Vahballat).

A determined woman, Zenobia wanted to restore Palmyra's fortunes and looked westwards to do so. In 269 she conquered Egypt, and following this success, took much of Asia Minor and Antioch. Her ambitions were great, and Aurelian, the new Roman Emperor, was prepared to grant the victorious queen some concessions. But these were not sufficient to satisfy her aspirations and in 271 she titled herself *Augusta* and proclaimed Palmyrene independence. All this was too much for Aurelian. He sent an expedition to retake Egypt, and he himself reconquered Asia Minor and Antioch.

Zenobia captured

At Emessa (Homs) the Palmyrene army was routed, and

Queen Zenobia attempted to flee and enlist the support of the Sasanians. She was captured crossing the Euphrates and taken as a prisoner to Aurelian, and Palmyra surrendered.

Installing a garrison to secure the city, Aurelian left for home. Before he got too far a revolt overwhelmed the garrison forces. Furious, he returned with a vengeance, and with the full force of Roman power allowed his troops to slaughter and loot the whole city.

from the desert to an Italian villa

Zenobia and her two sons were taken to Rome as captives and displayed through the city when Aurelian entered in triumphal procession in 274. What happened to her sons is not known, but Zenobia lived the rest of her life in a villa in Tivoli.

If this was the end of Palmyra as an important trading centre, it was not altogether the demise of the city. Diocletian who succeeded Aurelian constructed an area to house a large garrison and gave the city fortified walls. With the ever-present threat from the Sasanians, Palmyra was the main post along the Strata Diocletiana, a paved road which ran from Damascus to Sura on the Euphrates.

Palmyra in decline

In Byzantine times churches were built, and Justinian reinforced the defences in the 6th C, but by this time Palmyra was just a frontier city of the Empire.

In 634 it was taken by the Arabs under Khalid Ibn Walid. After a rebellion in 745 against the last Omayyad Caliph, much of the defences were destroyed. Except for the construction of Qala'at Ibn Maan on the hill, the city faded into obscurity.

The site visit

General tips

As the site covers a wide area, a visit to the ruins of Palmyra will require a lot of walking. Depending on how much you want to see, one or two days will be required. If your trip coincides with the hot time of the year, try not to be out at the site during the heat of the day. Be sure to take with a large bottle of water, and wear a hat!

sunset over the ruins

The best time to arrive is 2 or 3 hours before sunset. You will then have time to settle into a hotel before visiting the fortress of **Qala'at Ibn Maan** to the north west of the site. The setting sun over the ruins from this vantage point is magnificent, and something every visitor should try not to miss. The energetic can walk and scramble up the hill to the citadel while others can either drive or hire one of the colourful three wheel "taxis". To go up there in the morning is rather a waste as the sun will be in your eyes and the citadel itself is in quite a ruined state.

If you are unable to arrive in the evening then I suggest getting to Palmyra as early in the morning as you can and begin visiting the ruins right away.

▸ Temple of Bel

Start your tour at the **Temple of Bel**, situated on the east side of the highway facing the **Triumphal Arch**. This is the closest relic to the actual oasis, and a huge walled edifice which is easy to find. Apart from the museum, the Temple of Bel is the only place with an entrance fee in Palmyra and this is very modest. Also, because it is a closed enclosure there are visiting times: May-Sept 08.00-13.00/16.00-19.00; Oct-April 08.00-16.00; Ramadan 08.00-16.00.

Bol, Bel or Baal?

The main god of the Arameans of Tadmor was called Bol. This soon assimilated with Bel, the god of Akkadian and Babylonian origin who controlled the movements of the stars. Bel was associated with Yarhibol and Aglibol, the sun and moon gods. The Canaanite god Baal-Shamin (Master of the Heavens) was also associated with Bel. The deity was likewise linked with the Greek Zeus and the Roman Jupiter via the Semitic god Hadad.

The temple enclosure is huge — some 200 metres square. Still surrounded by walls, these have been modified on several occasions since they were first erected in the 2nd and 3rd C and what we see now is mainly the result of the defences built during Arab times.

striking sight

An outer row of columns ran inside the walls on all sides except the west. Of these only two are left standing in the south side. Inside this row, another row of Corinthian columns ran on all four sides. A fair number of these are standing on the south with a lesser number in the east. As you emerge from the dimly lit ticket office into the expansive courtyard, the dazzling sunlight reflecting from the pale limestone ruins, combined with the sheer size of the temple, can be overwhelming!

sacrificial entrance

To your left (N) as you exit the ticket office are seven massive columns which made up part of the inner row. Underneath them, below ground level, you will see an arched opening through which

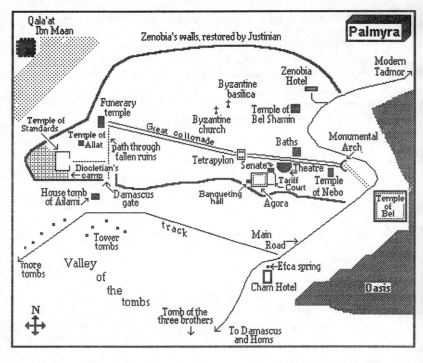

a sloping passageway provided entrance into the compound from outside and below the walls. Sacrificial animals were led into the temple via this entrance.

To the right (S) of the ticket office are the remains of the monumental entrance. This comprised of a trio of gates of which the two smaller outer ones are clearly discernable, the central main section being less well preserved. This gateway was extensively modified in the 12th C when the Mamelukes fortified the enclosure. (It is also worth viewing the gate from the outside when you leave the temple.) In front of the gateway are further surviving pillars of the inner colonnade.

altar to the gods

Continue past the gate to the south side, where the surviving stretches of this colonnade are impressive. From here there is a fine view of the *cella,* or **central sacred hall**, framed through these columns. Walk into the centre of the compound and approach the *cella* via the wide slope and steps. To your left (N) are the remains of the **sacrificial altar**.

The *cella* was dedicated in 32 AD but the site was probably used for religious devotions for 1000 or more years before that.

Rather unusual for this type of building, the entrance is on one of the longer sides of the rectangle, and slightly off centre. The stone frame and lintel of the entrance is extensively carved and decorated with leaves and bunches of grapes. The lower portion, restored by the French in 1932, is of smooth stone and looks badly out of place. To the right of the entrance are large chunks of limestone carved on both sides, and to the left a further carving depicting a scene with people and palm trees.

Passing through the gate you enter the main chamber, about 30 metres long and 10 wide. The reason for the entrance on the long side now becomes apparent: instead of the normal arrangement of a single altar to a particular deity at the short end opposite the entrance, the chamber has a niche at each end, most likely for effigies of the different gods who were included in the Semitic notion of Bel.

heavenly bodies

The stone roof of the northern niche has a carving of the planets surrounded by the 12 signs of the Zodiac. In the roof of the southern niche, approached by gently sloping steps, is an intricate carving of a central rosette surrounded by smaller replicas.

The whole edifice was originally surrounded by Corinthian columns, several of which survive on the eastern (far) side.

▶ The Colonnaded Street

Across the road from the Temple of Bel is the beginning of the great **Colonnaded Street**. About 1.2 kms long, it runs in a roughly east-west direction from the Temple of Bel to the Funerary Temple, which is situated near the western wall.

monumental arch

The first part of the street crosses the main highway and is in ruins, so for our purposes we begin at the monumental or triumphal arch, an effective entrance to so imposing a route. The arch was built around 200 AD during the reign of Septimius Severus at the height of Palmyra's affluence.

The street itself, which is 11 metres wide, is flanked on either side by porticos which contained shops and public offices. Columns from these porticos are still standing and some incorporate a pedestal (towards the top of the column) that was used to mount statues, probably honouring a dignitary. Perhaps to make the passage of horses and camels easier, the main boulevard was not paved.

Just beyond the arch, on the left, is the **Temple of Nebo**. This deity is the Babylonian god of wisdom and was akin to Apollo with whom he was eventually assimilated. A little further along on the right are the **Baths of Diocletian**. These are difficult to discern, but are identifiable by the tall columns in red granite.

Past the baths on the left you will see an arch at the corner of a colonnaded cross street. Here is the **theatre**. Recently restored, it finds modern-day uses during the Palmyra Desert Festival held annually in May (see below). The restoration work on the outer wall leaves something to be desired — the stones are too smooth and creamy-yellow, lacking the porous texture and rosy hue of the bulk of Palmyra's remains. Perhaps time will mellow the effect.

discovery of Palmyra Tariff

Around the rear of the theatre is the ruined **Senate** building. Here was enacted the famous Palmyra Tariff which was a list of the tariffs caravans had to pay on the sale of goods or their passage through the city. The stone inscribed with these tariffs was found in the adjacent courtyard, the Tariff Court, and is now in a museum in St Petersburg. It is from this stone that we have learned the type of goods the caravans carried and that they came from lands as far away as India.

Just by the courtyard is the **agora**, a large public area dating from the beginning of the 2nd C. Since it was excavated in the late thirties the agora has been partly restored. The open area was surrounded on all sides by a columned portico, part of which still stands on the south side. At the northern end of the eastern side is an opening which gave onto the Tariff Court. This was the Senators' Gate, decorated with statues of Emperor Septimius Severus.

Bordering the agora in the southwest is the **banquet hall**. Here, the rulers or religious leaders would recline on the benches around the wall.

concrete restorations

Returning to the colonnaded street, the huge structure in the middle is the main **tetrapylon**. This is a group of four sets of four columns which marked an important street crossing. Only one column — in the southeast group — is original, the rest being restorations made of concrete! From here the street veers off at a slight angle, continuing a further c500 metres to the **funerary temple**. There is nothing of specific interest in this section and you will have to pick your way carefully over the broken artefacts of bygone eras. The funerary temple, which dates from the late 2nd C, was probably a temple tomb. It had a grand frontal portico, some of which was still standing in its original form before the authorities decided to refurbish it with concrete!

vanished street

The route now takes us left (S) along a 2nd C street, starting at the funerary temple, once also flanked by columns and which led to the Damascus Gate. You will search in vain for this street! In spite of being clearly marked on the local tourist office map, it is now just an area of fallen masonry and it is difficult to identify the line of the street.

From here to the south and slightly east you can see on a small rise the **Temple of the Standards,** the temple which served the soldiers of Diocletian's camp and where the legion's standards were kept. Make your way there as best you can; a path through the remains does exist. The temple is preceded by a flight of steps in bad condition. At the top was the *cella* which housed the standards. From this elevated position you will see about 75m to the east, the remains of the **Temple to the goddess Allat,** identified with the Greek Athena.

Further south you reach the southern part of Justinian's walls built in the 6th C. Here was the **Damascus Gate** — like the street leading to it now long since gone. Some vestiges of the arcading inside the gate still survive.

You can now continue your tour outside the walls to visit the valley of the tombs (see below), or return the way you came, and tour the valley later from another, less tiring route.

► Temple of Baal-Shamin, and vicinity

The **Temple of Baal-Shamin** is located just south of the Zenobia Hotel close to the town.

Baal-Shamin (Aramaic for Lord of the Heavens) was the deity responsible for rain, thus in a desert land a god of extreme importance. Of the whole complex only the *cella* remains. This *cella* was built in 130 AD and was restored by the Swiss in the 1950s. In front of the building six Corinthian columns lead to a vestibule. The courtyards to the north and south were once colonnaded.

About 150 metres behind the temple (E) are the ruins of **two Christian churches.** Don't expect to see much.

Beyond the Zenobia Hotel you can see the remains of the north wall, built as part of the Roman defences. In the 6th C the Byzantines under Justinian rebuilt the walls and strengthened them.

► The Valley of the Tombs

The valley runs between the hill of Qala'at Ibn Maan and the hill of Umm al-Qais. You can reach the valley by walking, driving, or taking a three-wheel "taxi" to the Cham Hotel and then following the track west.

There are tombs scattered everywhere. They consist of three basic types: tower tombs of up to 4 storeys in height, inside of which are narrow niches where the bodies were stacked; house tombs in which the bodies were laid in niches around the walls; and underground tombs.

Some of these tombs were family mausoleums but many were built on a commercial basis, each space being sold.

An interesting house tomb to visit is the **tomb of Ailami** which is on a ridge almost facing the Damascus Gate and below a row of tower tombs. This building had elaborate decoration, some of which can still be seen. The burial niches were originally closed with stones carved with faces of the deceased. Some of these are in the local museum.

Above the tomb of Ailami are a number of tower tombs, the most notable being the **tower of Jambique**.

Almost facing the Cham Hotel is the **Frescoed Tomb of the Three Brothers**. This was a commercial affair and, as its name implies, is decorated with frescoes. The tomb is often locked and the keys are held in the museum.

It is very fascinating to explore the tombs properly — you can climb to the top of some and wander among the underground tunnels and vaults in others. But if you want to do this you really need the services of an official guide complete with keys, and this can be arranged at the museum.

▸ Palmyra Museum

At the entrance to the town is the **Palmyra Museum**. Not over-exciting, it does offer a collection of statues and examples of Palmyrene art found all across the site. A few mosaics have also survived but most have been transferred to Damascus.

▸ Efca Spring

Just by the Cham Hotel is the **Efca Spring**, the source of water for the oasis. The water, slightly sulphurous, has a constant temperature of 30°C. Access is via a building next to the hotel which has a bath with associate facilities, but you can just go in for a visit. The attendant will show you a long water-filled cavern where he says Queen Zenobia used to bathe. The spring emerges from under the hill of Umm al-Bais and feeds into the oasis.

▸ Qala'at Ibn Maan

Situated about 150 metres above the Palmyra ruins this castle affords a magnificent view over the entire area.

It was built in the early 17th C by Emir Fakir al-Din who tried to rebel against the Ottomans. His attempt failed and he was executed in Constantinople in 1635. The castle is today in poor condition, but it is impressive from the outside and it is primarily for the view that the ascent is worthwhile. It will take a fit person about one hour to get up by foot. The road journey which approaches the hill from the rear takes about 15 minutes.

As mentioned above, the best time to be up there is late afternoon when the sun is behind you. Another alternative (which I haven't tried) is to be there when the sun rises over the site. I am told it is truly spectacular. But you'll need to be up very early!

► Palmyra Desert Festival

The Palmyra Desert Festival with theatre performances is held here in early May. At that time hotel rooms are difficult to get unless booked well in advance.

7. THE EUPHRATES VALLEY

Location

For touring purposes the Euphrates valley can be divided into two sections: north and south of Deir al-Zor.

South of that city there are two main sites, Doura Europos (Salihiye) and Mari (Tell Hariri). Doura Europos is c100 kms from Deir al-Zor, and Mari a further c25. You could visit these on the same day as you depart Palmyra, provided you leave very early in the morning — it will mean driving close to 500 kms. The road from Palmyra to Deir al-Zor, a desert road, can be traversed in 2-2½ hours but the road south, passing as it does through many villages, is much slower. In spite of this, it should not take you more than 4-5 hours from Palmyra to Doura Europos. The limiting factor is that in doing so you will be visiting the site in the heat of the day, and there is no shade. It will also mean that by the time you get back to Deir al-Zor for the night you will have been on the road for perhaps 7 or more hours. As the next phase of the journey, Deir al-Zor to Aleppo, also has to be done in one day, and there will be at least two places to visit en route, it could all be too much.

less tiring itinerary

Far better, if you have the time, is to drive from Palmyra to Deir al-Zor (say after a morning exploring Palmyra) and stop there, spending the following day visiting the two main sites to the south (and you could also add one more, such as a visit to the village of al-Mayadin or the al-Rabha fortress - see below). You would then return to Deir al-Zor for a second night. This will allow you to take in the sites at a more leisurely pace.

Those without a car will have no alternative but to go to Deir al-Zor first and travel south the following day.

▸ DEIR AL-ZOR

As explained above, in order to visit the sites along the southern stretch of the Euphrates you will have to spend a night or two in Deir al-Zor, the only town with suitable accommodation in the region.

Deir al-Zor is a sprawling noisy town. The main part of the town is on the southern bank of the Euphrates, which divides into two channels as it flows through the town. Between the main part of the river and the narrower secondary channel is an island which is mainly a residential quarter. It is the secondary part of the river which flows through the town. Once a small sleepy township, the discovery of high grade oil in the area has turned Deir al-Zor into something of a boom town, with a population of over 80,000, and the resultant ugly development. During my last visit in late 1994, the secondary part of the river was being dredged and a new bridge was being constructed over it.

There is nothing of note to see in the city except possibly the long, narrow suspension bridge built by the French to aid in their military control of the area. As it is built in three separate sections, it is not a true suspension. Being narrow, probably just wide enough for a small armoured vehicle, it is only used now by pedestrians and bicycles.

Rich vegetation grows along the river banks on either side of the bridge, and this is the most attractive part of the city, with parks to sit in and al-fresco restaurants.

▸ SOUTH OF DEIR AL-ZOR

The route

For the sites south of Deir al-Zor you need to take the main road for Abu Kemal, a small town on the Iraqi border. Bus travellers need to get any bus going to Abu Kemal, and ask to be put off at al-Salihiye.

Along the way

Although the road runs parallel to the Euphrates, the river is not always in sight. Often you will pass Bedouin shepherds leading large flocks of sheep which kick up clouds of dust as they make their way along the sandy tracks.

If you do the journey in the autumn you'll see lots of cotton-picking combines as well as trucks piled impossibly high with sacks of the cotton being transported to storage points. Cotton, you will quickly realise, is a very important crop in this area.

▶ QALA'AT AL-RABHA

About 45 kms from Deir al-Zor is the town of **al-Mayadin**, a typical market town with a bustling souk. About 2 kms south of the turn off to al-Mayadin you will notice on the right (west) **Qala'at al-Rahba** high on a hill. If you are travelling by car a brief detour to visit it is worthwhile (especially if you started early from Deir al-Zor).

Qala'at al-Rahba was built in the 12th C, during the reign of Nur al-Din. It could not have had any great importance as the construction was far from rugged. It certainly did not have a long, useful life and was all but destroyed during the Mongol onslaughts of the 14th C. Looking very dramatic (and photogenic) from the outside, the interior has crumbled away and there is no safe admittance. However from behind its perch atop the steep hill you have a striking panorama of the desert to the west as well as a broad vista towards the Euphrates.

scattered villages

The villages and rural settlements you pass through along the route are noticeably scruffy. One, in particular, just before you reach Doura Europos, comprises recently built block and mud homes erected over a wide area on bare sandy ground, with not a blade of grass or tree in sight, no sign of shops or amenities or any obvious reason why it should be there at all!

▶ DOURA EUROPOS (al-Salihiye)

Even if (as at my last visit), there is no signpost pointing off the main road to Doura Europos, or even to Salihiye, you can hardly fail to notice it if you have been watching your car oedometer. The walls and the Palmyra Gate are quite plain to see from the top of the approach road.

If you arrive by bus, request to be put down at al-Salihiye. The approach road is less than 1km.

History

Doura Europos lies about 100 kms SE of Deir al-Zor on the west bank of the Euphrates. Although it was known from historical sources that a city called Doura existed on the Euphrates, the precise whereabouts was in doubt until discovered by chance by a British army patrol during the First World War. Originally a Babylonian city, Doura (Semitic for fort or fortified wall) came into the domain of Seleucus I Nicator after the division of Alexander's Empire. At the beginning of the 3rd C BC it was rebuilt as a fortress city intended to be a bulwark against Parthian and Persian intrusion.

Nicator added the name Europos (after his native city in Macedonia) to the earlier Semitic title. A grandiose plan for the city was never completed and from about the beginning of the 2nd C BC, with Seleucid power in the area weakening, Doura came under Parthian control. During the Parthian period Doura was a prosperous city on the caravan route and had extensive links with Palmyra. After the Roman conquest of Syria in the first century BC, Doura remained outside Rome's borders.

Roman perseverance

In the early 2nd C AD Trajan entered the city in his attempt to occupy all Parthia but was unsuccessful and Doura reverted to the Parthians. In about 160 AD the Romans entered the city again and this time it was incorporated into their dominion, continuing to flourish as a caravan and trading centre and important link between east and west.

With the growing threat of attack by the Sasanian Persians, the Romans invested heavily in strengthening the city, its walls and the garrison. This proved to no avail and in 256 AD Shapur I, after a major assault, occupied and destroyed it.

The site visit

Excavations at Doura Europus were commenced in 1922 by a French team and were continued from 1928 to the late 1930s by a Franco-American group of archaeologists.

Though very little remains above the ground a visit to this once important fortified city is fascinating. The walls are still largely intact and the position overlooking the Euphrates is quite superb. Most of the interesting items excavated here are now in museums, including the National Museum in Damascus.

rifle practice

Entry to the city was on the west side through the Palmyra Gate, but this is now closed and you will enter through an arched opening about 25 metres to the south. A Bedouin with an ancient rifle is usually on duty to collect the usual entrance charge. (He is happy to demonstrate that his firearm works — and he may try to sell it to you for some outrageous price!

The Palmyra Gate is still impressive despite the ravishes of time. Dating from around 16 BC it has a bastion on each side linked by an arched passageway. It was the only entrance to the city from the landward side. The other gateways faced the river. From inside this gate the main thoroughfare, a colonnaded decumanus, proceeded towards the river.

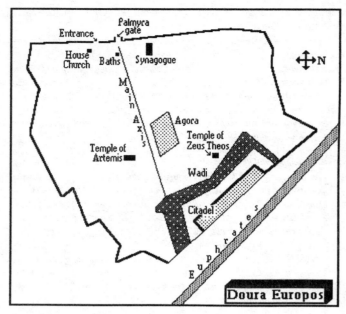

discovery of the frescoed synagogue

Two of the most important finds in this site lie just inside the Palmyra Gate. About 100 metres to the north (on your left as you enter) is the **synagogue,** perhaps the most remarkable find. Uncovered virtually intact in 1932, an inscription found on the roof dates it to 245 AD. From the size of the building it seems the Jewish community here must have been quite small and probably arrived at Doura in the late first century AD after the Roman destruction of Jerusalem.

The synagogue was discovered to be decorated with the most beautiful frescoes and as these had been totally covered since 256 AD, their state of preservation was very good. What makes this most unusual is the fact that Jewish houses of worship are never decorated with human or animal likenesses and these frescoes depicted just that — mainly biblical scenes.

preserved by sands of time

The synagogue lay just inside the city wall and the Romans, considering the inhabitants of Doura expendable, attempted to strengthen the walls of the city against the advancing Sasanians by ripping off the roofs of the buildings parallel to the walls and filling them with the desert sand. The synagogue was consequently buried and totally protected by the sand. The paintings had been completed only some five years earlier, and they emerged from the sand after 1700 years almost as fresh as when painted.

The synagogue and its frescoes have been removed virtually in their entirety to the National Museum in Damascus (you may have seen them prior to leaving Damascus). They should definitely not be missed. (See the National Museum section of the Damascus chapter.) A complete copy was reconstructed at Yale University in the USA.

Regrettably, the remains you see on the site today are hard to discern. The excavations and removal of the frescoes caused much of what was left to collapse. What can be made out are the bare vestiges of a pillared courtyard and two rooms adjacent to the main hall. There is some talk of a restoration effort, but today there does not look like much to restore.

ruined chapel

About 50 metres to the south of the Palmyra gate are the remains of a Christian **chapel**. Originally a house church it was dedicated as a church in 232 AD, according to an inscription found there. Like the synagogue, the baptistry was decorated with elaborate frescoes in the same style, and these have made their way to Yale University.

destroyed by the elements

The remains of the church are very scant, but a Syrian guide told me that only a few years ago it was a clearly identifiable building with some entire walls intact, as opposed to the difficult-to-make-out remnants you see today. But with the sand covering removed there is no longer anything to protect the building from the elements, and each year sees a further sad deterioration.

Along the main street some 60 metres east of the gate on the south side are the remains of **baths** but you will have to look hard to make them out. A further 250 metres on the north side, remains of the **agora** have been excavated. Unlike the traditional Greek agora of an open space surrounded by a colonnade, this one acquired an oriental character with small shops being constructed in the arches around it in a khan-like configuration. This was probably the result of Parthian occupation.

a variety of temples, too

Elsewhere on the site, and especially in the vicinity of the agora, were various **temples** including ones to Artemis and Zeus, but practically nothing of them is discernible. Their co-existence with a church and synagogue in apparent harmony is worthy of note.

wonderful view from citadel

What does merit a visit are the remains of the **new citadel** across the wadi overlooking the Euphrates. On a hot day it may be a hard walk to get there, and even harder to return. Pass through one of the surviving arched gates and climb up as far as you dare. You are now high above the river and your effort is rewarded by a magnificent view of the river and valley. These were once very extensive fortifications but most have been swept into the river long ago.

► MARI (Tell Hariri)

Twenty-five kms past Doura Europos stands Tell Hariri, site of the very ancient city of Mari. Dating back to the 3rd millennium BC, Mari was only discovered in 1933. While certainly a dramatic and significant find, unless you are a real archaeology buff there is not too much of visual interest here.

History

From earliest history Mari flourished as an important mercantile centre linking Mesopotamia with the Syrian desert and coast. Its inhabitants were first Semites and later Sumerians from southern Mesopotamia who brought to the city their culture and writing. In c2340 BC Mari yielded to the Akkadians under Sargon I.

At the beginning of the 2nd millennium, migrations brought another Semitic people, the Amorites, into the area. These people settled all over Mesopotamia and in parts of what is now Syria. As a result, Mari was ruled by a sequence of Amorite princes or kings, each of whom lasted only a few years. At the end of the 18th C BC the Assyrians under Shamsi-Adad took control, but were soon ousted by Mari's most famous ruler Zimrilin.

the great palace of Zimrilin

Although he only reigned for about 15 years the city reached its peak during that time. The great palace bearing his name was not entirely completed during his reign, many additions having been found dating from a later period, possibly even centuries later.

In 1777 BC the Babylonian ruler Hammurabi attacked the city, and destroyed it.

During excavations at the palace a host of cuneiform texts with all manner of information came to light.

The site visit

In spite of Mari's past and the promise of something spectacular from the palace, your visit may be a bit of a let-down! Little remains standing and the treasures found there have long been on display at the museums of Damascus, Aleppo and Paris. Yet for the dedicated, the crumbling walls of what is left will evoke the mystery of long-departed civilisations. The centrepiece, **the palace**, does offer something more tangible and a glimpse of former grandeur — in spite of being protected under a plastic roof! Possibly the most excavated site in Syria, the palace has yielded a trove of treasure. The vast structure contained about 300 rooms. The entrance was from the north and after opening out into a small courtyard, a web of zigzagging passages reached through to a larger court and then continued to zigzag in all directions.

The Tower of Babel?

To the southeast of the palace are the remains of a red brick **ziggurat** constructed about the end of the 3rd millennium. This is a staged tower, platform above platform. A considerable number of these towers have been discovered in Mesopotamia.

► NORTH OF DEIR AL-ZOR

The route

The distance along the main road from Deir al-Zor to Aleppo is c320 kms, not including the detours to the sites, so be prepared for a long day! Bus travellers who wish to visit both Halebiye and Resafa will have to spend the night in Raqqa (see below).

drive along the valley

The road north from Deir al-Zor passes, for the first part, through well cultivated (mostly cotton) land. At harvest time, early autumn, the fields are full of women at work. Some of the cotton is harvested by combines, but much is still picked by hand.

Soon the road veers away from the river and the land becomes more desolate. This sets the pattern for the whole valley: close to the river almost everything is green, but only a few hundred metres away the desert takes over. Motorised traffic, quite heavy close to Deir al-Zor, soon thins out, giving way to the donkey and occasional bicycle. Many villages are set in the arid land and, as on the trip to Doura Europos, one is left perplexed as to why the villagers choose to build their settlements on such barren ground when the fertile valley is so close at hand.

The first detour along this route is to the site of Halebiye. Its impressive walls and citadel, combined with it's marvellous location on the banks of the Euphrates and exceptional views from atop the citadel, make a visit here extremely rewarding, despite the scanty remains within the walls.

► HALEBIYE

Location

Situated 66 kms from Deir al-Zor, getting to Halebiye is no problem for those with a car. Take the road north (for Raqqa and Aleppo). About 10 kms north of the sandy village of al-Tibne, turn right at the small signpost and follow the road to the site. Along this road you soon join up with the Euphrates, and for a short distance the narrow road literally hugs the steep bank — there are not even a few centimetres of shoulder!

Passing through a squalid village in which ancient ruins have been adapted by the villagers for their own use, the site of Halebiye appears dead ahead. Even from a distance the walls look solid and impressive. The road crosses the city along what was once the main north/south axis.

Park just inside the walls.

For bus travellers the only practical way is to catch a bus to Tibne and negotiate with a vehicle owner there. You could also try to hitch, but this would only be practical in the main tourist season.

History

Previously called Zenobia in honour of the Palmyrene Queen in whose domain the city originally stood, Halebiye was built by •the Palmyrenes in the early/mid 3rd C, probably to safeguard a strategic crossing point on the Euphrates. After the fall of Palmyra in 273 the city, like the rest of the Palmyrene lands, was absorbed into the Roman Empire.

The city was regarded as being of strategic importance because it guarded the eastern frontier of the Empire from the Persian threat. The Emperor Justinian (527-565) resolved to turn Halebiye into a fortress city capable of withstanding any Persian onslaught. He despatched one of the greatest architects of the era, Isidorus of Miletus, to supervise the work. The end result was indeed formidable — evidence the walls which survive to this day — but even so the city and its garrison were unable to withstand the violent onslaught of Chosroes II in 611 who captured and sacked it.

The site visit

What we see today are essentially the remains of the Byzantine city. Being far from population centres the walls have fared quite well. They are reasonably intact and present a formidable aspect in this otherwise lonely area.

Nothing remains inside to the untrained eye, but archaeologists have unearthed the remains of a basilica, a church and the arcaded main streets. You will, however, see little apart from the walls and the citadel high on a hill to the west. Built by Justinian, the citadel was reinforced by the Arabs who made use of the fortress to watch movement on the river. Climb up to it for a magnificent view all around.

massive city walls

The walls are the main focus of interest. Thick and massive, constructed of hewn blocks of grey gypsum, they can be explored and in some parts entered and climbed. The river side has some interesting arches and a view through them towards the citadel is quite impressive.

About a kilometre north of the city are remains of Roman tower tombs, but these are not particularly remarkable.

Continuing north

a stop at a Bedouin market

Return to the junction and continue north. The road now is just too far away from the river for any signs of cultivation to be seen and the landscape is totally desolate on both sides of the road. After about 20 kms at the village of Ma'din Jadid cultivation resumes with fields of cotton covering the ground.

About 15 kms further on, just as you reach the beginning of the village of Abu Hamad, there is an extremely colourful Bedouin souk on the left-hand side of the road — definitely worth a short stop.

welcome to Raqqa

A further c40 kms will bring you to the turn-off for Raqqa, an important town just across the river and the junction for southern Turkey. You can't miss it — a large blue sign on the roadside bidding you "WEL.KOMTORAQQA" heralds the approach of the town!

Unless you need to stay here the night you can miss al-Raqqa without great loss. If, however, you have planned a stopover here or just want a brief visit, a broad road leading across a bridge takes you there. A mammoth statue of President Assad dominates the square as you reach the edge of the city.

► RAQQA

History

This can be called a new-old town. Little, however, remains of the old! Sited on the left bank of the Euphrates which is crossed by the main road to Urfa in Turkey (160 kms), Raqqa has developed over the past 20-30 years due to the general development of the Euphrates Basin. There are a few budget hotels which may be of use to bus travellers.

Raqqa was founded in either the 4th or 3rd C BC by one of the Seleucid rulers, probably Seleucus II Callinicos (it was called at one time Callinicum). During the Byzantine period it was, like other places in the area, a fortress against Persian incursions. After the Muslim conquest the Omayyad Caliph is said to have built a palace there. Around 770 the Abbasid Caliph al-Mansour redesigned the town in a semi-circular plan in the manner of Baghdad. Towards the end of the 8th C, Caliph Haroun al-Rashid made it his summer residence, and called it al-Rafiqa.

over-restoration

A great mosque was built by al-Rashid, and rebuilt in 1166 by Nur al-Din. Hardly anything of this remains. All there is to see are parts of **the walls** and **the Baghdad Gate** which have been so totally renewed that they are of very little interest; and another site, **the Qasr al-Banat** (Maidens' Palace), also in the process of restoration, is again too new-looking and so full of pestering children that it is best avoided.

but don't miss the next stop!

As already stated, for most people Raqqa can be bypassed without loss! Our next stop, however, is a different story!

Situated in starkly barren desert some 30 kms west of the Euphrates, the first sight of Resafa, with its magnificently preserved walls of light-reflecting gypsum is startling.

► RESAFA (al-Rasafeh)

Location

Continue north from Raqqa for about 25 kms until you reach the village of al-Mansurah, named after the Roman town of Sura situated a couple of kilometres south. Sura was where the Strata Diocletiana ended, the road which stretched from Damascus through Palmyra and then north through the desert past Resafa to the Euphrates.

From al-Mansurah a road on the left (signposted) reaches Resafa after a drive through the desert of about 30 kms. Bus travellers will have to spend the night in Raqqa, and then take a northbound bus and alight at al-Mansurah. If you then wait at the junction you should be able to negotiate with a driver to take you to this slightly out-of-the-way site, or perhaps get a lift.

History

Resafa, under the name Rezeph, is mentioned in the Old Testament (II Kings 19:12 and Isaiah 37.12 in which the Prophet records how the Assyrians destroyed the city). Ancient Assyrian writings also mention a city with the same name.

In spite of these early references Resafa did not acquire any prominence until Roman times when after the fall of Doura Europos in 256 Diocletian built a fortress here because of its strategic position on the Strata Diocletiana.

saga of St Sergius

This was the period of Diocletian's persecution of Christians. A certain Roman soldier serving in Resafa, one Sergius, was martyred because as a Christian he refused to worship the Roman god Jupiter. When Christianity became legal in 313, Sergius was made patron saint of the city, and around the end of the 5th C the Byzantine ruler, Anastasius, renamed it Sergiopolis. It became a point of pilgrimage, and the town expanded to cope with the flow of devotees who flocked there.

At this time new walls were constructed and the city was greatly fortified to counter the growing threat of Persian invasion. But nothing could stop the advance of Chosroes II and in the year 616 they took the city and sacked it. When Resafa later became part of the Omayyad empire, Caliph Hisham had the city rebuilt and constructed a palace for himself. An earthquake in the 8th century damaged much of the city but it continued to maintain a population, though much diminished, many of whom were Christians. Gradually, Sergiopolis became depopulated and by the time Hulagu's hordes entered the city in 1260 it was deserted.

The site visit

One of the most striking features of Resafa is its location in the middle of nowhere! You'll probably wonder why any town was built so far from the river, but the answer remains a mystery. As you approach it, its formidable walls loom up from the flat surrounds. A good idea is to drive around them before entering. They are well-preserved and you will obtain an impression of the size of the city and the strength of its fortifications. Outside, on the southern side, is a small modern village and closer to the walls a few Bedouin tents.

stupendous gateway

Entry is via the double-gated **north gate**, a magnificent piece of Byzantine architecture, and the most outstanding of Resafa's remains. The sheer size and beauty of this gateway is completely unexpected.

The outer gate, long gone, gave way to a forecourt where an inner triple gateway entered the city. This inner entrance, mostly intact, comprises three rectangular openings, the central and largest one

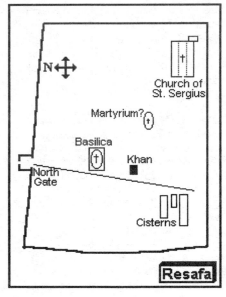

being over 3 metres high and the wall above it rising at least the same again. Each opening is flanked by two columns surmounted by a span of richly decorated arched friezes which together frame each of the 3 entrances.

colonnaded walls

Passing through the gate to your right (E) you can see the colonnaded inner wall which is largely well preserved. If you stand on some high ground you can survey the arched colonnade that passes all around the walls, and also get a fairly good idea of the spread of the remains.

The bulk of the site has not been excavated, resulting in high ground above walls and depressions where roofs once stood.

The main street, which runs from inside the north gate, has been excavated and is presently below the ground level. Walking along it you come, after about 120 metres, to a **basilica** — a beautiful piece of Byzantine architecture.

The three naves are divided with curves, while the arcaded and pillared interior give the building great charm. The three naves terminate at the eastern end with a central apse and two rectangular side chapels, a common Byzantine design.

water storage in the desert

About 100m further along the main street, the remains of a **khan and market** are visible. After another 100m or so, on the west side you will see the arched openings of enormous **cisterns**, vast underground caverns which when full were capable of holding sufficient water for the entire city for 2-3 years! The cisterns were supplied from a huge open reservoir outside the walls which filled up during winter rains. An aqueduct then fed this water into the cisterns. Take great care if you approach them closely.

Slightly southeast of the khan you can see what is left of the **Martyrion**. Built in the 5th C this served as the focus of pilgrimage until the basilica was constructed a century later.

beautiful marble church

The best preserved building in Resafa is the **Church of St Sergius** in the SE corner. Making your way over to it across the craters of the buried city, the area somewhat resembles a lunar landscape. Sufficient is left of the church, including inner and outer walls, steps and columns, to appreciate its cathedral size and magnificence. Built largely of marble it has fared much better than the purely limestone structures elsewhere in Resafa. The lintel stone across the entrance, though, is perched rather precariously and looks like a good sneeze might dislodge it!

During the Arab occupation of Resafa the north chamber was turned into a mosque. If you look on the east wall you can still see the mirhab.

back to the future

In several places you can climb atop the ramparts, wide enough to walk upon, to survey the surreal fragments of this ancient civilisation set in the midst of the wilderness.

The 20th century feat of engineering on the waters of the mighty Euphrates, where we are heading next, could not provide a greater contrast!

► THE EUPHRATES DAM and LAKE ASSAD

Two of the most notable achievements of the independent Syria are the draining of the Ghab valley (Orontes basin), and the construction of the Euphrates dam at Tabqa. The former can unhesitatingly be declared a great success; on the latter, judgment will have to be deferred. There are certainly greater dams in the world, but the Euphrates dam at Tabqa is worth a visit if you are already passing by, if only as an example of one of modern Syria's accomplishments.

Location

From Resafa return to al-Mansura and rejoin the main road to Aleppo. You reach the junction to **Medinat al-Thawra (Tabqa)** after c16 kms. Turn right and drive straight through al-Thawra, a new and mainly dormitory town for the thousands who work in the dam and its hydro-electric plant. Keep going straight for about 7 kms and you will reach an army checkpoint at a roundabout.

tea in army barracks

Explain that you want to see "*mei Assad*", literally the waters of (lake) Assad, and you will be accompanied to a nearby barracks. Here, an agreeable official, probably with very limited (or no) English will, after examining passports and producing the

A DETOUR NORTH EAST OF THE GREAT RIVER

The part of Syria across the Euphrates is the least visited by tourists. There are no locations of great interest, and unless you have spare time this area can be missed.

The Khabur river, a tributary of the Euphrates, flows down from the Turkish border and its waters, combined with those from the great river, enable much of the land to be irrigated. In the extreme northeast the river Tigris, Dajleh in Arabic, flows from Turkey through Syrian territory for some 30 kilometres before continuing its course into Iraq. At this point it constitutes the border between Syria and Turkey.

The area between the Khabur and the Tigris is called the *Jezireh* (taken from the Arabic word for island, *jazira*). Formerly rough steppe, the irrigation projects have allowed considerable cultivation, cereals and cotton being the main crops.

Syria's first oil finds were in this region, but the fields discovered here produced only a very low grade crude, and it is the more recent finds near Deir al-Zor with higher quality oil which have contributed most to the Syrian economy.

The population in Syria's north east are, like those just across the border in Turkey, mainly ethnic Kurds. The demarcation line between the two countries was fixed, not according to peoples or other historical reasons, but by the railway line that eventually reaches Baghdad.

The main town of the area is **al-Hasakah**, 126 kms from Deir al-Zor and c75 kms south of the Turkish border. The other town of size, **Qamishle**, 200 kms from Deir al-Zor, is right on the frontier, and is the crossing point into Turkey.

The places of possible interest to see in this area are:

► Ain Dywar

About 115 kms east of Qamishle (making it a 600+ km round trip from Deir a-Zor) on the banks of the Tigris. Here there is a considerably impressive bridge. Originally a Roman structure, what is left today is mainly Arab. However, even if you do make the journey, you will need the permission of the Syrian Police, and the assistance of a local guide to actually reach it!

► Tell Brak

45 kms NE of al-Hasakah. This is an extensive tell, and excavations have revealed remains of Akkadian and Mitanni settlements.

► Ras al-Ain (Tell Halaf)

Though artefacts dating back to the 4th millennium BC have been found here, it was in the first that an Aramean city, Guzana, was established. Its independence did not last long, and it soon fell to the Assyrians. Remains of a palace and a temple are among the buildings unearthed, but nothing of note has been left on the site.

To the south, on the road to al-Hasakah are sulphur springs where during the French Mandate people used to come for health cures.

requisite — and very welcome — cups of tea, escort you to the **visitors' centre** at the dam. There he will attempt some explanation and show you a model of the Russian-made water turbine used to generate the electricity of which Syria still does not have enough. You will be allowed to photograph the dam, which is also a traffic bridge to the other side of the river, and the vast lake which it has created in the middle of the desert.

Turkey's share in the river

The dam, inaugurated in 1974 after about 10 years of construction, has created a lake 80 kms long and 8 kms wide. When full it is designed to store over 14 million cubic metres of water. However due to the construction of an even larger dam in southern Turkey (in which country the Euphrates rises), this volume cannot be achieved. The dam is 4.5 kms long, and at the base 512m wide. In the hydro-electric plant there are 8 turbines which are supposed to turn out 110 megawatts each. This capacity was expected to have solved the power problems which have plagued the country for years, and still do, if not quite so badly. It was also hoped that with the extra irrigation water over 1 million hectares of land would be reclaimed for agriculture.

plenty of power cuts

Neither of these expectations have been completely fulfilled. Whereas the reduced flow of water has undoubtedly had a detrimental effect, the poor quality of the Soviet-made turbines and the lack of proper maintenance have also been contributory factors. There are plans to purchase new and better turbines, but this will require a lot of hard currency which is in short supply in today's Syria. Until then, power cuts will continue and you will become very aware of them during your visit to Aleppo!

on to Aleppo

From Lake Assad return to the main highway and drive straight to Aleppo without any further stops. You now pass through totally arid wilderness — it is hard to believe such a massive body of water is so close by. About 100km before Aleppo vegetation reappears along with the usual assortment of villages. Some of the dwellings have sensibly been whitewashed. There is so much construction activity as you approach Aleppo — virtually every house has piles of stones and building materials outside, making it difficult to tell whether the buildings are being erected or demolished!

8. ALEPPO AND VICINITY

"Aleppo is a town of eminent consequence, and in all ages its fame has flown high. The kings who have sought its hand in marriage are many, and its place in our souls is dear ... Glory to Him who planned its design and arrangement, and conceived its shape and outline"

"The Travels of Ibn Jubayr", 1184

Introduction

You will not of course see today the same Aleppo that sparked the sentiments expressed above. Yet Aleppo lives on as one of the great Middle Eastern cities and one where you will come the closest to the exuberant Arab bazaar life of a bygone era. If you pick your way around, through the decaying buildings, the dirt and the 20th century sprawl, a great deal of the former grandeur can still be found.

Aleppo is situated on a plateau, 390 metres above sea level. In 1992 the estimated population was 1,500,000.

This city, built largely of slate-grey stone, was once one of the major commercial cities of the Orient, lying on the land route between Europe and the East. But the heyday of Aleppo is, sadly, past. The Suez Canal, the re-adjustment of borders following the collapse of the Ottoman Empire and the rise of Damascus as the largest Syrian city have all had their effect on the ancient metropolis.

Russian shop signs

But commerce has always been Aleppo's forte and trading activity in the extensive covered souks continues undiminished in traditional fashion, while Aleppo's newer shopping streets are not lagging behind in enterprise. You will notice many shop signs in Cyrillic — a vast business has sprung up in recent years with traders from the former Soviet Union flocking to Aleppo to buy and barter. Textile goods and shoes are among the most popular commodities.

children at work

A more regrettable feature of Aleppo life (more pronounced than in Damascus) is the large number of children who work rather than learn. Boys of 8 or 9 will sit on the pavement for hours with a battered bathroom scales or wander the streets peddling anything from a couple of packets of cigarettes to a "gold" watch. Seven year-old shoeshine boys drag the tools of their trade from teahouse to teahouse while others serve the tea or help out in their fathers' stores.

Yet the frantic bustle and chaos of Aleppo, together with the variety of peoples who live and trade there, only serve to enhance its vibrant Middle Eastern character. While the stone of its buildings may be grey indeed, Aleppo is anything but a grey city!

Aleppo's Old City

Unlike Damascus's Old City which is still clearly defined by the walls, Aleppo's historic part is not so clearly demarcated. Most of the walls have, unfortunately, been destroyed to make way for the city's expansion and new roads. All that is left are two sections (see plan below). One along Bab Antakya Street, at the west side of the Old city, and the other from Bab al-Maqam to Bab Nayrab to the south and south east. At other parts, particularly in the north and east, Aleppo's historic *intra muros* city merges into its *extra muros*.

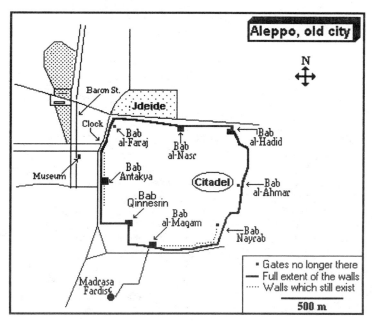

What to see

Rush visits can no doubt occupy less time, but ideally a minimum of two days are required to explore the city reasonably. This does not include any tours you will want to make to the surrounding areas which will be based in the city.

The main places of interest include—

▸ The old city with its 8 kms of covered souks, the oldest closed shopping centre in the world!
▸ The khans (caravanserais), mosques, and other medieval Arab buildings;
▸ the Citadel;
▸ the beautiful 18th and 19th century Ottoman houses of the Jdeide Quarter;
▸ and, of course, the spirited life of the inhabitants.

History

According to legend Abraham is supposed to have milked his flocks on the site of Aleppo. From this fable the Arabic name Halab, Aramaic for milk, is derived. History contends otherwise.

Settlement in the Aleppo area goes back to the 8th millennia BC but its first mention in history comes from texts of Mari around 1800 BC. The city, Halap, was the capital of the Amorite Kingdom of Yamhad. Lying at the foot of the Taurus mountains the state was strong enough to control trade between the Mediterranean coast and Mesopotamia.

When the Hittites launched a campaign against Babylon in the 17th C BC they conquered the Amorite Kingdom on the way, and soon after the area passed to the control of Mittani, a Hurrian kingdom centred east of the Euphrates.

advent of the Sea Peoples

The disastrous invasion by the Sea Peoples in the 12th C BC disturbed the entire region, and it was only later that the Hittites were able to restore their power. Small neo-Hittite states were established, some centred on Hama and Aleppo. This situation lasted until about the 8th C BC when the Assyrians dominated the area. In 539 BC the whole of Syria came under the control of the Persians until their defeat by Alexander at Issus in 333 BC.

On the death of the Macedonian, Aleppo with the rest of northern Syria passed to Seleucus Nicator, founder of the Seleucids. The name of the town was changed to Beroia after the city in Macedonia. What had till then been a small town was replanned on the classic Greek style. It continued to develop along similar lines after Syria came under Roman control in 64 BC.

rise in importance

With the construction of roads and the settling of the massif to the north and west, Beroia prospered as well as attaining importance in the control of the Roman imperial frontiers. It may never have reached the zenith of prominence or affluence enjoyed by Antioch on the Orontes to the west, but nevertheless its position as a trading city between east and west was firmly based. This status lasted with but a few interruptions until the last decades of the Ottoman Empire.

In 637 Aleppo was conquered by the Muslim Arabs. When in 661 Mu'awiya, the founder of the Omayyads, became Caliph and made his seat in Damascus, Aleppo was eclipsed by the splendour of Damascus, Islam's capital city. This was not changed by the rise of the Abbasids, as they ruled from Baghdad.

Aleppo becomes the capital

The weakening of the Abbasid dynasty allowed the Fatimids from North Africa to take control of Egypt and southern Syria. The Hamdanids, an Arab dynasty from Mosul, northern Iraq, expanded their rule into northern Syria and in 945 their leader Saif al-Dawlah captured Homs and Aleppo making the latter the capital of his emirate which stretched into present day Turkey. The area was constantly being threatened by Byzantium and in the late 960s Aleppo was temporarily lost to the Byzantine General Nicephorus Phocas, who invaded Northern Syria and despoiled the city.

Effectively squeezed between the Byzantines in the north and the Fatimids in the south, the Hamdanid state became a vassal of the Fatimids, although nominal rulers continued to govern.

Crusaders driven out

In 1070 Aleppo was taken by the Seljuk Turks and in 1098, following their capture of Antioch, the Crusaders lay siege to the city. The siege failed, but was renewed in 1124 under the forces of Jocelyn. Zengi, the governor of Mosul, came to the rescue, driving the Crusaders away. To secure Aleppo's continued protection Zengi became Governor, in effect ruler. He made Aleppo not only a key centre in the fight against the Crusaders, but one of the most important cities in the Muslim world.

Nur al-Din becomes Governor

Zengi was succeeded by his son, Nur al-Din, who besides continuing to harass the Crusaders was responsible for the construction of many mosques, madrasas and other public buildings. In 1186 after the death of Nur al-Din, his protege and the ruler of Egypt, Salah al-Din gradually took complete control of Aleppo and the rest of Syria. Thus was born the Ayyubid dynasty centred on Damascus.

Salah al-Din made one of his sons, al-Zaher Ghazi, Aleppo's governor, and the city profited greatly under his tenure. The city's fortifications were expanded and a moat around the citadel was dug.

Mongol defeat by Mamelukes

The Mongol invasion under Hulagu in 1260 devastated much of Aleppo and this inspired the Battle of Ain Jalud on 3rd September that year when the Mameluke leader al-Malik al-Zaher Baibars forced them to retreat. Aleppo now came under Mameluke control. During their rule, which lasted until 1516, Aleppo redeveloped as an important commercial city. The Mongol troubles to the north and east helped divert trade from the Far East away from the more northeasterly route that ran through Anatolia. Great khans (caravanserais) and souks were built to service this growing trade.

In 1516 Syria became part of the Ottoman Empire, and as the chief city of the area, Aleppo was made the seat of the Ottoman *wali*, or governor.

commercial hub

Despite the many failings of Ottoman rule Aleppo generally prospered. It became, together with Constantinople and Cairo, one of the main cities of the Empire. The great khans and souks which can still be seen today were constructed, and many enterprises flourished. In 1517 Aleppo was, perhaps, the first city in the world to have a resident consul when under the "Capitulations" Venice was given the right to appoint one. English, French and Dutch representations soon followed.

decline of land route

The beginning of Aleppo's decline probably commenced with the opening of a sea route to the east, around the Cape of Good Hope. The faster sailing ships of the 18th and 19th centuries compounded this and greatly reduced the flow of merchandise through Aleppo. Finally, the opening of the Suez Canal made the land route almost redundant. These developments caused a decline in the city's fortunes, but the influx of Christian and Jewish entrepreneurs helped maintain the commercial life.

Armenians bring prosperity

Armenians had lived in Aleppo for centuries, but in the second half of the 19th C more came there to settle. The Turkish persecutions of the First World War brought a large increase in their number. Their skills in commerce and manufacturing helped the city to maintain itself as the main commercial centre in Syria — a position it held until after independence.

Liberated from Turkish rule in 1918 Aleppo suffered the greatest blow in 1939 when the French ceded Alexandretta to the Turkish Republic. Already closed in by the establishment of the Turkish border in 1920, the loss of the historic port finally ended Aleppo's role as an international commercial city. However it remained the driving force in the Syrian economy during the first years of the Syrian Republic but, with the expansion and industrialisation of Damascus, was eventually relegated to second place.

Visiting the city

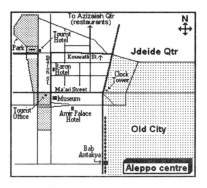

Any tour of the Old City will mean covering some ground more than once but a planned itinerary is necessary if you are not just going to go round in circles! In planning the walks for this chapter I have endeavoured to cover the points of most interest which the traveller with a reasonable amount of time available (two full days) will be able to see. The walks can be done separately or joined together. If you have less than two days in Aleppo they can be reduced according to your preference (and energy!).

The routes chosen are mainly aimed at the historical buildings and monuments of the city so that an overall perspective of its setting in history can be obtained. The walks are best enjoyed if not hurried, so that as you stroll from one place to another you will have time to savour the sights, sounds and smells of the bustling streets and alleys. And because the city, *intra muros*, lacks the modernisation seen outside, the atmosphere of perhaps the last remaining Ottoman bazaar city can be thoroughly enjoyed.

A tour of the wonderful covered souks should be done separately from the other tours (although some of the walks of necessity pass through parts of them), and a guide to these can be found in Walk No 5 below.

don't get lost!

As it is quite easy to lose your way even if you are studiously following instructions, I suggest that every now and again, especially after a change of direction, you check your bearings by enquiring of a shopkeeper. Just the name of where you want to go in a questioning manner is usually sufficient.

▸ Walk No 1

START: **Clock Tower;** MAIN FEATURES: **Bab Antakya (Antioch Gate) — Madras Moqaddamiye — al-Bahramiye Mosque — Customs Khan — Khan al-Nahasin — Hammam al-Nahasin — al-Adeliye Mosque — Maristan Arghun al-Kamili — Bab Qinnesrin;** TIME: **2-3 hours**

Follow the plan on page 118. **Remember, the streets traced with thicker lines denote the route to take.**

Enter the Old City via Bab Antakya, the Antioch Gate. To get there from the clock tower, proceed south on Bab al-Faraj St into Bab Antakya St, keeping straight all the way. Along Bab al-Faraj you can see on the left buildings with a typical Aleppo wooden construction on the upper storeys. This form of construction dates from the 19th and beginning of the 20th centuries, but some are in such an advanced state of dilapidation they appear much older! Many are clearly beyond repair but others are being renovated. Cross the busy intersection and you are in Bab Antakya street — you can see here on the left part of the city walls which are largely obscured by shops etc.

antique motors

Continuing straight, there is a street market-cum-taxi station on the right. If you are interested, cross over and inspect some of the taxis. Few will be less than 40 years old; many 50 and more. For those who are nostalgic about the 50s and 60s, here you can renew your acquaintance with perhaps the first car you ever had or the one you remember your father (or even grandfather) driving! More than a few are quite fascinating hybrids — bits taken from a variety of makes! Little is scrapped in Syria; recycling is everyday practice. (I have never seen a car dump in the country.)

Back on the left, you are now walking at the foot of the walls. This part of the street has a profusion of cobblers, some with nooks in the walls, others just plying their craft on the pavement. As cheap as you think shoes may be in Syria, they are expensive to most of the population, so everything that can be is repaired.

exit to Antioch

After c300 metres you reach **Bab Antakya**. As the name implies this was once the main exit to the Antioch road. The actual gate is, at first sight, hidden from direct view because of the shops outside. Built by the Ayyubid Governor, Yusuf II in the 13th C, the gate consists of two huge bastions. What we see today is mainly the Mameluke reconstruction from the 15th C. Entering the old city you are immediately assailed by a different atmosphere! Today the walls (what's left of them) no longer shut out the outside world, yet they do enclose a way of life and character unique to the oldest traditions of Middle Eastern commerce.

Aleppo's first mosque

Some 50 metres along the cobbled alley, where it splits, is the unusual **Mosque of al-Tuteh** (Mosque of the Berry). Built on the site of a 7th C mosque, reputed to be the first mosque built in Aleppo, it was reconstructed by the Ayyubids. Part of the outer wall includes remains of a Roman structure.

Take the right fork, along what was once the principal Roman decumanus (east-west thoroughfare) of Beroia, and you soon enter a covered souk. Count the turn-offs to the right, and turn into the third, which is about half way along the covered section. About 70 metres on your left is the **Madrasa Moqaddamiye**. Formerly a church, it is the oldest Muslim theological school in Aleppo, dating from the mid 12th C. This was the period when the Crusaders lay siege to Aleppo, and in retaliation a number of Christian properties were confiscated. The entry porch of this edifice is particularly noteworthy.

Return to the main alley and continue. You are now in the **souk al-Atarin**. This section of the souk is supposedly for food and household goods, but as each souk is no longer exclusive to one trade as it was in former years, you will see a sprinkling of other merchandise. A few metres along on your left is the small **Khan Titol**, the first you will come to of Aleppo's numerous khans. Note the ornamented balconies.

Turkish mosque

Take the next turning to the right, under an archway, into a narrow side alley. The large minaret on the left belongs to the Turkish style **al-Bahramiye Mosque** which dates from the late 16th C. If the entrance is closed, a few metres further along the main alley is a vaulted opening from where you can obtain a broad view into the mosque and courtyard.

the great Customs Khan

Proceed along the main alley, past the point where the street

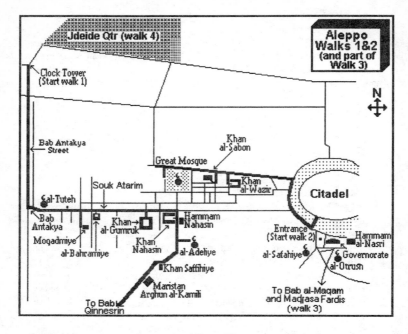

widens into a sort of square. After c50 metres a high dome over the souk announces the entrance, on the right, to the **Khan al-Gumruk**, the Customs Khan. This khan, with its beautifully decorated portal, is the largest of the khans in the city. Dating from 1574, it was where goods arriving in Aleppo were taken so that customs duty could be levied.

The Customs Khan was also the centre of foreign trading in the city, housing not only European financial institutions, but also the consuls of England, France and Holland. It covers a large area and is still very much a hub of commerce, with most of the trade being in textiles.

In the centre is a small mosque. Due to the buildings and piles of merchandise around it, the best sighting comes from the surrounding veranda from which you also get a good view of the entire khan. The steps up are at the rear of the courtyard.

world's first consulate

Exit from the khan and continue your tour. Turn right at the second street, which is reached after c80 metres. (You may wish to check your direction here by asking a shopkeeper the way to Bab Qinnesrin.) Thirty metres down on the right is the **Khan al-Nahasin**. This khan formerly housed the Venetian Consulate, the first consulate in Aleppo (and perhaps the first consulate in the world). For a long time the consulate building was owned by one Adolphe Poche, who until his death some years ago was one of Aleppo's most interesting characters. At various times he acted as Consul for the Austro-Hungarian Empire, Austria, Holland and, at the time of his death, Belgium.

hot baths

Opposite is the **Hammam al-Nahasin**. Now modernised, the baths were originally constructed in the 12th C, making them one of Aleppo's oldest baths.

Carry on down this street, passing some other, not too interesting, khans on the way. After c50 metres turn left up a narrow cross street. This leads to the **al-Adeliye Mosque**. Built in 1517 by the city Governor, Muhammad Pasha, it is the oldest Turkish mosque in Aleppo. Notice the outside is decorated with glazed, coloured tiles. Try to go inside and see the particularly fine mihrab.

visit to the asylum

Return to the street junction from where you turned off to visit the mosque, and carry on south. At the point where it bears right is the **Saffihye Khan** with its pleasant vine-shaded courtyard. Follow the road round to the left and after c50 metres on your left is **Maristan Arghun al-Kamili**. This is an asylum built by the Mameluke governor of that name (maristan means hospital) in 1354.

Entry is through an outstanding portal into a lovely ornate courtyard, with a central fountain and twin iwans. Across this yard a vaulted passage opens onto another more enclosed courtyard, also with a central fountain.

patients in chains

Around this initially enchanting setting are barred cells in which the insane were confined. Looking clean and peaceful today, the cells with their high ceilings and rings for chaining the patients are chilling. While commendable that a form of care was provided for the mentally ill in an unenlightened age, inmates were still kept here less than 100 years ago!

end of the tour

A couple of hundred metres further on brings you to **Bab Qinnesrin**. This is the best preserved of the ancient gates to Aleppo. Dating from the 12th C it was restored by the Mameluke, Qansaweh al-Ghawri in 1500.

You can return the way you came, or get a taxi.

> ▸ **Walk No 2 - The Citadel** and Great
> Omayyad Mosque

START: **Citadel;**   MAIN FEATURES: **Aleppo Citadel — Royal Palace — Great Mosque — Khan al-Wazir — Khan al-Sabon** TIME: **approx 3 hours**

This tour starts by visiting **the Aleppo Citadel**. The best way to get there is by taxi. It may appear you are outside the old city here, but you are in fact in its very centre (see plan of walls on page 111).

The hill on which the citadel stands is probably the *raison d'être* for Aleppo and was used as a defensive position as far back as the first millennium BC. It was fortified by the Seleucids and later the Romans during their respective occupations. During the period of Hamdanid it became the palace of the rulers.

The citadel was used during Ayyubid rule of Syria by al-Malik al-Zaher Ghazi, one of the sons of Salah al-Din who reinforced it with the moat and steep glacis. In 1260 most of the fortress was destroyed by the first Mongol invasion. Rebuilt by the Mamelukes, to whom much of its present appearance is due, it was devastated again in 1400 by Timur.

striking entrance

There is only one entrance to Aleppo's citadel, but what an imposing entrance this is! You must first pass through a 13th C tower some 20 metres high. An inscription on the tower commemorates some rebuilding in the 16th C. After passing through it you now cross a bridge supported by 8 arches crossing the moat and glacis. This leads to a massive second tower — a cleverly designed defensive gateway. Immensely fortified, it was meant to expose any attackers to the full thrust of the fort's defenders while they were attempting to gain entry.

However, in constructing this entranceway aesthetics were not neglected. Notice the windows above the entrance arch. The inscribed band running around it commemorates the rebuilding of the fortress by the Mameluke Sultan al-Ashraf Khalil c1290, after the first Mongol destruction.

Inside the gateway you have to negotiate 5 right angled turns and formidable gates prior to gaining access to the upper defences. After the turns of the entranceway you reach a rising passage off which are a number of rooms of Byzantine construction.

governor's palace

Continuing up, you come on the right to **the Royal Palace** built by the Ayyubid governor al-Aziz in 1230. Parts have been restored including the **throne room** and the **hammam** at the rear. A little further on and to the left is the **Mosque of Abraham** said to have been built by Nur al-Din in 1167. This site was once a church. The path terminates with the remains of the Great Mosque built in 1214 by the Ayyubid Governor al-Ghazi. To the east of this mosque are **the barracks**, built in 1834 by Ibrahim Pasha who governed Aleppo for a short while under Muhammad Ali, and which now serve as a refreshment bar.

Fine views of the city are obtainable from up here, but you do need a bright sunny day to compensate for the greyish monotones of Aleppo's buildings.

The Great Mosque

From the citadel, the itinerary takes you to **the Great Mosque**. To get there, walk around the citadel clockwise from the entrance to the main street on the west side, al-Jami al-Umawi Street (Omayyad Mosque Street). Turn left here and after c400 metres you reach a large square on your left. The mosque is at the back of this square.

Although called the Omayyad Mosque, this building never possessed the grandeur of its Damascus namesake. Established by the Omayyad Caliph al-Walid, the same builder, it was not completed until after his death.

another severed head...

Like the Damascus edifice it was built over a spot dedicated to Christianity, namely part of the Byzantine Cathedral of St Helena. For some reason the mosque acquired the title Jami Zakariye, the Mosque of Zacharia, the father of John the Baptist. This may have been simply an attempt to give the building extra status as there is no Christian evidence that any of his relics were interred there. Yet Muslim tradition, too, continued the association, and holds that just *his head* is buried there (as likewise it claims John's is in Damascus's Great Mosque)!

...and another fire

In 1169 the building, with the exception of the 45 metre minaret, was completely destroyed by fire. It was entirely rebuilt by Nur al-Din but the original, almost undamaged, Seljuk tower was retained.

Entry to the mosque is from the west and there is also an entrance from the souks directly into the prayer hall. The arcading around the expansive courtyard provokes echoes of the much grander Damascus structure. Inside the prayer hall take note of the 15th C carved wooden *minbar*. Near the *mihrab* is the room supposedly containing the head of Zachariah (see above).

outstanding Ottoman khan

Some 100 metres east of the mosque, on al-Jami al-Umawi Street, you will see a small square, used mainly as a car park. At the eastern end of this square is the **Khan al-Wazir** with its exceptional portal of black and white stone. This 17th C Ottoman khan is a really beautiful example of Ottoman architecture, but this may not be evident at first glance. It is currently undergoing restoration work which hopefully will enable it to be better appreciated. The windows above the portal are outstanding in their ornamentation. View them from the inside looking out.

unfulfilled promise

If you now enter the souk and almost immediately turn right you will notice the imposing entrance to the **Khan al-Sabon** (you may have to ask). The beautifully carved portal promises much, but the interior of this 15th C Mameluke structure is sorely neglected.

You could now visit the covered souks (Walk No 5) should you wish to continue further.

> ► **Walk No 3**

START: **Bab al-Maqam**; MAIN FEATURES: **Bab al-Maqam — Madrasa Zahirye — Madrasa Faradis — Madrasa Sultaniye — Hammam al-Nasri**; TIME: **1½-2 hours**

Refer to plan of Walks 1 and 2, SE corner (page 118).

The main purpose of this walk is to visit the Madrasa Faradis (al-Firdoos), one of the most elegant mosques in Aleppo. It is nearly 2 km south of the citadel, so some taxi riding will be in order. If you are pressed for time and just wish to visit this building you can take a taxi each way missing out the other sites.

The full tour starts from the **Bab al-Maqam**, south of the citadel, and you should take the taxi to there.

This gate was built by the Ayyubid Governor al-Zaher Ghazi in the late 12th C and rebuilt by the Mameluke Sultan Qait Bey in 1493. As you walk through the gate you will see a small square to the right. Take the street opposite which heads southwest. About 50 metres on the left is the **Madrasa and Mausoleum of Kheir Bey**. (Use its location to check that you have taken the correct street.) This edifice dates from 1514. A further c100 metres on the right (just before a fork in the road) is the largely derelict **Madrasa Adray**.

forbidding structure

Further on, where the road forks, to your extreme left you will see the bulky structure of **Madrasa Zahirye**. With a towering arched entranceway and virtually no windows, this building looks more like a fort or prison than a mosque from outside but it does have an attractive inner courtyard. The edifice is sometimes locked, but the caretaker may be around.

Return to the intersection and take the right fork along a street with a cemetery on both sides. At the end of the cemetery take the (unpaved) lane to your left and 70 metres down you will see the **Madrasa Faradis**.

finding the key

If locked (as it often is), you can easily arrange to have it opened and the mosque is definitely worth seeing inside. To find the custodian: almost facing the entrance is an alley (unpaved). Go to the end (about 50 metres), and turn right. The first door you come to has an iron grill and a high bell-push on the door frame. The keyholder lives here. His English is very limited, but just say *miftah jami* (key to mosque) and he will come and show you around.

School of Paradise

The Madrasa Faradis, School of Paradise, was built in 1235 by Daifeh Khatun, widow of al-Zaher Ghazi. She was Salah al-Din's daughter-in-law as well as his niece.

The portal opens out onto a courtyard with an ornamental pond. The vaulted iwan on the north side is now used for study. The arcading on the other three sides are supported by recycled ancient columns. The prayer hall, now quite ordinary, is covered by 3 domes. Perhaps more care could be taken in the upkeep and quality of restoration of the building. (In particular the artificial renovation of the two sets of double doors leading into the prayer hall, mars the sense of antiquity the building otherwise generates). Yet the overall effect is one of peace and tranquillity.

Walk back to the main road and return to the Citadel by taxi.

Across the road from the Citadel are a number of mosques, the most notable being the **Madrasa Sultaniye** (the closest one to the Citadel entrance), constructed in 1224 by a son of al-Zaher Ghazi. The edifice houses the cenotaphs of the al-Zaher Ghazi family.

beautiful Turkish baths

A little further east is the **Hammam al-Nasri**, the building with the dome. These are the most splendid baths in the whole country. First built in the 14th C they have been extensively reconstructed and modernised. If you want to try a bath but are reluctant to go to the ones in the Old City then these are for you. The proprietor will be happy to show you round in any event.

Between the Madrasa Sultaniye and the Hammam is the **Governor's office**. In the side street alongside is a row of aluminium booths housing clerks who help citizens overcome the bureaucratic mazes involved in completing official forms and typing up various applications, which in Syria can be endless.

► Walk No 4

START: **Jdeide Square**   MAIN FEATURES: **Beit al-Dalal — Beit Wakil — Beit Basil — Beit Balit — Beit Ghazale — Museum of Popular Traditions**   TIME: **1½-2 hours**

The **Jdeide Quarter** lies just north of the line of Aleppo's ancient walls. It first developed during the late Mameluke and early Ottoman periods. In this area are most of the main Christian churches, but these are comparatively modern constructions and the main interest lies in some of the Ottoman Arab houses. For anyone interested in Aleppo's architecture these beautiful structures should be seen.

Ottoman luxury

Formerly residences of rich families, mainly Christian merchants, they have survived in a manner which allows us to appreciate the gracious living of the period which money, and perhaps influence, could buy. The basic design of these

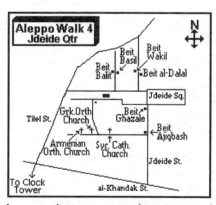

residences is the street door opening onto a spacious courtyard with a central fountain, dotted with orange, lemon and jasmine trees. On one side of the yard, inset into an outer wall, would be the iwan (or diwan), which was used for relaxing during the warm summer evenings. A door off the iwan led into the winter drawing room with a wood burning stove. This room would have had richly decorated ceiling and walls and, naturally, expensive carpets on the floors. Other rooms around the courtyard would have been a dining room and a guest salon where the owner would receive visitors. On the upper level were the sleeping quarters and, if the owner was a Muslim, perhaps a separate area for women.

This walk takes us to see some of these residences, now mostly taken over by institutions.

Armenian school

Take a taxi to Jdeide Square (Midan Jdeide). Walk to the north west corner of the square. Proceed down the lane for about 15 metres and turn right into a cobbled alley, Sissi Street, (under an arch).

The first house on our tour, **Beit al-Dalal**, is at the first door on your right (c25 metres). This is a 17th C house, now an Armenian elementary school. Ring the bell and you will be welcomed in. At the end of the lovely large courtyard is the spacious iwan. The rooms off the courtyard, now used as classrooms, were the living quarters of a very rich family. The teachers don't mind visitors and you are welcome to peep into a classroom full of cute little children at their desks.

A further 20 metres on the left is **Beit Wakil**, now owned by the Greek Orthodox Church.

Return to the main lane from which you turned under the arch, and continue along, past several handbag shops. Take the first street on your right, Zabbel Street. The first door on the right, number 14, is **Beit Basil** a Greek Catholic orphanage. This lovely home dates from the early 18th C. The iwan has been converted into a chapel, but the decoration is still there.

On the opposite side of the street, number 13, is **Beit Balit**, now an Armenian orphanage.

Return to Jdeide Square and cross it to the southwest corner. Fifty metres down Jdeide Street on your right is **Beit Ghazale**. Dating from the 17th C it is now also an Armenian school. This is, perhaps, the grandest of the Aleppo homes.

museum of traditions

Further down Jdeide Street is **Beit Ajiqbash**, now the home of the **Museum of Popular Traditions** (open 8.00 to 4.00 closed Tuesday), dating from the mid 18th C. The guest salon, facing the iwan. has a beautiful ceiling of gilded and painted wood.

Incidentally, no admission charge is made to visit these homes, but a donation is appreciated (though not requested) by the orphanages.

> ▸ **Walk No 5** - the souks of Aleppo

"As for the town, it is massively built and wonderfully disposed, and of rare beauty, with large markets arranged in long adjacent rows so that you pass from a row of shops of one craft into that of another...These markets are all roofed with wood, so their occupants enjoy ample shade..." Ibn Jubayr, Medieval Arab Traveller, 1184

While the vaulted roofs are now made of stone, this 800 year-old description of Aleppo's souks is still a fairly accurate portrayal of what you will find.

The labyrinthine souks of Aleppo twisting to and fro for some 8 kilometres are arguably the best in the Middle East and maintain the age-old traditions of Turkish and Arab commerce. Unlike the souks of some other Arab old cities, these are still the hub of everyday shopping for the people of Aleppo and its environs. There is no "tourist" area here, and while the business-minded Arab shopkeeper is always on the lookout for a foreigner with money to spend, there are no specialised shops catering to them.

The world's first shopping malls?

Centuries before we thought of having a vast covered shopping area to protect us from inclement weather, covered markets and bazaars were the norm in Ottoman and Arab cities. The lofty vaulted roofs keep the souks cool in the high summer heat and dry in the often torrential rains of winter.

stepping back in time

Here is a glimpse of a way of life virtually unaltered for hundreds of years — with perhaps the electric light bulb being the only major change. I have visited these markets countless times and never tire of it. Each visit is fascinating: the scented spices, colourful cloths, the glitter of gold and, most of all, the people; for here you will find a mingling of the whole gamut of Middle Eastern peoples — Arabs, Kurds, Turks, Armenians, Iranians.

As previously mentioned, the former exclusivity of each souk to a trade is not now strictly adhered to, although a particular craft often still dominates. Near the Khan al-Sabon (see end of Walk 2) you will find the gold souk. Gold is very important to Arabs. At marriage every woman acquires a quantity of gold jewellery, and many a young man has to save hard in order to provide it.

golden bangles for the bride

Note how the rough cobbles have given way in this

"expensive" area to smooth paving, even marble in some places. The tiny shops, each hardly big enough to hold more than two or three people, are brightly lit and sparkle with golden bangles, necklaces, and earrings. Plush red velvet seats take up most of the space in some. Watch how seriously the men, especially the Bedouin, take their gold purchases, usually with their wives or brides-to-be in tow. Assayers' scales are always used to determine the price, which may be haggled over for quite some time. And though there are so many shops, all selling seemingly identical merchandise, customers do not shop around much but know exactly where they want to go. Gold purchase for many is not a one-time activity, but rather on-going as and when money becomes available. Gold has always been a traditional way for Arabs to keep their money, and I would expect in an economy such as the Syrian this is by far the safest bet — and a legal one as the holding of foreign currency is not permitted.

rolling out the carpet

Also near the Khan Sabon is the carpet and rug souk. Every Arab home whether it be a palace or a tent has carpets. The bare floors are covered with them. So, of course, are the mosques. Shoes are always removed before treading on them, and the shopkeeper has endless patience as he unrolls carpet after carpet to tempt a would-be buyer. As the purchase of such an important article concerns the whole family, there are many to please and many cups of tea to be consumed.

enjoy a tea break

Then find the tailors' souk, the ropemakers' souk, the souk for bridal gowns. Just take your time and wander about. Merchants may try to induce you to buy, but few will be pushy and if you are invited for tea you can accept without any obligation to purchase. It may give you an opportunity to meet some of the locals.

heady aromas

The spice and nut markets are always enticing: the fragrances of cinnamon, cumin, coriander and the aromas of roasting nuts and coffee ground with cardamon. The array of nuts will tempt you — cashews, walnuts, watermelon and sunflower seeds, pine nuts and almonds. If you like pistachios (fistook), those from Aleppo, *fistook Halab*, have been world-renowned for centuries. There are vendors who sell nothing but large cakes of utility scrubbing soap next to purveyors of the finest Damask silks; carcasses of sheep hang next door to shops of shiny brass and copperware; whole streets sell nothing but shoes, others wool and yarn and yet others kefiya headdresses and galabiyas, the long loose Arab robe.

exotic atmosphere

All the while you have to shuffle through the milieu, while children thrust socks or towels at you, not to mention having to dodge out of the way for cars which somehow manage to honk their way through the crowded narrow alleys with millimetres to spare on either side! And just to complete the experience, the wailing strains of Arabic music waft everywhere, emanating from the various shops and cubbyholes, providing a permanent accompaniment.

THE BARON HOTEL

Whilst this guide doesn't dwell in detail on any particular hotel, the Baron deserves special mention as having secured a niche in Aleppo's modern history.

Situated on Baron Street west of the clock tower, it is, if no longer Aleppo's premier hostelry, certainly its most celebrated. When it was built in 1909 it was the first hotel outside the city walls and, amazing though it may seem now, faced the open countryside and trees. (The street was named after the hotel, not the other way round!) It was a luxury hotel offering everything the rich, early 20th century traveller desired: central heating, bar, restaurant and European style bathrooms, which perhaps the guest had not seen for days. Aleppo was then on the route of the Orient Express which travelled via Constantinople to Baghdad.

The Baron counts among its many distinguished guests Theodore Roosevelt, Charles Lindberg, General Allenby, King Faisal (of Syria), Moustafa Kemal Pasha (Kemal Ataturk), Agatha Christie and numerous members of European royalty.

The hotel has good reason to remember T E Lawrence's visit: for some reason he left hurriedly and neglected to pay his bill! You can see it displayed along with other memorabilia in a glass case in the TV lounge.

Sadly the heyday of this hotel has past. Once the epitome of good living it has now declined to such a degree that only nostalgia brings people to stay. The city that has grown around it is noisy and scruffy; the difficulties during the latter part of the French occupation of Syria and the austerity of the state post-independence have taken their toll. Unable to modernise without great investment, the Baron today is in sore need of general maintenance and the waiters could do with new suits!

For all that, I do recommend you try and stay in this legendary hostelry which was once the last word in elegance and comfort. Its huge, high-ceilinged, dimly-lit rooms with outmoded plumbing may no longer be suited to today's celebrity traveller, but for a sentimental glimpse of a lost era you could do a lot worse.

Other places of interest

► Public gardens

Just west of Baron Street are the public parks. Laid out during the French occupation they are a peaceful area for relaxation if the noise and bustle of the city gets you down. The leafy shade of the tall trees is very soothing, and the well-appointed lawns and pathways with benches to sit on are kept scrupulously clean.

► Aleppo Museum

Situated on the corner of Baron and al-Maari streets, the Aleppo Museum contains artefacts not only from the city itself but from all over northern Syria. As you enter you can see basalt statues from the 9th C BC found during the 1920 excavations at Tell Halaf, on the Turkish border in north-east Syria. There are also exhibits from Mari, which include some interesting statues.

Mari, one of the most important archaeological finds in the past 50 years, has much on show here. The site itself, on the southern stretch of the Euphrates (see Euphrates Valley chapter), is really quite dull, but if its history interests you it is here that your curiosity should be satisfied.

Also of interest is the section on Ras Shamra-Ugarit. Some of the jewellery from the 14th C BC is quite fascinating.

The museum is open from 9.00-14.00 and from 16.00-18.00 every day except Tuesday.

AROUND ALEPPO

► THE DEAD CITIES

The area around Aleppo, especially to the north and west, abounds with ruins which are termed by archaeologists "the Dead Cities". Most date from Greek and Roman times and are so decayed that they are of little interest to the touring visitor. Others exhibit more extensive remains and are worthy of a place on your itinerary. Excavations show that the building of these settlements began in the first century AD and peaked around the 6th C. By the 9th or 10th C, due apparently to the almost constant conflict between Byzantium and the Arabs, the area was virtually abandoned.

The most interesting of these sites to visit in the vicinity of Aleppo are the Church of St Simeon above Telanissos, today Deir Semaan — a must in every traveller's itinerary — and, to a lesser extent Cyrrhus, known as Nebi Uri in Arabic, north west of Azaz on the Turkish frontier.

► CHURCH OF ST SIMEON (Qala'at Semaan)

Location

About 40 kms north west of Aleppo, Saint Simeon or Qala'at Semaan should be visited from Aleppo.

There is a direct road to the site from Aleppo via Daret Ezzeh but it is not too easy to locate from within Aleppo's busy traffic maze. You need to get to the Pullman Hotel, and from there someone can guide you onto the road. If you have to ask, ask for Daret Ezzeh or Qala'at Semaan. Once you are on the road there are plenty of signposts.

For bus travellers there are quite frequent microbuses from the microbus station near the Amir Palace Hotel which reach Daret Ezzeh. From there you'll have to find a lift.

In the season there are daily tours which are reasonably priced. Ask at your hotel.

History

St Simeon the Stylite — he is sometimes called the Elder — (Semaan al-Amoudi or Semaan of the Pillar in Arabic) was born in 386 in Cilicia. When he was about 16 he joined a monastic community located on the slopes of Jabal al-Sheikh, Mount Hermon. About ten years later he moved to another community at Telanissos (or Deir Semaan, below the site of Qala'at Semaan, where he was to spend the remainder of his life).

over 40 years on a 40 foot pillar!

After some years he felt the need to isolate himself from people and erected a column 2 metres high on the hill above the village, with a platform on the top and took up residence there! Later, to achieve even greater solitude, he extended the height of the column to about 15 metres. His food was supplied via a ladder by fellow monks once a week and here he lived for 42 years (!) braving all kinds of weather on this very exposed hill until his death in 459.

no ladies please

During this period he attracted pilgrims from all over the Byzantine world, and it is said occasionally preached to them. He would take questions from the pilgrims and try to answer them. He would not, however, speak to women and refused to converse even with his own mother!

On his death the local Christian leadership wished to bury him near the pillar, but his remains were taken by Byzantine soldiers to Antioch, where they were interred in the Cathedral. There is evidence that they were later moved to Constantinople.

cult status

After his death a cult developed around his example and others emulated him, the most famous being Daniel al-Amoudi who sat atop a pillar near Constantinople around the end of the 5th C. St Simeon (the Younger) perched on his pillar near Antioch in the mid 6th C. Others continued this strange custom until about the 11th C, and odd cases did occur later.

Adherents of this peculiar form of monasticism became known as Stylites, after the Greek word *stylos*.

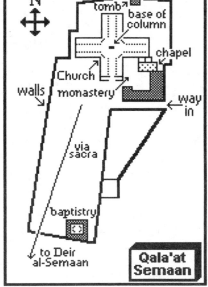

Even more so after his death than during his lifetime pilgrims made the journey to see the pillar, and in 476 the Byzantine Emperor Zeno began the construction of the great church complex.

Visit

Qala'at Semaan is a wonderful location to visit, set on a high hill overlooking the Afrin valley. The River Afrin, rising in southern Turkey, crosses northern Syria into Turkey again and waters the broad valley.

The remains are very substantial and it is easy to grasp how magnificent it must have been nearly 1500 years ago. So solid-looking are the buildings that it is no wonder the Arabs called it a *qala'a* (fort).

The road goes up to the summit where the entrance to the site is located. After paying the usual tiny charge you take a path which leads to the hill's flat top. To the south is the baptistry and a view over Deir al-Semaan (Telanissos). To the north is the church.

souvenirs of the pillar

The enormous **octagonal church** comprises four huge basilicas in the form of a cross. When it was finished towards the close of the 5th C it was, perhaps, the largest church in

Christendom. In the centre is a courtyard where **St Simeon's pillar**, now little more than a base, stood. (Over the centuries pilgrims have chipped away pieces for souvenirs.) The courtyard was most likely capped with a wooden domed roof. This would have been destroyed in the earthquake of 528 and no attempt was made to reconstruct it.

The **eastern basilica**, the largest, was used for services while the others served to receive the many faithful who flocked there. At the end of the **western basilica** is a terrace with views over the Afrin valley. This is an area well suited just for wandering about, admiring the remains and taking photographs. Much of the wonderful decoration is still visible.

Between the eastern and southern basilicas are the remnants of a **chapel and cloister**. It can be supposed that visiting priests were housed here, as were those who officiated in the church. At the far north of the hilltop is a small **mortuary chapel**.

the sacred way

At the south end of the site c200 metres from the church is the **baptistry**. Between the two parts is the *via sacra* or sacred way which commenced in Telanissos from where the pilgrims began their processional climb to the shrine. The baptistry has weathered the centuries remarkably well. A square building which encloses an octagonal interior, it was, like the courtyard of the main church, topped with an 8 sided wooden roof.

village in ruins

At the foot of the hill is the village of Deir Semaan, ancient **Telanissos**. Originally just an agricultural village it housed a monastery to which St Simeon attached himself in his early years. After his death, and with the building of the church, Telanissos grew in importance as thousands of pilgrims came to the Stylite shrine. Hostels were built to house them, as were churches to serve their spiritual needs. The scanty remains of some of these buildings can be seen amid the ruins.

▶ THE TEMPLE OF AIN DARA (Maabad Ain Dara)

Some 17 kms north of Deir Semaan in the Afrin valley is the Tell of Ain Dara, a Hittite temple dating from around 1200 BC.

If you have a car and the extra time it is worth a visit, especially in the spring when the surrounding countryside is beautiful. Without your own transport it can be difficult to get to, and I am not sure if the effort is really worthwhile.

black lion

Discovered in the early 1950s Ain Dara was initially excavated in 1956. The temple was built on a wide terrace of stone, and was surrounded by black basalt statues, many of which still cover the tell while others are on display in museums around Syria.

restoration?

Archaeologists from Japan are currently restoring the site and it looks more like they are building it as there is concrete everywhere! Perhaps they intend to paint it black afterwards! Of the basalt statues the most impressive left on the site is a huge lion lying on its side with incredibly clear markings.

From the hilltop there is a good view of the Afrin river as it flows towards the Hatay.

► CYRRHUS (Nebi Uri)

Location

Nearly 80 kms north of Aleppo, almost on the Turkish frontier, Cyrrhus is an interesting site to visit for those with transport. Follow the road north for the northern Turkish border to the town of Azaz. Cyrrhus is then another c30 kms slightly north west along a far from good road. (Try to confirm your route by asking for Nebi Uri.) This road passes over two 3rd C very humped back Roman bridges (see below). Negotiate them very carefully!

Those without transport have a problem. Although there are microbuses to Azaz there is no onward public transport to Cyrrhus, which means trying to get a taxi, but it may be expensive.

History

Built by Seleucus I Nicator around 250 BC, Cyrrhus lay at the northern edge of the Seleucid territories. In 64 AD it was incorporated into the Roman Empire and was used as a military base for campaigns to the north (against Armenia). The city was badly damaged by Persian invasions during the 3rd C. Under the Byzantines the city was rebuilt and renamed Hagiopolis. In the 6th C Justinian re-fortified it against the Persians. Cyrrhus fell to the Arabs in 637.

The Crusaders called the city Corcia and made it part of the Principality of Edessa (Urfa). After reverting to the Arabs at the time of Nur al-Din it faded into obscurity.

Visit

The most notable remnant is the **theatre**, somewhat restored by the French. This was a huge edifice and in its original rivalled the one at Bosra for size. To the west of the theatre is the **citadel** and if you scramble to the top your reward will be a fine vista of the countryside around.

A short way along the modern road, west, in the direction of Bulbul you can notice just south of the road a hexagonal **Roman tower tomb** with a pyramid roof. In the 14th C it was converted into a tomb for a Muslim holy man hence the Arabic name for Cyrrhus, Nebi Uri, the Prophet Uri.

The two **Roman bridges** on the road from Azaz are certainly worth noting. The first one crossing the Afrin river employs three arches, while the second, spanning the Sabun, has six. The fact that they have survived to this day is a tribute to Roman construction.

SOUTH OF ALEPPO

If your itinerary allows it, there are two places of interest to visit in an excursion south of Aleppo: the archaeological site of Ebla and the town of Maarat al-Numan.

► EBLA (Tell Mardikh)

Ebla is one of the most important archaeological discoveries in Syria in the past half century. Having said that it is not of great interest to most laymen, as there is hardly anything to see.

Location

Situated about 50 kms south of Aleppo off the main Damascus highway. Turn left at the signpost (to Tell Mardikh) 5 kms south of the junction for Latakia. Without your own transport, take any microbus for Hama and alight at the turn off. From there you will have a 45 minute walk.

History and visit

Ebla was one of the most important and powerful city-states in northern Syria during the third millennium BC. At the zenith of its power, between c2600 and 2240 Ebla's influence ran from Lebanon into northern Mesopotamia. When the site was excavated (1964+), as many as 15,000 clay tablets were discovered which, besides being informative about Ebla, provided a source of knowledge about the era which to some extent had hitherto been lacking.

worldwide traders

Ebla was prosperous and this prosperity was due to a number of factors. Situated in a fertile region of Syria, agriculture was intensive and with the raw materials that were under its control Ebla was able to conduct commerce with countries far beyond the bounds of Syria itself. These included Iran, Cyprus, Egypt, and lower Mesopotamia.

greed of the Akkadians

Ebla's economic power, however, proved to be its downfall. Wanting to seize it for themselves, the Akkadians under either their great ruler Sargon or his grandson, fired the city in c2240. The city survived that event but its heyday was over. In the early 2nd millennium it was taken over by the Amorites, a Semitic people who formed a new state. The Amorite state was unable to attain the prowess of the original Eblaite state and it was destroyed by the Hittites in c1600 BC.

Archaeologists have been at work since 1964 and have unearthed many exciting remains, but these have been transferred to museums. What you can see at the site are scant remnants of the palace, a temple and some royal tombs.

► MAARAT AL-NUMAN

Location

25 kilometres further south on the Damascus highway lies Maarat al-Numan with its typically oriental atmosphere. Known as Arra in Hellenistic and Roman times, no vestiges of that period remain.

History

Crusader cannibals

Maarat's place in the history books is ghoulish! In 1099 the Crusaders under Raymond de Saint-Giles, the Count of Toulouse and Bohemond, styled Prince of Antioch laid siege to the town. The townspeople were able to hold off the attackers for some weeks before the Crusaders offered to spare them if they surrendered. This they did and the Franks proceeded to massacre them all, men women and children. It is said that 20,000 Muslims were slaughtered. History records that the Crusaders were so famished that they resorted to eating the Muslims they had killed! Maarat remained in Crusader hands until retaken by Zengi in 1135.

Visit

Just off the centre of the town is a 16th C caravanserai, now the town's museum. The mosaics displayed there are from the surrounding sites and date from the 5th and 6th centuries.

The mosque in the main square has a 12th C minaret. The mosque stands on the site of a pagan temple and uses some recycled bits and pieces. About a kilometre northwest of the mosque are the remains of a citadel.

Route possibilities

Car drivers can continue to al-Bara (see below) which is c25 kilometres west of Maarat al-Numan, and drive on to Latakia for the night. If you plan to do this, as al-Bara is by far the most visually interesting site of the three described in this excursion, you should not linger too long in Ebla or al-Numan to avoid driving across the mountains at night. (You may even wish to skip one or other of them.) Without your own transport I don't recommend visiting al-Bara from Maarat al-Numan.

Alternatively, return to Aleppo from al-Numan and visit al-Bara on your way to the coast the following day (main itinerary).

▸ AL-BARA

Before setting out it is a good idea to buy some food for a light picnic as to have a picnic lunch at al-Bara is delightful.

Location

For bus travellers al-Bara is not easy to get to, and even if you do manage it, it may be difficult to sort out the transport problems, see the site and get to Latakia, or even back to Aleppo, all in the same day. But for the determined, I suggest taking a microbus (check the times in advance as they are not too regular) from Aleppo to al-Riha (Ariha), and from there try to get a taxi or other vehicle to take you. It will, however, be expensive.

Take the Damascus highway south for c70 kms to Saraqib. Here the road to Latakia branches off west. Continue to al-Riha (Ariha), about 24 kms. After another c5 kms you will come to Uroom al-Joz. Turn left here to al-Bara. Try to check with a local or passing motorist that you have the correct turn off. Al-Bara is another c15 kms.

When you reach the modern village of al-Bara you will see a sign post pointing right, to the ruins. Take this narrow road, and after 200m or so, where it curves right, another lane leads off it, slightly downhill and forking slightly to the left. Along this (asphalted) track, almost immediately you will see a pyramid tomb sitting in the middle of an olive grove. Find somewhere to park.

History

Al-Bara, Kapropera in Greek, is a prominent example of one of the "dead cities". Dating from the 4th C, during the 5th and 6th centuries it was a very flourishing city. It was a major olive oil and wine producing centre, and you can see to this day that olive groves are abundant. Many of its citizens must have been very wealthy, as the impressive tombs indicate. The Muslim conquest left the city quite unscathed, and the history of the town continued well into the Crusader period.

Visit

The setting of al-Bara is thoroughly pastoral. What was once a city is now a patchwork of olive groves and orchards. As the remnants of the city are scattered through these fields, to get to many of them you will have to climb over stone boundary walls, constructed largely from materials taken from the old buildings. To see al-Bara properly a guide would be very helpful as it is spread over several kilometres. I find it adequate just to roam around. If you do want a guide, ask in the village for the warden, who also has keys to some of the locked buildings.

tombs of the unknown

The **pyramid tomb** you arrive at is the smaller of two that still exist intact. Finely decorated on the outside, there are 2 sarcophagi inside. If you follow the lane around to the right you will be able to see the second, and much larger, mausoleum, also with a high, pointed roof. This tomb has much richer decoration, and contains 5 sarcophagi. It is not known to whom these tombs belonged, or if those buried there are all of one family. Time and neglect have affected the interior of the mausoleum, bird droppings and graffiti having made their mark while a few tenacious weeds have made it their home. This nevertheless only tends to enhance the sensation — evoked by the ruins as a whole — of having stumbled upon a remote page from the past.

The scattered ruins cover a vast area and include the remains of at least 5 churches. These can be located roughly 300 metres east and north east of the larger tomb.

combining the present with the past

Almost everywhere you look are building remnants, and because of the altitude it is very pleasant to wander about in the quiet of the olive groves, absorbing the sense of history and continuity contained within their walls.

9. LATAKIA AND VICINITY

TO THE MEDITERRANEAN COAST

From al-Bara return to the main highway to Latakia.

The road now begins to climb over the Jabal al-Zawiye before descending into the Ghab, a depression through which the Orontes flows northwards.

reclamation of swamp

Not so long ago the valley was useless marshland into which the river petered out. The draining of this swamp was the second major agricultural project undertaken by post independent Syria. This one, unlike the Euphrates dam venture, has proved an unqualified success and the Ghab is now one of the most fertile regions in the country. The numerous drainage canals can be seen from high up as you descend into the valley.

When the road reaches the valley it passes through the town of Jisr-al-Shugur. Known in Greek times as Seleucobelus it was then an important river crossing point. There is nothing of real interest left to see apart from perhaps the road bridge which incorporates elements of former structures and is said to contain bits of the original Roman one.

through the mountains

The road now climbs through the Jabal Ansariye.   Since ancient times the route through the mountains to the coast has been the same, naturally choosing the lowest and most negotiable passage, but it still goes over a pass at nearly 700 metres, twisting and turning the whole way.

treacherous night drive

You are advised to try to avoid making this drive during the hours of darkness. The road is not too wide and a large number of heavy vehicles rattle (and roar) along it, many with defective headlamps or no rear lights at all! Until the new autostrada is completed (this will take some years, I reckon), this road is probably Syria's most dangerous for night driving. The distance from Jisr-al-Shugur to Latakia is 75km.

► LATAKIA (al-Ladhiqye)

Syria's main port, and most atypical city, Latakia strives to put on a "Mediterranean" look and parts of it might just succeed. Until independence a town of little importance, it has recently grown tremendously, mostly in the past 20-30 years.

venue for Mediterranean Games

The city was overhauled in the late 1980s for Syria's hosting of the Mediterranean Games. Stadia of international standards were erected as were access roads and all the associated paraphernalia. The Games were a vast public relations exercise for Syria at a time when its global esteem was at a low ebb.

Such as it is, Latakia is Syria's premier seaside resort, boasting 2 five star hotels as well as chalet complexes. Nonetheless, much will have to be done before tourists from Europe select Latakia for a beach and fun holiday!

The main reason for staying in the city is to use it as a base to visit some of the nearby sites.

History

Until the fall of Ugarit (see next sub-chapter) the area of Latakia was part of that kingdom. After the division of Alexander's empire it became a major city and port of the Seleucids under Seleucus I Nicator. He renamed it Laodicea, in honour of his mother. Its name today is a corruption of this.

Laodicea came under Roman control in 64 BC and the Romans appended the words *ad-Mare* (by-the-sea) to its name. During the latter part of the first century BC, Mark Antony, who looked with some favour on the place, made it a free city (no or few taxes).

Biblical links

That Laodicea had an important early Christian community is attested to in the New Testament. Paul, in his letter to the Colossians asks for his letter to be read to the church there (Col 4:13-16). Laodicea was also one of the Seven Churches mentioned in John's Revelation (1:3), and its believers were recipients of a special message (Rev 3:14-22).

During the 2nd C Septimius Severus undertook major construction, making Laodicea, for a while, capital of the province.

In the late 5th and mid 6th centuries the city was devastated by earthquakes but was rebuilt and fortified (against the Persians) by Justinian. In the 7th C it was taken by the vanquishing Arab armies.

For the next few centuries the city see-sawed between Arabs, Byzantines, Seljuk Turks, and the Crusaders who renamed it La Liche. In 1103 Tancrede incorporated the city into his principality of Antioch. Taken briefly by Salah al-Din in 1188, the Crusaders regained control and it remained in their hands until the last years of the 13th C when the Mameluke Sultan Qalaun drove them out.

During the Ottoman period the city, mostly ruined, fell into obscurity. One hundred years ago the population was less than 8000.

French quasi-state

The French, during their rule in Syria, tried to divide the country by establishing separate Druze and Alawi French-protected states. Latakia was the "capital" of the latter.

Before the French handed the Sanjak of Alexandretta (today's Hatay) over to the Turks in 1939, Alexandretta (Iskenderun) was Syria's main port. Since independence Latakia has steadily been built up to replace it, and also to avoid dependence on the Lebanese ports.

Visit

Practically nothing has survived of ancient Latakia. The couple of Roman columns that still stand are hardly worth the trouble of locating them.

If you wish to sample the beach life of Latakia you will have to visit the "Côte d'Azur" past the Games complex. The large hotels here (including Le Meridien) have access to fair (not great) beaches, while the small houses along the shore are vaguely reminiscent of a Greek-style coastal village.

AROUND LATAKIA

There are two sites and a mountain village to visit north of Latakia. They can all be visited by those with cars, but I suggest bus travellers limit their excursion to the nearest — and most important — site, Ugarit.

▸ UGARIT (Ras Shamra)

Location

Head north past the huge sports stadium towards the Côte d'Azur Cham and Meridien hotels. Just before the former, at the circle, turn right and continue for c5 kms. The site, called Ras Shamra in Arabic, is signposted. Those travelling by public transport can get a bus from the microbus station going north. Request the driver to stop at the *Khirbet* (ruins).

History

One day in 1925 a local farmer, Mahmoud Mela al-Zir, while ploughing his land near a bay called Minet al-Beida, the White Port, which the Greeks named Leucos Limen, unearthed a stone slab. From this incident attention was drawn to an adjacent hill known as Ras Shamra, Headland of Fennel, and which had the appearance of a tell. Thus was uncovered Ugarit, an ancient Canaanite city and sea port, whose importance in archaeology cannot be overestimated.

revelatory finds

As a Canaanite civilisation it was the forerunner of the Old Testament world, and its hitherto unknown language has had a marked effect on our knowledge of early religion, literature and on Biblical studies.

The site has been excavated almost continually since 1929 and the artefacts found can be seen in the museums of Damascus, Aleppo and the Louvre in Paris.

Ras Shamra was settled from as early as the 6th millennium BC, but it was during the 2nd that it developed into an important urban centre. Between 1600 and 1200 BC it was the capital of a small but prosperous kingdom which had strong ties with the Egypt of the 18th dynasty. Trade relations were maintained with Cyprus, Crete, Mesopotamia, and Anatolia.

Canaanite gods

Religion played a very important part in the daily life of Ugarit. Two temples have been uncovered on the high ground of the city. One was dedicated to Baal and the other to Dagon. Both these deities are familiar to readers of the Old Testament as gods of the Canaanites. A royal palace has also been excavated, and this contained almost 100 rooms.

earliest language?

Particularly significant was the discovery of an unknown language and script. This has been called Ugaritic. The language was written, as were others from Mesopotamia, in cuneiform signs, but unlike them Ugaritic was alphabetic and not syllabic. The alphabet comprises 30 signs with the consonants in the same order as they appear in Hebrew. A vast quantity of inscribed tablets have been unearthed, and besides giving details of life in the city testify to a people who had extensive literature. The availability of such material has been of great importance to scholars in understanding certain linguistic aspects of the Old Testament.

Ugarit was destroyed in 1200 during the major upheaval caused by the invasion of the Sea Peoples. (This was about the same time as the Israelites were moving into the area.)

Site visit

Entry to the site is from the west. Nearby is the fortified entrance to the city, the only surviving part of the walls that surrounded Ugarit. Note the thick stone glacis which was a feature of the walls along their entire circumference.

Just south of the entrance is the **Royal Palace** which was so magnificent that the King of Biblos, Rib-Addu, described it in a letter to Amenophis IV, Pharaoh of Egypt. It dates from the 14th or 13th C BC and has been thoroughly excavated and you'll have to visit the museums mentioned above to see the treasures it yielded. The two temples are on the high ground to the east.

► KASSAB

High in the mountains, 65 kilometres north of Latakia, Kassab lies in the forests of Jabal al-Aqra, the Mount Casius of history, astride the Syrian-Turkish frontier. There are no historical sites to visit here but it is an attractive summer resort, with refreshing mountain air. A number of small hotels cater to the needs of guests.

10.   THE CRUSADER ROUTE

THE CRUSADERS

era of destruction and construction

On 26th November 1095, in a fervently delivered sermon   at Clermont in France, Pope Urban II called upon believers to *"retake the holy places of Christendom from the unbeliever! It is God's will!"*

Thus the Crusades, with their bloodletting and slaughter, burst upon the Levant. By 1118 the entire Levantine littoral, Jerusalem and parts of what is today southern Turkey were in the hands of the Franks (as they are often called).

To reinforce their hold on these territories, the Crusaders fortified cities and built massive fortresses and castles. It took the Muslims over two hundred years to finally dislodge them from the lands they had conquered — and the positions in the brilliantly engineered citadels were the last to fall.

superior remains

During the ensuing centuries many of these intrepid fortresses scattered across the Middle East have crumbled into almost unrecognisable ruins, but of those that have survived, some of the finest and best preserved are in Syria. On visiting them, one can only be astounded at the enormity of the task involved in their construction and the stark beauty of their design. Though little else remains of the bloody Crusader episode, these mighty strongholds testify in stone and mortar to the drive and determination of the enterprise.

▸ The Crusader Castles of SALAH AL-DIN and MARQAB

Both these magnificent Crusader castles lie east of the Latakia-Tartous highway and can be visited from Latakia or en route to

Tartous in the same day. The castles are open every day except Tuesday from 9am-4pm.

▸ QALA'AT SALAH AL-DIN (Saône, Sahyoun)

Location

The castle is situated in the mountains some 25 kms from Latakia. Those without a car can take a microbus from Latakia to Haffeh. From there it is about an hour and a quarter's walk or take a taxi, remembering that you'll want to get back (you might get a lift for this).

By car, take the main road south for Tartous. Just outside the city it passes under a railway bridge and c2 kms further is an exit road to the right, signposted (amongst others) to Haffeh. Take this road and it will lead you under the highway and east.

Follow all the signs to Haffeh, and when you get there (it's a hilltop town), make for the top. There, at a junction to your right there should (but may not) be a sign pointing to Qala'at Saladin. (The last time I was there the sign had been knocked down and was lying on the side of the road. In Syria, it could take a long, long time before it is put back!) If there is none just ask the way. Everyone will know what you are looking for! After about 1.5 kms turn left (try to check again) and this will lead you via a precipitous, winding road down into a steep gorge.

dramatic setting

As you descend, stop where suitable to get a dramatic vista of the castle high on the opposite side of the gorge. Continue down into the gorge and across a small bridge over a stream, and you arrive at the castle through a narrow canyon with almost vertical sides — incredibly mostly man made — with a rock pillar some 28 metres high in the middle of the road. The castle defences rise as if in one piece from the sheer canyon wall. Park at the end of the canyon.

History

Given the name Qala'at Salah al-Din only in 1957 in honour of its illustrious captor, the historical (and Crusader) name for this castle is Saône (or Sahyoun), after Robert of Saône, a vassal of the Frankish Prince of Antioch who took over and enlarged the castle in the early 12th century.

Spectacularly set on a ridge below the loftiest peak of the Jabal Ansariye (over 1500 metres) and with a commanding view down to the coastal plain, the suitability of the site for a fortress had been obvious for more than a thousand years before the

Syria

Sites with distances

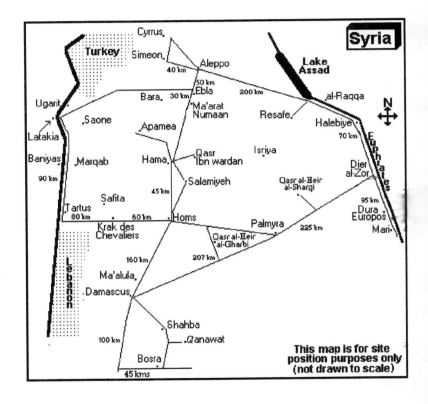

THE LIFE OF SALAH AL-DIN

Salah al-Din Yusuf ibn Ayyub (Righteous of the Faith, Joseph son of Job), known to the west as Saladin, is arguably the most illustrious of Muslim rulers. Also called al-Malik (the King) al-Nasir Salah al-Din Yusuf I, he preferred to be known as Sultan.

Salah al-Din was born into an important Kurdish family. His father, Najam al-Din Ayyub, entered the employ of Zengi the Turkic governor of Aleppo and northern Syria.

Although he showed a preference for religious studies, he joined the army under his uncle al-Din Shirkuh, who served under Nur al-Din, son of Zengi, and soon to succeed him. Salah al-Din was sent to Egypt to prevent that land being taken by the Latin King of Jerusalem. In 1171 he abolished the (Shi'ite) Fatimid Caliphate there, and returned the country to Sunni Islam. He was appointed ruler of Egypt, under Nur al-Din, with the title al-Malik.

On the death of Nur al-Din in 1174 he marched into Syria to ensure that Nur al-Din's young son succeeded to the throne. However his ambition to unite all Muslims caused him to abandon this and he became ruler himself. He soon developed a reputation as a generous and benevolent leader. With his Muslim piety he encouraged the growth of Islamic religious institutions and he sought the company of scholars and preachers.

Determined to drive the Crusaders from the area, his exceptional military skill was devoted to this purpose. Until then the Crusaders, with their tremendous military prowess, had succeeded in holding the Muslims at bay.

His greatest triumph came on 4 July 1187 when he was able to draw a thirsty and exhausted Frankish army into battle just west of the Sea of Galilee. (At that time of the year the area is stiflingly hot and humid.) Beneath a towering cliff known as the Horns of Hittin he trapped and destroyed a parched and heat-crazed army. So great was the victory that all of Crusader Palestine soon fell to him. On October 2 the same year Jerusalem surrendered to him, thus ending nearly 100 years of Crusader rule.

Unlike the Christian conquest, when the Crusaders barbarically slaughtered the inhabitants, Salah al-Din and his army behaved in a civilised and generous manner.

The shocked European world, determined to regain Jerusalem, launched a third Crusade. They were, however, unable to recapture the city or any of the interior, and the Crusader holdings were confined to the coastal areas. Although Salah al-Din did not live to see the final departure of the European Christians from the region his campaigns broke them in such a way that they were never to recover.

Although those around him, including some of his relatives, enriched themselves, Yusuf never sought or asked for worldly benefits. He died in Damascus on 4 March 1193, penniless. The most unselfish ruler the Muslim and Arab world ever had did not even have enough money to pay for a tomb!

Crusaders built their stronghold here. It appears that the first fortifications on the ridge were constructed by Phoenicians, probably from Arwad Island (see Tartous, below). Others after them must have also made use of such a naturally advantageous location.

The site was taken by the Byzantine Emperor John Zimisces around 975 and whatever fortifications he found there were expanded. The Crusaders apparently took possession early in the 12th C, as in 1119 the castle is recorded as being in the hands of Robert of Saône, whose name it bore until recently.

Saladin seizes command

The work the Crusaders invested in strengthening the fortress must have been considerable even though their undertaking was a reworking of the former Byzantine citadel. Yet in spite of its seemingly impregnable location and formidable bastions, it did not survive very long in Crusader hands.

Salah al-Din, fresh after his rout of the Crusaders at Hittin and recovery of Jerusalem in 1187, proceeded to eliminate the Crusader presence from the Syrian coastal area. In the summer of 1188 he took Latakia and then moved on Saône to which he laid siege. Within a few days he had overwhelmed the castle's defences and it surrendered without much opposition. It was never retaken by the Crusaders.

Qa'alat Salah al-Din was subsequently occupied by different Arab leaders who added to it here and there. So large was its area that a small town grew up within the walls, eventually abandoned.

Visit

Minus the bits added by the Arabs, Saône is one of the best examples of early Crusader castle building. The castle area is vast: about 700 metres long and 120 wide at its broadest, and it is built on the top of a narrow buttress which extends from the mountains.

You enter the castle from the south side via a long stepped path, leading gradually upwards through pine-wooded slopes. The path passes along the foot of three huge **square bastions**, part of the Crusader rebuilding. The entry gate is via the third of these towers and was once secured by a portcullis. The entry chamber (where you pay and are offered the usual selection of postcards) leads to the castle interior which is in a ruinous state.

On the south side, just east of the first of the square bastions, is a **cistern**, one of a number which were necessary for the fortress's water supply. The two-storey **main donjon** (keep) is on the east side and between that and the cistern are the large

stables. The walls of the donjon exceed 5 metres in thickness and with its massive base it was supposed to be the redoubt-of-last-resort. You can gain access to the terrace for a superb view.

man-made gorge

To the north of the keep was the drawbridge, which utilised the rock pillar in the canyon below as support. The canyon was mainly excavated by the Crusaders but there is every possibility that some sort of trench had been dug there by the Byzantines earlier. We can only wonder how such a gorge was carved out of the rock, leaving just the pinnacle, without the use of mechanical tools or explosives.

Facing the entrance were the Arab-constructed **baths** and to the right a **mosque** erected in the 11th or 12th C. On the higher ground to the west are the remnants of the **Byzantine citadel** constructed in the 10th C and in front of that, the **Crusader church**.

easily overran

To the west of this elevation is an uncompleted ditch dug out of the rock. This ditch separated the main castle from the lower courtyard. Here the walls were weaker, and the ditch was supposed to act as an inner moat to forestall rapid advancement of the attackers should the walls be breached. As it happens, Salah al-Din was able to gain entry fairly quickly, and the unfinished ditch presented no obstacle to him completely overrunning the fortress.

Near the western extremity of the lower court are the remains of a **Byzantine chapel**.

▸ QALA'AT MARQAB

Location

Situated 6 kms east of Baniyas (roughly halfway between Latakia and Tartous), Qala'at Marqab can be visited from either city, or en route. If travelling by bus, there is a microbus from Baniyas which goes almost to the castle. There is nothing of note in the town of Baniyas itself, but there are a couple of hotels that may prove useful.

To get to Marqab when driving south from Latakia, take the exit into Baniyas (as there is no left turn from the highway) and drive into the town, turning left (S) just before the sea front. Continue south through the town until you see a signposted left turn. Follow this ascending road over the highway for about 6 kms. Just before the castle, the road forks. Either way will bring you to the entrance on the west side, but if you follow the left fork you will gain a good appreciation of the castle's position and will also get an excellent view of the southern — and most important — defences. The right fork (with a sign pointing to the castle cafeteria) takes you along a particularly hair-raising stretch, with a shoulderless road hugging the vertical mountain edge.

spectacular setting

The castle looks stunning! Sitting on the edge of an extinct volcano at an altitude of 360 metres, the black basalt ramparts stand out in dramatic relief against the pastels of the hills and the brilliant backdrop of blue sky. Far below, stretched out before you, are the Mediterranean sea and town of Baniyas in the coastal plain — which is at its narrowest point here.

The citadel's position is clearly strategically as well as scenically superb. From the ridge on which Marqab stands all movement along the coast from Antioch into Palestine could be monitored.

History

First erected by the Muslims about 1062, Marqab was seized by the Frankish Prince of Antioch around the same time as Saône, between 1120 and 1140. An important French family, the Masoirs, were installed there and proceeded to rebuild and strengthen the castle. In 1186 it was given to the Knights Hospitallers who with their large resources and expertise turned it into an almost impregnable bastion.

too formidable for Saladin

So formidable was Marqab that Salah al-Din, after his victories in Palestine (1187) decided not to attack it when he passed by in 1188. Other attempts to take it in the 13th C were repulsed. In 1285, fourteen years after the surrender of the Krak des Chevaliers, and after being besieged by the Mameluke Sultan Qalaun for some 4 weeks, it eventually capitulated.

The defending Knights were given safe passage to the last Crusader strongpoints on the Levantine coast, Tartous, Tripoli, and Acre.

Visit

The ridge on which Marqab stands allowed for the castle's triangular design, with the sharp edge pointing towards the most vulnerable southern aspect where it is joined to the main mountain mass. To provide extra defence from this quarter a deep trench was cut, effectively severing the castle from the surrounding mountains. The road skirting the castle (the way which brings you to the castle via the left fork), follows the line of this trench.

You enter from the west side up an ascending path and through an arched **tower gate** into a **vaulted entrance lobby**. Here you pay the small entrance fee. Turn right and you are between the castle's outer walls (on your right) and a second defence wall (to your left). Continue another 25 metres or so to reach an **inner entrance gate** (a barbican gate) with towers on either side. Inside is a vaulted, three-directional hall. Follow the stairs leading upwards into the castle's **courtyard**, off which most of the castle's facilities were located.

Gothic edifice

To the north and northeast were the **storerooms** capable of storing 5 years' supplies. At the southern end is the **chapel** which was built by the Hospitallers in the late 12th C. Note the two admirable doorways. This example of austere Gothic architecture is perhaps the best preserved item in the castle.

Just south of the chapel steps is the **Great Hall** and to the east of that the three-storeyed **round donjon**, or keep, with walls up to 5 metres thick! Together with the south tower this was the most heavily fortified section of the whole fortress. Coupled with the massive double walls these defences could not have been taken by storm — maybe not even by missile bombardment! It was by mining under the southern tower that Sultan Qalaun was able to persuade the defenders that further resistance would be fruitless.

► TARTOUS (Tartus)

Location

Situated at the northern end of the Syrian coastline, 17 km north of the Lebanese border, Tartous was a sleepy fishing port until about 20 years ago. Today it is the second port city of Syria, and is expanding rapidly. As the city grew much of the medieval city was built over or left to decay. Now, somewhat belatedly, but happily not altogether too late, this is being rectified and a fair amount of restoration work is being carried out.

For relaxation there are coffee houses along the corniche, the road running parallel to the sea. In late afternoon and early evening the corniche is crowded with the local populace strolling up and down, escaping the heat and humidity of their often crowded homes.

picnic on the beach (but not a swim)

Groups of young people gather together on the beach (which unfortunately is not really suitable for bathing), sometimes with small primus stoves for making coffee. The atmosphere is very friendly, and you should expect to be stopped by a student or other wanting to practice English (or French) with you.

History

Tartous was originally founded by the Phoenicians as a mainland colony for the offshore island of Arwad (Ardus). In Seleucid and Roman times it was used as a supply point for the island. The Romans called it Antaradus (anti-Aradus). Emperor Constantine bestowed on the city separate status and its name was changed to Constantia.

miraculous icon

Constantia soon became mostly Christian, and in the 4th C a chapel dedicated to the Virgin was erected. According to local tradition, an icon said to have been painted by the Evangelist Luke which was kept in the chapel, miraculously saved the altar following an earthquake in 487.

The city was occupied by the Muslims in the 7th C and retaken by the Byzantines in 968. In the last years of the 10th C the Fatimids occupied it when they pushed into Syria.

construction of cathedral

The year 1098 saw the arrival of the Crusaders who recognised in the city a port with close proximity to Cyprus. Raymond of Toulouse reinforced it and changed the name to Tortosa. In 1120 the Crusaders constructed the Cathedral of Our Lady of Tortosa on the site of the original chapel in order to accommodate the revered altar which attracted the devotions of many pilgrims.

stronghold of the Knights Templar

Around 1160 the Knights Templar were put in control of Tortosa, and it became their main bastion. Parts of the city were occupied for brief periods by Nur al-Din and later by Salah al-Din, but the Knights Templar never lost overall control of Tortosa and the attackers were forced to withdraw.

Tortosa's hinterland was protected by the great castles of Marqab and the Krak des Chevaliers which helped the city to remain in Crusader hands despite the attempts by the Mameluke Sultan Baibars in 1267 and 1270 to wrest control from them.

sea escape of the Knights

The end, however, eventually came in August 1291, less than 3 months after the Templars' main fortress at Acre was overrun. The Krak had finally fallen in 1271 to Baibars, and Marqab capitulated to his successor Sultan Qalaun in 1285. Further resistance by the Knights of Tortosa was useless, and under cover of darkness they slipped into their boats and sailed the few kilometres to the tiny offshore island of Arwad where they managed to maintain a presence for a further 12 years. The fall of Tortosa effectively marked the end of the Crusader episode in mainland Syria.

Visit

▸ The Cathedral

Of the pre-Crusader city nothing remains, and it is the Crusader city of Tortosa, the "old city", where the interest lies.

The **Cathedral of Our Lady of Tortosa** is easy to locate, just north of the main shopping area. Its austere, fort-like exterior hides a simple, three-aisled basilica design which is marvellous — "*the most beautiful interior from the Crusader period in Syria*" (Johannes Odenthal, Syrie).

After the Crusader withdrawal from the city, the building fell into decline, and apart from serving as a mosque for a short time it found no serious usage. During the French mandate it was extensively restored to its original design and the Syrians have turned it into a quite interesting museum.

severe aspect

Apart from fragments of recycled masonry, there is nothing of the early Byzantine chapel left. As mentioned above, initial construction of the cathedral took place in the first half of the 12th C, but it was badly damaged when the city was partially occupied by Salah al-Din in 1188. When it was rebuilt in the 13th C it acquired the somewhat dour, severe appearance we see today. The towers at the east end were added at that time to reinforce it as a defensive position. Originally there were towers in each of the four corners. Now the only remaining complete ones are at the eastern end.

Entrance is from the western end and the door here may have been preserved from the Byzantine edifice. The interior is uncomplicated: a three-aisled basilica, each aisle ending with an apse. The second pillar down on the left stands on a piece of masonry with a passage through it which may well be a remnant from the original chapel.

interesting exhibits

The small museum has some interesting items, but most of the exhibits carry either no description or a barely legible, faded one in Arabic only. On the right as you enter is a black stone carving of Baal, the chief Canaanite deity, dating from the 7th C BC. It was discovered at Baniyas, north of Tartous. In front of the middle pillar on the left (N) side, the one with the opening in it, is a large 4th C BC Phoenician double jar found at Amrit. The Phoenicians stored their oil by burying an outer jar in the ground to about two thirds its depth, then breaking it to level it off. The second jar full of oil was put inside this as a cool, safe storage facility. There are also some interesting mosaics in the central and eastern apses and a fresco found at the Krak des Chevaliers.

A number of empty marble sarcophagi lie to the north of the church entrance (on your left as you enter). All but one were found at Amrit. The exception was discovered very recently in Safita.

► The Old City

The old city of Tartous is the former Crusader stronghold. The best way to get there is to walk down to the sea-front road and follow the few signs that point to it. As you walk along the landward side you can easily recognise the vestiges of the city walls which form the lower parts of the buildings. In Crusader times this wall was lapped by the sea, the modern road having been built upon reclaimed land. Along this stretch you will see a blue and white sign pointing between the walls to "Old Tartous City" and this leads you directly into its main square.

restoration in progress

Until recently the old city area was in a state of total decay. Families had moved into the old buildings making additions as they pleased and destroying anything which got in the way. As is common in this sort of situation, most of the dwellers were poor so the area took on the appearance of a slum rather than an historical site. Not too late (hopefully), the authorities have begun to rectify matters. Some parts have already been restored and work is continuing. In the meantime, more than a little imagination will be required to see this as a Crusader fortress!

One of the nicest parts is **the chapel**, but you will have to close your eyes to the dirt as you visit it (perhaps by the time you are there it will have been cleaned up)! You'll find it in the north-east corner of the square, through an arched opening with a clearly church-like façade. The high-domed hall is now partially open to the elements, and around it people have made their homes. Despite this it is easy to imagine how it once looked.

Back in the square you may be able to approach **the donjon** on the west (sea) side. At my last visit this was being restored and access was difficult. On the sea side of the donjon, remains of the **talus** with a small rear gate can still be seen. From here the Knights Templar entered their boats and abandoned the fortress.

homes on top of the walls

Around the old city perimeter, on the north and east sides, a deep moat separates the old from the new. All the old walls have been utilised for building upon and are lived in; one tower has even been converted to a mosque complete with minaret.

► ARWAD ISLAND

Three kilometres offshore is the island of Arwad. Today just an appendix to Tartous, time was when the positions were reversed.

A shuttle boat service operates from the small fishing harbour on the sea front esplanade. The trip takes 15-20 minutes. You pay on the way back.

History

Arwad, or rather its people, are mentioned in the Bible, Genesis 10:18, when the "Arvadite" is referred to as being descended from Noah's son, Canaan.

Under the Phoenicians the island acquired importance, and its rulers even founded settlements on the mainland, as far inland as Hama. The seafaring nature of the islanders made it an important trading centre with other places in the eastern Mediterranean.

help for Xerxes

Although Arwad was able to secure its independence throughout much of the area's turmoils, the Assyrians, and later the Persians, eventually brought it under their control. According to Herodotus, the islanders' seafaring skills were used to advantage by Xerxes at the great sea battle of Salamis in 480 BC.

In the mid 2nd C BC the island became part of the Seleucid domains, and in 64 BC was incorporated into the Roman Empire. With the increase in importance of Tartous, Arwad's influence waned, to be briefly revived a thousand years later when it became the last stronghold of the Crusaders following the fall of their mainland citadels.

Visit

Potentially a very picturesque island, much of Arwad's attraction is marred by litter and dirt! But don't let this deter you from visiting.

car-free island

You can spend an hour or so wandering around the alleys that seem to twist and turn all over the island. You will not encounter any traffic; there are no cars! Measuring no more than 800 metres long and 450 wide, a broad promenade runs round most of the island and this, kept cleaner than the interior, makes an enjoyable stroll. The fact that the island was once a fortress is plain to see from the great walls which remain in many places, albeit with various additions. Fishing boats are moored all around and you will pass many Arvadites repairing and stowing their nets.

shipbuilders since Phoenician days

Arwad could be one of the world's oldest shipbuilding yards, and while many far newer and greater ones elsewhere are closing down, Arwad continues in this tradition that goes back at least to Phoenician times. You can see the boat builders at work — most are on the south side of the island.

The **castle** dates from the Crusader era, but when captured by the Muslims it was rebuilt. It is of little interest, and even the small **museum** does not have much to offer. Arwad's chief charm is in its location and its history.

Back at the main harbour there are some restaurants and cafes, where you can enjoy a drink or lunch while watching the typical activities of a fishing harbour.

► AMRIT (Marathus)

About 6-7 kms south of Tartous is an ancient religious site probably founded by the people of Arwad, originally called Marathus and known today as Amrit.

Location

This Phoenician site lies just off the old road to Tripoli (Lebanon), along the sea. Leave the Tripoli road to the right after about three km; you will find the site just over the bridge across the River Amrit. A bus is supposed to go that way — ask at the ticket office.

Visit

An extensive Franco-Syrian redevelopment and restoration project is currently underway and the 3 x 2km large site is enclosed by a concrete wall. There is not too much to see at the present, but quite probably as the work progresses this situation will alter.

healing waters

The item of chief archaeological interest is a **temple** situated not far from the entrance, by the main tell, but little of this is visible above ground. The locals call the temple al-Maabed and it dates from about the 5th C BC. It was dedicated to the god Melqart and built around an artificial lake some 50 by 40 metres in size. The waters of a nearby spring were supposed to have healing powers and a **channel** brought this water to the pond. The channel is currently one of the few clearly identifiable remains of the temple complex. Almost facing, on the other side of the river (N), there are signs of a **stadium** which dates from Hellenistic times.

About half a kilometre south-east of the temple is a **rock-hewn house** and some 300m south of the house is an interesting necropolis with two circular **funerary towers** dating from about the 4th C BC. One is 7 metres high and the other 4. The local name is Maghazel.

► SAFITA (Chastel Blanc)

Location

In the hills between Tartous and the Krak des Chevaliers the Crusader fortress of Chastel Blanc sits atop the small mountain town of Safita.

Safita can be visited either from Tartous, or en route to the Krak. It's about 30 kms west of the city and once you are guided onto the right road you can't go wrong. Most taxi drivers or policemen will point out the way. There is a direct microbus service from Tartous.

attractive countryside

The drive takes you through the foothills of the Jabal Ansariye. The entire area is covered with olive groves and dotted with small villages and is really quite lovely, especially during the springtime.

You will see the square donjon of the Chastel Blanc jutting into the skyline long before you reach the town.

At an altitude of nearly 400 metres, Safita has a pleasant climate, especially during the hot summer months. Not surprisingly it is a resort and there are quite a few hotels including a 4 star Cham Palace and some in the budget range. Once an Eastern (Greek) Orthodox town, Safita today has a mixed population.

History

The first castle was built in Safita almost as soon as the Crusaders took control of the region around 1115, probably as a defence post for Tartous. When Nur al-Din occupied Tartous for a brief period in 1168 he destroyed this first castle. Later, perhaps around the turn of the century, the area was turned over to the Knights Templar, and they rebuilt it, constructing the donjon that has survived until now.

The castle fell to the Mameluke Sultan Baibars just before he seized the Krak.

Visit

To get to the donjon take any ascending cobbled lane off the circular main street. As you ascend you pass many well-kept, stone houses with attractive courtyards. The cool mountain air is refreshing, particularly if you have come from the summer humidity of Tartous.

The donjon was protected by two series' of walls and entered through a **gateway** from the east. Part of this gateway can still be seen. The keep itself, of which the bottom level houses the Greek Orthodox **Church of St Michael**, is entered up a flight of stairs from the west. If it is locked ask at one of the shops around the square and someone will open it. You enter directly into the nave of the church which is a vaulted hall with an apse at the end. In the corner to the right of the entrance, a narrow stone staircase with steep steps well worn by centuries of feet, leads up to a **gallery** divided by 3 cruciform pillars. This second floor is wonderfully designed and was most likely the living quarters for the Knights.

roof with a view

A further flight of stairs opens out onto a terrace, from where there are fantastic views. To the west Tartous is visible on a clear day and the Krak des Chevaliers, to the east, can be seen perched on its spur. With the two castles in sight of one another it must have been possible to send messages between them.

the way to the Krak

There is a route from Safita through the hills to the Krak, but it is complicated to find, and you could lose your way. It would be better to join up with the main Homs-Tartous highway and approach from that direction.

▸ KRAK DES CHEVALIERS (Qala'at al-Husn)

Location

The Krak des Chevaliers can be visited from Damascus (a long day, and only recommended if there is no other choice), Homs or Tartous.

From Damascus take the Homs/Aleppo road north. Before Homs, take the bypass around the city to the west and continue in the direction of Tartous. After c40 kms the turn off to the Krak is signposted. Exit under the highway and continue north, following the road all the way until you see the castle.

From Homs proceed in the direction of Tartous, and follow as above. Most travellers without their own transport will find it easier to get to the Krak from Homs as there are frequent direct buses, especially in the morning. You'll need to get one going to **al-Husn**, the village below the castle.

From Tartous take the Homs highway and exit after c55 kms at the sign. Continue as above. By bus: take the bus to Homs, and ask to be let off at the road to al-Husn. Then cross the main highway and walk to the small road leading to the village. Wait there till a minibus comes and it will take you. The return journey may be more difficult, as when you return to the main road you could have a long wait for a suitable bus to Tartous.

History

"The castle is one of the finest buildings of the middle ages I ever saw", wrote the explorer Johann Lewis Burckhardt (who discovered, among other sites, Petra and Abu Simbel) in 1810.

in command of the Homs Gap

The fortress is built on a ridge of Jabal Khalil which rises to almost 800 metres, and is part of the Ansariye range. The castle itself stands at 300 metres above the plain below, the Homs Gap. This is the only significant break in the mountain ranges of Jabal Ansariye and Jabal Lubnan which traverse the whole of Syria and Lebanon. From earliest times this route was the most important between the coast and the inland regions.

Recognising this, the Emir of Homs built the first recorded stronghold here in 1031. He garrisoned Kurds there and it acquired the name Husn al-Akrad, the fortress of the Kurds.

In 1099, Raymond de Saint-Giles, Count of Toulouse, briefly occupied it on his way to Jerusalem, and in 1110 it came under the control of Tancrede, the Frankish Regent of Antioch.

strengthened by Hospitallers

The castle was given to the Hospitallers, Knights of St John in 1144 when it first acquired the name Le Krak des Chevaliers (the origin of the word Krak is not really known). Under the Knights it was extensively augmented and fortified until it evolved into more or less what we see today. So mighty was this bastion that two of the era's greatest warriors failed to take it: in 1163 Nur al-Din was forced to withdraw following an arduous seige and in 1188 Salah al-Din, in the mood for further conquest after his momentous victories at Hittin and Jerusalem, inspected the defences. Deciding that an attempt on the stronghold would be futile, he directed his warriors to less awesome projects such as the taking of Latakia and Saône (see above).

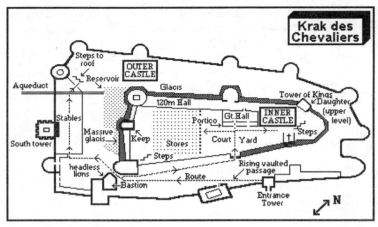

taken by trickery

In fact the great fortress never succumbed to assault. Its end came by deceit, not by battle, in the year 1271 during a siege by the Mameluke Sultan Baibars. After a month of sustained attack in which Baibars was unable to compel the defenders to yield, he resorted to chicanery to achieve what force could not. A letter purporting to come from the Knights' Grand Master in Tripoli instructing them to surrender was delivered to the castle. Believing it was genuine the Knights rode out, having been granted safe conduct to Tripoli. Normally garrisoned by at least 2,000 warriors, only a few hundred were holding it at the fall.

Crusaders reach the end

Thus began the last chapter for the Crusaders in Syria and the Holy Land. By 1291 they had totally withdrawn.

The Mamelukes made some additions to the castle. These consist mainly of the towers in the outer walls. However the Krak did not continue in use very long and was eventually abandoned.

The castle today

The Krak des Chevaliers has remained in a remarkable state of conservation over the centuries. When visited by Burckhardt in 1810 he wrote in his journal that it was "in perfect preservation". Initially the French and subsequently the Syrian Antiquities Department have undertaken what restoration works have been necessary to maintain its intact condition and safeguard tourist access.

I have visited the Krak many times and at different seasons of the year; each time it offers a fresh aspect: in spring, when the grassy hills bloom with a riot of red anemones it assumes an almost fairy-castle appearance; in summer the grey ramparts stand in lonely splendour against the clear skies and sunburnt hills, whilst in winter a towering backdrop of dark, swirling clouds furnish it with a dramatic, defiant countenance. Whatever time of the year you choose, all that is required to complete the scene (as Robin Fedden so admirably puts it), is *"the babble of medieval French...to reach one from the guard room and the chanted Latin Mass from the 12th century chapel"*.

Visit

The castle is open every day of the week (except public holidays) from 9am till 5pm. There is a small admission charge. If you do not like crowds try to get there as early as possible — around noon coach tours from Damascus arrive and may spoil your photo opportunities.

A visit to the Krak des Chevaliers, perhaps the grandest and best preserved medieval castle in the world, is indeed one of the high points on any tour of Syria, one you will remember long after other images have faded. It is so superbly constructed, so perfectly set that not even photography can convey the full impact of its stature.

The Krak des Chevaliers or Qala'at al-Husn (which translated means Castle of the Fortress), is built on a protruding ridge which drops on all sides except the south. To have had any chance of success, an attack would have had to come from that direction. Consequently the fortifications on the southern edge were the heaviest. Unlike other castles (such as Marqab) the Krak is built on solid rock, so mining was impossible.

Before entering the castle I recommend you walk or drive to its southwestern exposure in order to get a good perception of the fortress with these formidable defences from its most vulnerable point. From here you can also see the **aqueduct** which carried water from the hills above.

slippery slope

The Krak is built in 2 parts: the outer wall with its round towers and the inner section, built around the keep and protected by a glacis.

The Crusaders were already renowned as great castle builders and all their know-how, with additional help from Europe, went into the redesigning of this fortress.

The **square tower** to the left of the entrance is Mameluke, while the tower immediately in front of the entrance-way is Crusader — though the inscription on it commemorates the Mameluke conquest. The main entrance, leading to the inner castle, is imposing: a long, gently rising, vaulted passage with low, widely spaced steps for comfortable negotiation on horseback. Once inside, (following the route marked with arrows on the site plan on the page 158), the first entrance on your left as you ascend this passage leads via the **guards' tower** into a long hall which was possibly used as a stable.

headless lions

Further along, the passageway twists back on itself (U turn) before continuing. At this point there is an opening through a bastion. Pass through the opening (we will return to the passageway later) and you come out at the water-filled **cistern** or moat (on your right). Also to your right is the sloping **glacis** which protects the massive towers of the keep above. You are now facing the southern wall and its defences. Glance back the way you have come and you will see **two headless lions** above the passageway.

As you approach the southern wall you will notice a hall about 60 metres in length. This was most likely the **main stable**. Walk through the length of the hall and exit by a stairway. These steps lead up to the roof where you can see the tower which was the mainstay of the southern defences and get a clear view of the inner castle and the line of the outer walls.

For an even better perspective, climb the steps of the tower. From this vantage point you will clearly understand why the only possibility of attack would have come from the south. The tower was rebuilt by the Mamelukes on the original Crusader base which was probably badly damaged during Baibars' assault in 1271. The towers at each end of the southern wall are also Mameluke.

Gothic portico

Now return the way you came through the main stables to the vaulted entry ramp and continue upwards to the end. Turn left and proceed through an arched entrance-way which was formerly protected by a portcullis. You now pass through the inner walls to a **courtyard** and the inner castle. Directly facing is the **Great Hall**, preceded by a very beautiful portico. Gothic in style it was built in the 13th C, perhaps in the final decade of the Crusader occupation. The front is divided into 7 arched niches, 2 of these are doorways and 5 are decorative windows. The vaulted ceiling is covered in intricate carvings.

Two doors lead from the portico into the Great Hall. This 27 metre long room, which has a gloomy appearance despite the windows, was probably the Knights' banqueting hall and also used for ceremonies. The opening in the vaulted ceiling was for ventilation purposes.

kitchen facilities

Behind this hall is another, much longer one (120 metres), which must have had various functions. (If you brought a torch, it will be useful here.) The central part was certainly a kitchen — you can see an oven and to its left, a well.

Back in the courtyard, to the right (S) as you exit the hall, is a large, almost square area divided by five rows of thick arched pillars. This was used for stores and refectories. At the opposite end of the courtyard (N) is the **chapel**, dating from the mid 12th C. After the Muslim occupation it was converted into a mosque.

a rest in the Tower of the King's Daughter

Outside the chapel, steps lead to the upper area. On the northwest is a tower which bears the enigmatic title of the **"Tower of the King's Daughter"**. This is now a cafeteria and you may well be in need of a cold drink by now!

Walk across the roof to the southern end and this brings you above the cistern and near to the towers protected by the talus you saw from below. This is the castle's **keep** and was the most heavily fortified section of the Krak. In the three towers the upper ranks were quartered. They are of immense strength, especially the central one and are three storeys high. The southwest tower has circular rooms with a cross-vaulted ceiling, while the southeastern tower comprises a large square hall (this is the tower with the headless lions on the façade, which you saw from below).

You can climb the towers and from the roof of any of them you will have tremendous panoramas of the Krak and the entire area.

11. HAMA AND VICINITY

"It is a city renowned through the lands, and a long companion of time ... you will find her beauty concealed until you have spied out her most inner parts and scrutinised her shades ..."

"The Travels of Ibn Jubayr", 12th century

Introduction

Hama (Hamah, Hamath) is situated between Homs and Aleppo on the banks of the Orontes. The river's Arabic name is *Nahr al-Assi*, meaning Rebel or Rebellious River. It earned this title because it flows from south to north as opposed to all the other rivers in the region which flow from north to south.

Hama ranks among the oldest of Syrian cities, and is frequently mentioned in the Old Testament.

The medieval traveller Ibn Jubayr, arriving at Hama in the summer of 1184 described it thus:

"... I saw a large river that in its strong course spreads out and branches, and on its banks observed water-wheels that faced each other. Along these banks are disposed gardens that hang their branches over the water, the green leaves appearing like down on its cheeks as it flows through their shade ..."

For once, the words still aptly portray parts at least of Hama as you will find them today. To enjoy it without rushing, one full day is required — more if you wish to use it as a base for visiting nearby sites.

restful scenery

The town has a relaxed atmosphere, due in large measure to the extensive gardens along the banks of the Orontes. It is Syria's fourth city, being an important agricultural and industrial centre and is the capital of the *muhaafaza* (province) of the same name which extends over an area of about 9000 sq kms.

MEDIEVAL TRAVELLERS

Three voyagers, a Moor from Valencia, a Jew from Tudela, and another Moor from Tangier were among the great travellers of medieval times. Because of their chronicles we have a fine picture of life in the places they visited, which for two of them were as far as China!

Rabbi Benjamin of Tudela may have been the first European to reach the frontiers of China. He travelled throughout the Middle East, recording details of Jewish life he encountered and describing the cities which he passed through. He visited Damascus around 1175. The full journal of his travels is contained in a book, *"Massa'ot (Travels), the Itinerary of Benjamin of Tudela"*.

Abu al-Hussein Muhammad ibn Ahmad ibn Jubayr was born in 1145 in Valencia, then part of the Moorish kingdom of Grenada. He made the *haj* in February 1183, and afterwards travelled extensively throughout Muslim lands. He kept an almost daily journal, published as *"The Travels of Ibn Jubayr"*, and his fascinating accounts of Aleppo and Damascus, which he visited in 1184, are unique, dating from 100 years before the Mongol invasions. The glory of the Omayyad Mosque was still to be seen and Ibn Jubayr describes it in detail.

Ibn Batutta (his full name would take up several lines!), the third traveller, born in Tangier in 1304, was perhaps the greatest of them all, although his record was not written until after he returned to North Africa. Ibn Batutta was a very educated man with a passion for travel. He travelled just for the pleasure of it, and was able to earn as he roamed by teaching.

The list of places he visited is amazing. The most ardent of wanderers today would be hard put to match his exploits. His journeys east took him to Delhi, where he sojourned for some time, then on to Sumatra, Ceylon and the Maldives. He sailed down the African coast to what is now Tanzania. He stayed some time in Damascus where he was highly regarded by Islamic scholars. One of his last trips was across the Sahara to Mali, then a great Muslim Empire.

His book, *"Rihlar"* (Travels) is an important document of the era.

To the west of the city and along the watercourse agriculture is productive but east of the city the land is arid and not much grows.

Besides agriculture, which covers a variety of produce including cereals, the *muhaafaza* has become prominent industrially, especially around the city of Hama itself. Steelworks, Syria's only tyre factory, cement and textiles all contribute to the province's economy.

traditional city

For centuries Hama has been noted for its conservative Muslim piety. This has continued through to the present — in 1982 it became the centre of a Muslim Brotherhood uprising which ended with much bloodshed and damage to the old town (see below).

picnic time

In his book "Dar ul Islam" Mark Sykes wrote in 1904, *"Hama is, excepting Damascus, by far the most picturesque city in Syria..."*, and you may wish to take time out just to relax in the attractive gardens along the river banks. The best day for this is Friday, the Muslim day off, when crowds of people from other towns and cities visit Hama. Arriving in the morning by the bus and truck-load, whole families, young and old, gather for a picnic brunch in the gardens. They spread a cloth on the grass and lay it with all manner of goodies: huge mounds of flatbread and sesame rolls, a variety of white cheeses, olives, tomatoes, eggs and more. And in no time at all they have tea or coffee brewing on a primus.

If you are strolling by, expect to be invited to participate! During one visit I was treated to a spontaneous performance of Arab dancing by some young people.

History

Excavations show Hama to have been settled since the Iron Age. Evidence of Hittite occupation has also been found by way of a hieroglyphic inscription.

In the Book of Joshua, Hama is mentioned at the time when the land was divided up between the 12 tribes of Israel:

> *"and the land of the Gebalite, and all*
> *of Lebanon toward the east, from Baal-*
> *gad below Mount Hermon as far as the*
> *entrance to Hamath."* Joshua 13:5

Hama became the capital of an Aramean kingdom at the beginning of the first millennium BC. At that time there were intermittent conflicts with the Kingdom of Israel, then ruled by David. At the height of its power Israel stretched as far as Hama but never actually included it. In the 9th C BC Hama fell to the Assyrians, as did Israel (the Northern Kingdom).

After depopulating the cities of Israel the Assyrians settled them, partly with people from Hamath. This is also narrated in the Old Testament:

"And the King of Assyria brought men
...from Hamath...and settled them in
the cities of Samaria in place of the
sons of Israel. So they possessed Samaria
and lived in its cities. " II Kings 17:24

When the power of Assyria and Babylon waned, Hama came under the control of the Persian Empire until that was defeated by Alexander. In the Seleucid period, Antiochus IV Epiphanes renamed the city Epiphania in the 2nd century BC.

Under Byzantine rule the city was called Emath, a corruption of the original name. During this era it became largely Christian and many churches were erected.

Arab conquest

In 637 Hama was captured by the Arabs, who transformed the principal church into a mosque. Nearly 500 years later, in 1108, the city was captured by the Crusaders, but only briefly, the Muslims retaking it in 1115.

An earthquake badly destroyed Hama some time in the 12th C. According to the Jewish traveller from Spain, Rabbi Benjamin of Tudela, 15,000 people died in one day leaving only 70 survivors. However by the time Ibn Jubayr visited in 1184 the city must have recovered for him to have made the observations quoted above. Later, the city became part of the domain of Salah al-Din. Thus it remained for over a hundred years until 1299 when it passed to Mameluke sovereignty, becoming the seat of the governor.

After the Ottoman conquest Hama was incorporated into the sanjak of Tripoli. The city then followed the general course of Syrian history.

uprising against the Ba'ath

Hama's latest claim to fame occurred in 1982, when the Muslim Brotherhood (a Sunni fundamentalist organisation), in an uprising against Assad and the Ba'ath party, seized the city. After intense fighting with government troops the rebellion was put down, but only with great loss of life and much damage to the city including the complete destruction of the Great Mosque.

As brutal as Assad's response to the rebellion was, it must be looked at from a background of Muslim Brotherhood fanaticism in which they had assassinated many people, especially Alawi army officers and cadets. They were waging a war of attrition and eventually a showdown had to come.

It is unwise to talk to anyone about any aspects of this event.

Visiting the city

► Norias (water-wheels)

The chief attraction of Hama are the great norias, or water-wheels which originated in Byzantine times. The oldest surviving wheels we see today probably date from the 12th or 13th C.

The norias, which all have given names, were used to raise water from the river into aqueducts which then supplied the water to irrigate the orchards or for drinking. As these functions are now carried out by modern methods, the purpose of the wheels is today purely decorative and of historical interest.

moaning noises

Of the once very many norias only a few remain, and these are carefully maintained. With a diameter that can reach up to 20 metres, they are made entirely of wood. As the blocks on which they turn are also made of wood, the friction creates a peculiar moaning or creaking sound which can be heard some distance away. On visits to the city I have seen carpenters at work cutting and replacing various parts, in particular the paddles or scoops, which gradually become rotten.

Unlike the river that Ibn Jubayr saw, the Orontes of today is not a very swift flowing river, and if you look carefully you will notice that channels have been constructed to propel the water past the norias with greater force.

The first wheels you see will probably be the ones on opposite banks in the park right in the centre of town. The setting is attractive, each one flanked by a stretch of the aqueduct into which it feeds. The more distant wheel is the larger of the two, and the beginning of my suggested walk leads behind it.

► Walk No 1 (downstream)

From the park walk in the direction of that noriah which follows the river downstream (roughly north) — follow the route of the thick line on the plan on the next page. An **aqueduct** crosses the street ahead of you. Just before the aqueduct turn to the right and follow the road under the arches, taking the short alley to the right, (altogether a distance of only a few metres) and you come up behind two noriahs. The largest, **al-Nawa'ir Aj'jisriyeh**, is the one which you could see from across the park. The top of the smallest, **al-Ma'amouriyeh**, is immediately in front of you, and you can see exactly how it operates, dropping the water lifted from the river into a channel.

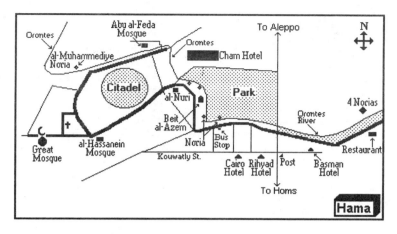

the pasha's house

Continue under the big archway to the left, along an alleyway which is part of the old city, until you reach the **Beit al-Azem** which houses **Hama's museum.** The Beit al-Azem (Azem Mansion) was the 18th C residence of the then Governor of Hama, Assad Pasha al-Azem, who later became Governor of Damascus (1743-1757). As sumptuous as this residence is, the one he built in Damascus is even more splendid (see chapter on Damascus). Badly damaged in the 1982 fighting, the building is now being extensively restored.

lady musicians

After entering and paying the small charge you find yourself in a large, well laid out courtyard, the *haremlek,* with a central fountain. At one end is the diwan with a mosaic on the wall. Off the courtyard is the museum which displays various items found in the Hama area. There are also some lovely mosaics, the best of which is displayed with prominence in the far left corner. Dating from the 2nd half of the third century it depicts a group of pretty young women playing musical instruments while another maiden, on the right, dances. The border is richly decorated with likenesses of deities hunting wild animals and winged cherubim.

profusion of fountains

Out in the courtyard are steps leading upstairs. Here there is another attractive yard with central fountain. To the left are a number of rooms with wax model displays of various aspects of Syrian life in days gone by. Facing, preceded by an arched portico, is a magnificent hall with its own fountain. As it is currently being renovated it can only be viewed from the entrance, but this is sufficient to appreciate what a splendid room it is.

Note the richly decorated wood ceiling with its cupola (under restoration).

Returning downstairs you can visit the **hammam** complete with wax models showing how it was used. The other side of this is yet another courtyard with marble flooring and on the right is a further exhibit room. Upstairs are additional rooms with fine wood-panelled walls. These rooms still require restoration.

Leaving the museum, continue the walk, bearing right past the Palestine Language Institute. You will hear the moans of three norias up ahead before you actually come to them, just under the aqueduct arch. The way now leads through an arched tunnel-like passage and you exit to find the river and a bridge across it to your right. The **al-Nouri Mosque** is on the corner to the left.

Roman remnants

This mosque was built in 1172 by Nur al-Din. The interior does not live up to the expectations raised by its attractive outer appearance, but the *minbar,* a gift of the revered ruler, is worth looking at. Probably constructed on the site of a former Roman temple, odd remnants of that era are incorporated into the building, with one somewhat incongruous-looking column forming part of the otherwise plastered portico around the courtyard.

Cross the bridge (the Aphamia Cham Hotel is on the other side) for a few minutes to obtain a beautiful view embracing the mosque and the river, with the three norias on one bank and a fourth on the other.

from palace to fortress

Return across the bridge and proceed straight on past the al-Nouri Mosque to the main road at the top. Almost opposite is the steep hill of the **citadel** (qala'at Hama), once the site of a royal palace at the time of the 11th C BC Aramean kingdom of Hamath, and much later a Muslim fortress. Nothing of the past remains and the summit is now a park affording excellent views over the city.

Continue straight to the southwest corner of the citadel. Across the road on the left is the small **al-Hasanein Mosque**. Rebuilt on the site of an earlier mosque by Nur al-Din there is nothing remarkable about it. Beyond this mosque you will see a modern **Greek Orthodox Church**. Go west down the road to the side and you will see the tall minaret of the **Great Mosque.** Almost totally destroyed in 1982 it is now being rebuilt by the Department of Antiquities in its original plan.

recent destruction of Great Mosque

The original building was of Omayyad construction and, like the Great Mosques of Damascus and Aleppo, was built on the site of a Byzantine Church which was itself constructed on the spot where a pagan temple once stood. The original Byzantine basilica plan was incorporated into the mosque with the 5 domes in the form of a cross. Around the courtyard were vaulted porticos. The structure in the courtyard standing on pillars is the treasury and was the only part of the complex to escape destruction in 1982. It is supported on 6 recycled Roman pillars, some bearing Kufic inscriptions. At the time of writing, the prayer hall and surrounding buildings were filled with busy workmen. Vestiges of Byzantine masonry and decoration have survived and can be seen on the outer side walls of the prayer hall, particularly the side of the black and white square minaret.

4th century church

Walk back now to the Greek Orthodox Church, a very modern building. To its left is the seat of the Metropolitan (Orthodox Bishop). Adjacent to that is a deep excavated plot. Remains of a **4th C church** were discovered here when preparing the foundations for the new church building.

Christians in Hama comprise about 14% of the population. Most are Greek Orthodox and there are smaller congregations of Syrian Orthodox and Catholics. On Sundays this church is crowded, many of the worshippers being young people.

If you continue to proceed clockwise around the citadel mound you will, after about 200 metres, see on the left 2 norias. The larger one, **al-Muhammadiye**, dates from the early 14th C and supplied water to the Great Mosque. Walking now east parallel to the river notice the decorated mosque with twin cupolas on the opposite bank.

The Serpents' Mosque

This is the **Mosque and Mausoleum of Abu al-Feda** who died in 1331. He was an Arab historian and geographer who was made governor of Hama by the Mameluke Sultan. The mosque is also called Jami al-Hayyat, the Serpents' Mosque, because of a window in the prayer room decorated with columns carved with an interlaced, snake-like design. To reach this mosque cross the river by the lower, old bridge, and not the new main road one.

On the corner of the slip road that leads down to the old bridge is the **Izzi Mosque**, built in the 15th C by the Mamelukes.

► **Walk No 2 (upstream)**

All the main points of interest are downstream from the town centre. However, for an agreeable stroll you can walk upstream through the gardens which flank the west side of the river. On the opposite bank of the river are the vestiges of the once renowned Hama orchards.

About 1.5 kilometres along, you will come to four norias together, called **An'nawa'ir al-Arba** (literally the four norias). Next to them there is an attractive, though largely overpriced, restaurant.

AROUND HAMA

Base for touring

As Hama offers virtually the only accommodation in the region, it makes a good base for touring the surroundings, although some places can be visited en route. If you have your own vehicle, these journeys present no problem; if not, then you may be limited to those sites you can reach by bus.

► APAMEA (Aphamia, Afamia) (Qala'at al-Moudiq)

Location

About 50kms west of Hama, Apamea should definitely be visited. If you are going by car, take the road to Mhardeh after exiting Hama from the northeast. Due to the dearth of signposts and the ongoing construction, you are strongly advised to ascertain that the road you are on is correct. This may be bothersome but will avoid trouble later! From Mhardeh continue northwest to Sheizar (5 kms) (as you drive through this village you can see on a ridge to your right the ruins of Qala'at Sheizar—discussed later), and then carry on to Suqeilibiye (22 kms). The newer village of Qala'at al-Moudiq is a further c5 kms, at the foot of the rise on top of which is the citadel (the old village of Qala'at al-Moudiq) and the ruins of Apamea. To get to the ruins take a sharp right turn just through the village. The road from Hama is badly signposted (in any language), but this sharp turn is clearly marked in English.

If travelling by bus, take the quite frequent microbus or service taxi via Suqeilibiye to the newer village of Qala'at al-Moudiq. From there either walk or find a ride to the upper part of the village which is actually inside the citadel and which in turn is a few hundred metres' walk from the ruins of Apamea.

the good earth

The journey from Hama passes through a thriving agricultural region with rich, dark soil that is intensively cultivated. Tent-dwelling families live and work in the fields, creating many a picturesque scene as you drive past. Tobacco is an important crop here as are corn and cotton.

Enjoying a favoured location in the valley of the Orontes, about 80kms southwest of ancient Antioch (Antakya), Apamea was surrounded by this fruitful land. Over the centuries neglect turned the whole Orontes valley into a swamp, and it is only in the past 20 years after a massive draining and reclamation project that the area has been returned to its former state.

History

great Seleucid city

While probable that some sort of settlement may have existed here in pre-Hellenistic times, we do not hear of Apamea until after the Greek conquest of Syria. Founded by Seleucus I Nicator in the early 2nd C BC and named after his wife, Apamea was, along with Antioch and Seleucia, one of the great cities of the Seleucid Empire. To avoid confusion with Apamea Cibotos in Anatolia, the name *Apamea ad Orontem* (Apamea on the Orontes) was often used.

Of the Seleucid Empire's three major cities (Antioch, Apamea and Seleucia-on-the Tigris), Apamea was the most important militarily. Here the garrisons were kept prepared for despatch to any troubled area.

Antiochus's elephants

By all accounts Apamea was a very beautiful city, and was an oft-used residence of Seleucid rulers. It is said that Antiochus the Great used to train and graze his elephants in the surrounding countryside. The thousands of horses needed for his cavalry were also pastured in the surrounding farmland.

Apamea was very prosperous, with a population of about 120,000. In 64 BC it became part of the Roman Empire and continued to flourish. Under the Byzantines it was made the seat of a Bishopric. The city was destroyed by Chosroes II, the Persian ruler, in the early 7th C AD. The Persians occupied the area until 628 when it once again became Byzantine until falling to the Muslim Arabs just eight years later.

decline and fall

Apamea fell into decline and eventually came under the rule of the Egyptian Fatimids. In 1106 the famous Norman leader of the Crusades, Tancrede, took the city and renamed it Femia and it became a Latin Archdiocese. Nur al-Din conquered it in 1149. After being stricken by an earthquake in 1157, Apamea lost all importance. However, in the 13th C the fortifications on the acropolis were used by the Mamelukes to build the Qala'at al-Moudiq fortress.

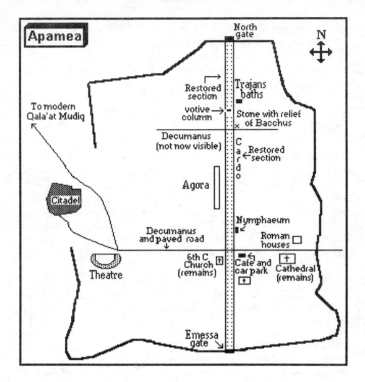

The site visit

The approach road from the Qala'a cuts through the ruins of Apamea and was in fact an east-west Roman decumanus, bisecting the north-south cardo maximus. Park on the right in front of the cafeteria at the junction of the cardo.

Start your tour by walking north along the cardo or **Great Colonnade**. Try to imagine this long thoroughfare lined with columns on both sides for its nearly 2 kms length. For most of this, each side was flanked by porticos. Under these porticos hummed the everyday life of the city: public offices, shops, houses, baths and other facilities common to a Greco-Roman metropolis. The columns were Corinthian, with the superstructure in various styles, the shafts smooth or carved with vertical or spiral fluting. As you can see, many still stand or have been re-erected.

a sense of grandeur

The street is paved with large, irregular flagstones. Thanks to sustained restoration work, the large number of re-erected columns along the cardo help to create a wonderful sense of the grand ancient city. True, careful examination of some of these pillars reveals signs of pre-stressed concrete and other building methods unknown in the classical world, but provided — as in this case — the overall result is enhancement, I believe the means are excusable.

In springtime the ruins carry a lively melody of colours from the seasonal wild flowers and flourishing greenery. In late summer and autumn they tend to assume a starker aspect, with dry scrub and thorns pushing through fallen capitals and around pillar pedestals.

beware of antique salesmen!

As at so many sites in Syria one is struck by the sheer quantity of decorative masonry and remains just lying around everywhere. It lends credence to the claims of local villagers who ply the site, purporting to have hoards of antiques for sale in their homes — to which you are of course cordially invited! (Some of these antiques may be genuine, but I have yet to see one that is!)

About 40m north of the asphalted road along the Great Colonnade are, on the right, the remains of a **nymphaeum** or water fountain, recognisable by its curved exedra. Roughly 150m further down on the left was the **agora**, which was long and narrow. Entrance into the agora was via a traverse street to the south and a monumental gateway to the north. The traverse street at the southern end was lined with seven columns on each side. This led through a **tetrapylon** into the market. Climb the bank to view the remains of all this.

In the next stretch intensive restoration work was under way during my last visit, and this may now be complete. At the end and on the right of this newly reconstructed section is the **plinth of an honorific column**, imbedded below street level. This marked an intersection.

the pipes of Pan

A little further along, past the next (as yet) unrestored portion, was another intersection where the remains of a **pillar** which supported an arch across the portico are on the right. The stones carry a relief from the legend of Bacchus: Lycurgus restrained by Bacchus in the stalks of a vine, and Pan with his pipes and flock of goats. The tall, **votive column** in the centre of the street, which has been re-erected on its original base, marks another cross street. Some 150m past the votive column, on the right, are the remains of **Trajan's baths**. Climb the embankment to view them. These baths were very palatial and had a splendid entrance.

the oldest and the best part

The final stretch of the cardo leading to the northern or

Antioch gate is truly impressive. Restoration work combined with the already present remains have captured its dignity and magnificence. Built during the reign of Trajan, it is the oldest section, dating from 116-117.

the southern section

Return now to the main (tarmac) decumanus and cross the road in order to visit the southern part of the cardo. The remains on this side are much less substantial than on the north side.

Almost immediately on your right (W) are the remains of a **6th C church**. Slightly further to your left (E) are the remains of another **church** with a large courtyard. The thoroughfare then continued to the southern or **Emessa Gate**.

If you return to the tarmac road and turn right (E) and walk (or take your car) for about 400 metres you'll see on the left (in the northern section) remains of **3 Roman residences**. One has a reconstructed façade.

On the south side of the decumanus are the remnants of the **cathedral** which opened to the road through a monumental portal. This cathedral was supposed to house some relics of the "True Cross". Little is left of the former, and nothing of the latter.

way to the theatre

Drive back now past the intersection of the cardo along the modern road in the direction you originally came, until you reach a line of houses on the left. The **theatre** is in a dale behind the houses and slightly to the west. You can't miss it though little remains now, much of the seating etc having been used for other purposes over the centuries. It is best viewed from afar where the outline is still very clear. Looking up, you have an excellent view of the Qala'at al-Moudiq citadel, perhaps the best you'll get.

squalor in the citadel

The road now leads up to Qala'at al-Moudiq, the medieval fortress built on the site of the Seleucid citadel, made use of nowadays by the local villagers. Inside the walls of the fortress filth reigns supreme so there is no need to wander about. From outside the gate there is a magnificent panorama over the region, and the lay-out and size of the theatre become more apparent.

► Museum in a caravanserai

Down in the village is a museum with some interesting exhibits, housed in a renovated caravanserai. Descend to the main village and turn south (way back to Hama). After a short distance you should see, almost directly beneath the southern end of the ridge, a sign on the left pointing to the museum.

The walled compound of this typical example of an Ottoman caravanserai has a spacious courtyard entered by a gateway with a large arched entrance porch. The courtyard is dotted with sculptures, pottery and inscribed stones. Practice your Latin or Greek! Inside the rooms leading off the yard are displays of various artefacts and mosaics.

▸ QALA'AT SHEIZAR

Location

As it is situated on the Hama-Apamea road, you may care to visit Qala'at Sheizar. This can be done on your way to or from Apamea, but I recommend you do it on the way back to ensure sufficient time at the far more interesting site of Apamea. Bus travellers will have to break their journey, so make sure there will be another bus.

History

Situated at an important crossing point of the Orontes it is thought that the hill on which this castle stands may have been the acropolis of the long-vanished Roman city of Caesarea. (There was more than one city with this name.)

The castle was built by the Fatimids and conquered by the Byzantines in the last years of the 10th C. They held it until 1081 when it was seized by a local chieftain. Its position was so commanding that repeated attempts by the Crusaders to take it were to no avail. In 1108 the Crusader leader Tancrede was unsuccessful, and in 1138 another attempt by John Comnene met a similar fate.

destruction by war and earthquake

What the Crusaders were unable to accomplish, nature did for them, and in the earthquake of 1157 much of the structure was destroyed. The Crusaders then occupied what was left but were soon driven out by Nur al-Din. He repaired much of the damage, but not many years later it was again damaged by earthquake. It then came under the control of Salah al-Din (1174).

In 1233 the Ayyubids constructed a new keep and under the Mamelukes further re-construction was undertaken. This was its final form, as seen in the ruins today.

Visit

little left but the view

The spur on which the castle sits is ideal for a bastion. The entrance is from the northern side near the old bridge (built in 1290). The structure appears very impressive from below, but little is left of the castle today apart from one gate and the main tower. A good view is to be had from the top.

► QASR IBN WARDAN

Location

You can only visit this site if you have your own transport, though no doubt a taxi will take you there for a price. It is situated about 60kms northeast of Hama in the desert steppe. Take the road to al-Hamra and continue another 10kms. Try to be there about a couple of hours before sunset as the desert hues can look beautiful in late afternoon, lending a mystical touch to the ruins. It's about a one hour's drive.

beehive houses

The journey is along a typical desert road, with some very interesting villages along the way. The majority of the dwellings in these villages are now either concrete or pressed blocks, but the older "beehive" mud houses still exist, used now mainly as storerooms or the like. These were once the normal village home in the Syrian desert as well as southern Turkey (the Harran plain). The design is supposed to be cool in the hot summer months. The smaller, usually whitewashed, egg-like "beehives" are ovens used for baking bread or roasting meat.

The site

Qasr ibn Wardan is reached quite suddenly, the buildings almost isolated in the desert although a small modern village lies to one side.

The original complex consisted of three main buildings, the palace, a church and barracks. Only the first two are still standing with just a chunk of façade with an arched window remaining of the barracks (more clearly lie beneath the mound from which it protrudes).

Constructed at the end of the reign of the Byzantine Emperor Justinian in 546 AD, Qasr ibn Wardan was built to garrison soldiers who had the task of keeping control of the desert peoples and to guard against invasion from that quarter.

materials re-used

The ruins certainly present a remarkable aspect in an otherwise barren environment. I have only visited the site since their restoration so it is difficult to convey an impression of how they looked previously. The recent restoration tends to make the buildings appear rather "new", in spite of the re-use of the original materials. Nevertheless the complex is very impressive and well worth a visit if you have two or three hours to spare.

Both the palace and the church are built mainly of brick and basalt in alternate layers which create an unusual striped appearance. In restoring the buildings some concrete has had to be used but this is only really noticeable when you climb onto the roof of the palace.

Governor's palace

The two-storey palace, built presumably to house the governor, forms the largest section. The entrance is through a fairly well preserved façade leading into a dim vaulted hall. On each side are vaulted chambers, which were used for ceremonial occasions.

The rooms off the large courtyard were used for the everyday life of the palace such as the kitchens, storerooms etc. Upstairs the (now) solid roof affords an extensive view over the area and the church.

columns from Apamea

The church has not (as yet) been so thoroughly renovated as the palace but work is still being carried out. It has a basic square shape with a huge, high dome, now collapsed. Perhaps there are plans to rebuild this. Like the palace, much of the fabrication is of brick and locally found stone. Columns and capitals taken from other sites, perhaps Apamea, are also incorporated.

You can go upstairs to the **triforia** or gallery which runs on three sides. This was used by the women, who in a traditional Byzantine church sat separately from the men. (This custom is still preserved in some Eastern Churches).

Custodian's home

If the buildings are closed the custodian will be happy to open them for you. He can be found in the house closest to the site, which has a plaque over the entrance saying **Maison de la Mission National**. The doorframe and lintel are made of black rock, most probably recycled from the ruins. The custodian and his family live here. As befits dwellers in the desert, they are Bedouin.

The entrance to their modest home opens onto a spotless courtyard decorated with potted plants, leading to a second yard off which is the main part of the house. Inside this second yard you may glimpse the custodian's wife (or one of them) dressed in typical north Syrian desert dress (also common in southern Turkey).

Bedouin hospitality

On the left of the first courtyard is a salon beautifully decorated in Bedouin style with coloured rugs on the floor and richly embroidered cushions and leaning bolsters around the sides. Any member of the family will invite you in to rest (remove your shoes first). If people are already inside they will rise to greet you. A woman should not hold out her hand to greet a man unless he first holds out his. In Bedouin society men do not shake hands with women. They do not generally sit with women for coffee either, but here they are happy to make an exception to accommodate western customs, and female guests will be welcome to join in and need not feel embarrassed to do so.

bitter coffee and sweet tea

You will be offered a sip of caffeine-loaded, bitter, black, Bedouin coffee from a tiny cup. This is the Bedouin pick-me-up, similar to a shot of whisky (alcohol, of course, being forbidden to Muslims). This will be followed by sweet, almost syrupy, tea. Even if you don't speak Arabic, with his very few words of English and the few (hopefully!) you do know in Arabic, your host will manage to find out where you come from and what you think of Syria; a stay of about 10-15 minutes is sufficient to be courteous.

driving off into the sunset

If you timed your trip as I suggested, the sun will now be setting and the ruins silhouetted against an apricot sky.

Drive back carefully, taking your time: Syrian drivers tend to use lights (if they have them!) very sparingly.

► SALAMIYEH

If you are driving and can afford a detour of about 2 hours, a visit can be made to the town of Salamiyeh, southeast of Hama. The distance to Homs on the Autostrada is 50 kms, while the route via Salamiyeh is just under 80 kms.

Location

To get there take road number 45 out of Hama. After about 23 kms, on the left (north) you will see Qala'at al-Shmemis, or al-Shams (either way the name means Castle of the Sun). To reach it you will have to park your car and trek for about 1.5 kms. The castle, built inside the cone of an extinct volcano, was constructed by the Ayyubid governor of Hama in the early 13th C. Although it appears rather stunning from the distance, close up it is little more than rubble.

History

The area of Salamiyeh was once ancient Salamais, a Roman/ Byzantine outpost town. From here a road continued north east to Resafe and the Euphrates. Today it is only a track, but quite passable with a four wheel drive vehicle. An oil pipeline which originally terminated at the port of Tripoli in Lebanon parallels this track. Some 90 kms along this desert road (in Roman times the area had a fruitfulness that belies its barren appearance today!) are the ruins of Isiyeh, ancient Seriana. Seriana was an important caravan crossing point on the Palmyra-Aleppo route. A 3rd C Roman temple in a fair state of preservation stands here amidst the ruins of the ancient town.

An important Ismaili centre, Salamiyeh was where the first Fatimid Caliph, 'Ubayd Allah al-Mahdi was born (see box Divisions of Islam on page 26).

Salamiyeh was destroyed by Timur in 1401, and the Ismailis fled to the Jabal Ansariye where many of their sect already lived.

In the mid 19th C rivalries broke out between various Ismaili factions, and some started to move down from the mountains. At the same time the authorities wanted to settle people east of the Orontes to provide a bulwark against repeated Bedouin raids. To encourage the Ismailis to move to Salamiyeh they were offered a few incentives which included no taxes, and no compulsory military service. Thus the town was slowly rebuilt, mainly from the black basalt rock found in the area.

Today Salamiyeh and the surrounding area has a population of over 70,000. Far from being an outpost on the fringe of the desert, this rather liberal town provides many educated people for the Syrian economy. One of the founders of the Syrian Ba'ath party hails from this town as does the Syrian poet Muhammad al-Maghut.

Visit

Modern Salamiyeh has no historical sites, but the basalt buildings typical of the town are interesting to see and the drive is pleasant. The people are very welcoming of foreign travellers — not too many get there — and you are almost certain to be offered hospitality if you stroll about the town.

► HOMS (HIMS)

Location

Homs is situated 168 kilometres north of Damascus on the main Damascus-Aleppo highway. It is 80 kilometres east of Tartous on the Damascus-Latakia route. Homs is a very busy city and quite frustrating to drive through due to the hectic traffic conditions and one-way streets. If you do not intend to make a stop here there is a bypass road which circuits the city to the west. All buses travelling between Damascus-Aleppo and Damascus-Mediterranean coast stop here.

Being a centrally located city, all tours of Syria have to pass through (or right by) it. As there are a couple of churches and a mosque worth visiting, a useful two hours or so can definitely be spent there. And for those who wish to break their journey, there are of course hotels in a city this size.

> *"It is of broad extent and of oblong dimensions. Its spectacle is a refreshment to the eyes because of its gracious beauty."*
>
> "The Travels of Ibn Jubayr", 1184 AD

Present day Homs may still be of broad extent but you will search in vain for its gracious beauty — as an industrial city of over 600,000 people, Homs offers little for the tourist.

History

Some remains have been unearthed showing that settlement on the site of Homs goes back into antiquity. Its history as a city dates from Roman times when it was called Mesa. On the edge of the desert, Mesa was used by the Romans as a base to safeguard caravans on their way to Palmyra and beyond.

the beautiful Julia

In 187 AD the Roman commander of Mesa, Septimius Severus, married Julia Domna, daughter of the High Priest of the city. Gibbon described Julia as having *"the attractions of beauty...united to a lively imagination, a firmness of mind, and strength of judgment, seldom bestowed on her sex."* In 193 Septimius Severus was appointed Emperor — the African Emperor, as he became known — and his charismatic wife, together with her considerable talents, proved a force behind the throne.

the mad emperor and the black stone

Some of Julia's descendants became emperors, the most famous — or infamous — being Elagabalus, who was appointed to the high office while still a youth. He was a priest of the sun god which at that time was worshipped in Mesa in the form of a black stone. The stone was taken from Homs and transported to Rome where it was venerated. The strange young Elagabalus became increasingly insane and his reign sank into depravity. He was eventually murdered by the Praetorian Guard and the sacred stone found its way back to Mesa.

A later emperor, Aurelian, was also an adherent of this sun god and prior to his victory over the Palmyrenes in 272 he visited the temple in Homs to pray.

Christianity then Islam replace sun worship

Under Byzantine rule the city became mainly Christian and many churches were built there (see below). In 540, in spite of the efforts of Justinian, the city was sacked by the Persians under Chosroes and a century later, in 635, Homs fell to Khalid and the advancing Muslim armies.

Although close to the Crusader fortress of the Krak des Chevaliers, Homs never came under the Knights' control, and around 1130 the Emir of Mosul, Imad al-Din Zengi who had taken Aleppo in 1128, added the city to his realm.

In modern times Homs is the home of the Syrian military academy and was influential in the formation of the Ba'ath party.

Visit

Two ancient churches and a relatively recent mosque are worth visiting. The eastern part of what was once the walled area is the traditional Christian Quarter, and even today a good proportion of Homs' Christians (about 8% of the population) live here. Both the churches are located in this part of town.

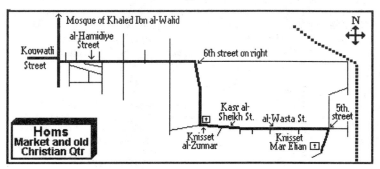

▶ Knisset al-Zunnar

The Church of the Virgin's Girdle (Knisset al-Zunnar) is situated to the east of the market area. To get there follow the continuation of Kouwatli Street, right in the centre of the city, (where it becomes al-Hamidiyeh Street), east into the souk area. Count the streets on the right (including alleys) and at the 6th, turn. The church is at the end of this street. From the corner of Kouwatli Street to the church is c700m.

181

discovery of the Virgin's belt

A Syrian Orthodox church, the Church of the Virgin's Girdle gets its name from a textile girdle said to have belonged to Mary, which was buried under a slab in the church as far back as the 4th C. (It is claimed with some authority that a house church has existed on the spot since 59 AD.) The story of this relic had been known by the church for centuries but it was not until 1953, during excavations to extend the building, that the belt was actually found. It is now displayed in a showcase in a special room. The story behind the discovery is quite interesting, and the church has a booklet which records the history surrounding it.

► The Church of Mar (Saint) Elian

The Church of St Elian, the most interesting building to visit in Homs, is located a little further east. After exiting the Church of al-Zunnar turn right, and follow Kasr al-Sheikh St, keeping left the whole way. The street changes its name to al-Wasta after a short distance but carry on straight. Turn right at the fifth street (the one before the end), and you'll see the church on the left about 75 metres down. (In total, c550m from the Church of the Girdle.)

The church is Eastern (or Greek) Orthodox and is dedicated to Elian, the son of an important Roman official who was martyred in 284 for refusing to renounce his Christian faith. In 432 a church was erected on the site where he died, and his remains were interred in a sarcophagus in the crypt. Over the centuries, either by warfare or earthquake, the Church was reduced to a pitiful condition.

early paintings revealed

In 1969 it was decided to renovate and redecorate the entire building and this was when the significant discovery of the ancient frescoes occurred.

While working in the crypt workmen, scraping old plaster off the walls, uncovered mural paintings dating back to the 12th C and some fragmentary mosaics of probably much earlier origin. Paintings of Christ with the Virgin Mary and Mary Magdalene adorn one side of the crypt while John the Baptist and perhaps Elian himself are on the other. In the corners are the four evangelists, Luke and John on the left, Matthew and Mark on the right.

Romanian iconographers

After rebuilding, the church was completely re-frescoed in bold colours in 1973 by Romanian iconographers, the brothers Gabriel and Miha Morasan. Many scenes from the life of St Elian are included in their work.

▸ The Mosque of Khalid Ibn al-Walid

Half a kilometre north of Kouwatli Street, on the Hama Road is the Mosque of Khalid Ibn al-Walid. The mosque was built in the early 1900s and, as its name implies, houses the tomb of the military leader who conquered Syria for Islam.

12. THE HAURAN

THE HAURAN PLATEAU and AL-ARAB MOUNTAIN RANGE

History

Some 90 kilometres slightly south east of Damascus lies the Hauran Plateau and the Jabal Druze, now called Jabal al-Arab.

The first mention of the name Hauran (as Hauranu), is found in an account of the Assyrian Shalmaneser's attack on Aramean Damascus in 841 BC. Hauran is mentioned in the Old Testament — Ezekiel 47:16 and 18 refers to it when talking about the borders of the Land.

Fought over by the Seleucids and the Ptolomies, it eventually came under Nabatean and then Roman rule. In 23 BC Augustus gave the Hauran, or Auranitis as the Romans called it, to Herod the Great. In 34 AD it was incorporated into the Roman province of Syria, but by 70 AD the southern part was again in the hands of the Nabateans who made Bosra the capital.

a fertile land

In 105 AD the whole area was assimilated into Provincia Arabia. During the Roman era the Hauran prospered, and on account of the fertility of the black lava soil and ample winter rains, became one of the breadbaskets of the Roman Empire.

From the 2nd C Christianity flourished in the region; by the 4th and 5th centuries the faith had become deep rooted, and the region abounds with the remains of churches.

Under Muslim rule the area declined and over the centuries was significantly depopulated.

In the early 18th C Druze from Mount Lebanon began to move there, and following riots in 1860 Druze settlement in the area increased rapidly.

The region today

No less fertile now than in Roman times, the Hauran's rich farmland yields abundant produce. The main crops of the plateau are wheat and cotton. Other crops such as barley and tobacco as well as fruit are also plentiful. The region's farmer's seem to be prospering from their fruitful land, judging by the array of futuristic villas sprouting across the countryside.

inaccessible mountains

Towards the east, where the plateau rises to the Jabal al-Arab, the soil cover vanishes leaving a bare landscape. These mountains, which soar to almost 2000 metres and where the Druze originally fled, were until recently quite inaccessible and isolated, enabling the inhabitants to both politically and socially ignore the rest of the country. Only since the establishment of the Republic has this situation changed.

Besides residing in the hills, Druze inhabit the plains, and in some towns and villages comprise almost 100% of the population. They can easily be recognised by their distinctive dress, which most of the women and some men continue to wear.

What to see

You may wish to confine your visit of the Hauran to Bosra, the main site and a highlight of any tour of Syria. In this case you should then use the main Damascus-Jordan highway to Deraa which is 100 kilometres from Damascus; just before the frontier, turn east (signposted). Bosra is reached after 40 kilometres.

Bus travellers should take the bus to Deraa, and from there another to Bosra. Alternatively there are direct buses and microbuses from Damascus. Tour operators run daily tours.

There are, however, a number of other very interesting places to visit in the region. The Swiss explorer J L Burckhardt was one of the first Western travellers to come across many of the fascinating sites of the Hauran and he recorded in detail what he found. Partly as a result of his journey, Bosra was drawn to the attention of Europe and has since been extensively excavated and restored. But many of the lesser known sites remained obscure, and as a result they have retained an off-the-beaten-track appeal.

It is easy to reach the main sites of interest if you have a car, more difficult by bus, but still possible if you allow two days, one to visit Shahba and Qanawat, and one for Bosra. Details of buses to the first two are given in the text.

THE DRUZE

Called Duruz in Arabic (or Darazi, singular), the Druze are a small Levantine people whose faith is, to put it simply, a very remote form of Islam. They are an extremely cohesive people and throughout their 1000-year history have been able to cling to their identity and unusual faith in the face of much turbulence. There is no conversion to the Druze faith, and intermarriage is not allowed. Truthfulness and mutual support are among the basic duties imposed upon them.

They keep the tenets of their religion secret while at the same time making sure that they are identified as Druze.

So secret is the faith that only certain individuals, called *uqqal* (knowers), participate fully in the ritual and have deep knowledge of the *hikmah* (religious doctrine). The laity, termed the *juhhal,* have no knowledge of this doctrine.

The Druze got their name from one of the founders, Muhammad bin Ismali al-Darazi. Generally not thought of as Muslims, their background certainly is, though they have moved very far away. It is not known if the first adherents were already a distinct ethnic group prior to adopting the present faith, but this is likely.

The faith spread from the teaching of Hamza ibn 'Ali. Living in Cairo in 1017, he and a group of followers, who included al-Darazi, announced a doctrine in which elements of many trains of spiritual thought flowing around the Middle East at the time were all mixed together.

These included utopianism, re-incarnation, transmigration and other concepts. All were united under the redemptive divinity of al-Hakim bi-Amr Allah, Ruler at the Behest of God, the sixth Fatimid Caliph al-Hakim, who ruled from 996 to 1021. Followers believed that al-Hakim did not die, but only "disappeared from sight", and that he will return to herald a messianic age.

There may have been other groups at the time who held similar ideas, but only the Druze have survived.

The main religious text of the Druze is called the *Kitab al-Hikma* (the Book of Wisdom). This is a collection of letters written by al-Hakim and Hamza.

They have tended to live in mountainous areas where they would be isolated and could feel safe from local rulers. Most of their number are found in Lebanon, although because of riots etc many moved to the Syrian Hauran and the mountains to the east in the 18th and 19th C. These mountains acquired the name of Jabal al-Druze, but this has now been officially changed by the Syrian Government to Jabal al-Arab.

There is also a large Druze community in Israel, where they have tended to identify with that State. They are also the indigenous population on the (Israeli occupied) Golan Heights, but here they have remained fiercely nationalistic towards Syria.

► SHAHBA (Philipopolis)

Location

Shahba is situated on the Hauran plateau some 90 kms south of Damascus. Follow the signs towards the airport, keeping your eye open for the right turn to Sweida. Microbuses make the journey from Damascus starting from the south bus station. The trip takes about an hour and a half.

The first part of the journey is unremarkable, but as you near Shahba you will see the black volcanic earth and the basalt rock which is used in much of the local building.

Shahba is an almost completely Druze town and if this is your first visit to a Druze district you'll quickly notice that their style of dress is different from the customary Muslim Arab garb.

History

Shahba, or its vicinity, was where Philip, who became Roman Emperor from 244 to 249 was born. Known as Philip the Arab it was he who built the city which he named Philipopolis, in honour of his birthplace and with the hope (unfulfilled) of the city becoming a second Rome. It was the only new city built by the Romans in Syria (as opposed to the many they altered or rebuilt). The Roman remains are situated in the centre of the present town, and for a small city are really quite extensive. Today, Shahba has a definite rural character, which together with its traditional Druze population, makes an unusual setting for the Roman ruins.

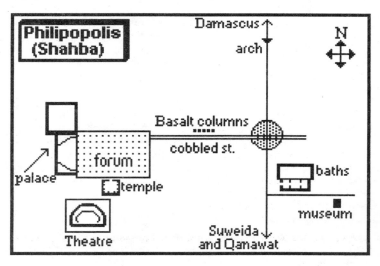

Visit

The road (from Damascus) takes you into the town past the remnants of an arch which was one of the gates of Philipopolis, the walls only existing in profile. Yet when the explorer Johann Burckhardt visited the town in 1810 he wrote, *"The walls may be traced all around the city, and are perfect in places; there are 8 gates, with a paved causeway leading to and from each into the town. Each gate was formed by two arches, with a post in the centre"* ("Travels in Syria and the Holy Land" 1822). It is a sad fact that the last century has managed to obliterate these walls which were able to survive virtually intact during the preceding 1500 years.

Follow the road into the town until you come to a roundabout in the centre. Park in a side street.

Druze handicrafts

Walk up the street that leads off the roundabout to the right (W). This street is paved with large black basalt cobblestones. On your right, slightly raised on a terrace are five basalt Corinthian columns, which are the remains of a **temple portico**. On the left are small shops selling traditional Druze handicrafts.

relics destroyed

When Burckhardt visited in 1810 this street ran from the east gate, which he reckoned to be the principal one. He described it thus:

"[It] leads in a straight line through the town; like the other streets facing the gates, it is paved with oblong flat stones... Following this street through a heap of ruined habitations on each side of it, where are many fragments of columns I came to a place where four massy cubical structures formed a sort of square, [the roundabout today] *through which the street runs... Farther on to the right, upon a terrace stand five Corinthian columns..."*

In the intervening years, as the town expanded and was rebuilt, many of these structures, like so much else, were lost. (As a general rule, non-Islamic relics were not preserved in Syria prior to the French occupation. Indeed it is only very recently that the Syrian Government has started attending to the fabric of many of the historical sites.)

At the top of the street, to the left, is what must have once been the **forum**. Almost facing, on the west side, are the remains of the crescented **façade of the palace** with an area of niches in front (these were also noted by Burckhardt). On the left (S) is a small **temple** with a wide and high doorway. The inside is square with double closed arches on the three (non-entrance) walls.

well-preserved theatre

Behind the temple (to its south) is a **theatre**, which Burckhardt called *"the principal curiosity of Shahba"*. (It should be noted that he was not aware of the origins of the town.) This theatre, though small, is very well preserved. In this case Burckhardt's description of 1810 is identical to what we see today, indicating a rare instance of an unplagiarised monument.

extensive baths

Return to the roundabout and walk along the road heading south (a direct continuation of the way you came). After a few metres on the left (E) are the extensive remains of the **baths**. These are especially large for a city the size of Philipopolis and are currently being renovated. They have two high arched entrances with statue niches on either side. Here, the remains found by Burckhardt in 1810 were far more complete than what can be seen today. He records finding the aqueduct which brought water into the town and to the baths, with at least six arches remaining at that time. Today practically nothing of this is left.

beautiful mosaics

If you turn left into the street by the baths, about 75 metres down on the right is a small **museum** which is worth visiting for its display of lovely 4th C mosaics discovered locally. They include, among others, the Three Graces, the Wedding of Ariadne and Bacchus, Tethis, Goddess of the Sea and Aphrodite and Ares.

► AL-QANAWAT

Lying at the foot of the Jabal al-Arab massif, al-Qanawat is, perhaps, the most enchanting of the ancient cities of the Hauran. Al-Qanawat's quiet rural setting, off the main routes conceals its rich ancestry.

Location

Continue south from Shahba for 10 kilometres, and turn left (E) at the signpost. Carry on to the village and at the T junction turn left (N). A microbus runs between Shahba and Qanawat taking about 25 minutes. It terminates at the top of the village by the Seraya (see text).

History

The settlement first comes to light as Kanut (or Kenath). It was taken by the tribe of Manasseh (Old Test. Numbers 32:42 and I Chron 2:23) and renamed Nobah after the leader of one of the tribes. Later, like most of the area, it was captured by Tiglath-Pilesner III. (No ruins of the pre-Roman period have been found.)

Decapolis city

In Greco-Roman times it was known as Canatha and was the site of a battle between Herod and the Nabateans. Canatha was one of the Decapolis cities, a loose federation of 10 cities under Roman suzerainty. Later it was incorporated into Provincia Arabia, and Septimius Severus gave it the name of Septima Canatha.

During Byzantine times Canatha was a bishopric and had a mainly Christian population. The town fell into decline after the Muslim conquest, and when Burckhardt visited in 1810 he described it as *"the ruined city"* and states that he found but two families living there.

In the meantime a lot more people, mainly Druze, have chosen to live in this large village.

Visit

Continue for some 250 metres until you see high on the left the pillars of the **temple to the sun god Helios**. Built in the 2nd C it had 31 columns, and stood well-elevated in the centre of a public square. To reach it, park, and walk down the narrow alley. Climb up to the platform on which the temple stands. From here you can obtain a broad view of the surrounding countryside with the peaks of Jabal al-Sheikh (Mount Hermon) in the distant west.

Back at your vehicle you can either follow the road, bearing to the right along the banks of the wadi, or take any other preceding right turn to get to the main ruin which is known locally as the Seraya. Anyone will direct you. Down in the wadi you can see extensive remains of the ancient city scattered everywhere.

palace among the oaks

The **Seraya**, which means Palace, is at the top of the village, and is charmingly set. A couple of huge oak trees with abundant foliage frame the southern part, growing out of the now roofless courtyard.

The palace has been partially restored and normally there is a guardian around who speaks some English and French. The area comprises two basilica type buildings, one to the west and one to the south. A courtyard separates them, but as the whole is walled it appears as one unit. Entry is into the west basilica and then, via the court into the southern. The original purpose of the west building was most likely a praetorium, or governor's palace whilst that of the second is not clear. Both were converted into churches in the 4th C when Qanawat became a bishopric. Notice the carvings and inscriptions on almost everything, both standing and fallen.

To the south of the Seraya up a side lane are the ruins of a **Temple to Zeus**.

charming locale

Qanawat as a whole is just a labyrinth of ruins. If you have the time walk down some of the streets and you can see that almost everything is built or partly built of recycled stones and blocks. The streets are steep and picturesque.

► BOSRA (Busra ash Sham)

Bosra is a premier site in Syria, and should not be missed by anyone. While it is principally for the magnificent theatre that Bosra is visited, I consider the other parts of the site just as interesting, even if they lack the dramatic impact of the theatre.

Location

From Qanawat return to the main Sweida road and continue south through Sweida in the direction of al-Qrayya. At the major crossroads, c22 kms south of the town, turn west for Bosra c10 kilometres. Check your compass through Sweida to ensure that your direction is southerly. (It is easy to get confused, and asking someone may not be too reliable.)

History

Muhammad's visit

According to a traditional story, a certain Muhammad ben Abdullah occasionally passed through Bosra with caravans. He would take time to consult with a revered Christian monk, Bahira, on theological matters. Bahira, it is said, prophesied the future course of this man's life. Thus Bosra chronicles its connection to the founder of Islam.

attacked by the Maccabees

Mentioned in 14th C BC Egyptian writings as Busrama, Bosra was a town of little significance until Seleucid times. Like much of the Hauran, Bosra came under Seleucid control after the division of Alexander's Empire. When Judas Maccabeus had driven the Seleucids from Palestine he attacked Bosra in the summer of 165 BC:

> *"Judas and his army at once turned off the desert road to Bosra; having captured the town he put the entire male population to the sword, plundered the town and set it on fire."*
>
> 1 Maccabees 5:8

Trajan legions

Later, Bosra became the capital of the Nabatean presence in the area, developing into a great city from 105 AD when the Emperor Trajan created Arabia Provincia and incorporated into it all Nabatean territory. He constructed a major Roman highway from Bosra to Aila (today Aqaba on Jordan's Red Sea coast), the Via Nova Traiana. Trajan stationed the Third Legion in Bosra and the city was renamed Nova Trajana Bostra. The city expanded, and many new buildings typical of a Roman city were constructed. Around 230 Bostra was made a colonia by Severus, and during his reign Philip (the Arab — see Shahba above) elevated the city to the rank of metropolis. The city was very prosperous, maintaining trade links with Persia and Arabia.

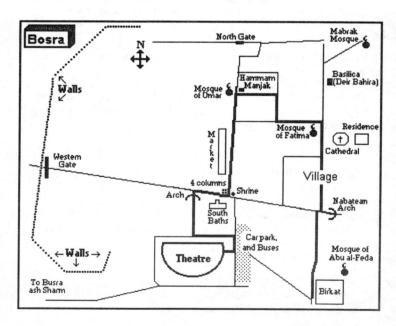

seat of archbishop

Bostra became an important Christian centre and Arch-bishopric and had a noted cathedral. (Besides the ruins of this and of a basilica, bare remains of at least 3 more churches have been found).

In the 5th C it became the capital of a Ghassanid principality (a Christian Arab tribe) under Byzantine suzerainty.

Being close to the Arabian desert the city was one of the first to be taken by the Muslim armies. During the first centuries of Muslim rule the city declined. The Crusaders twice tried, unsuccessfully, to capture it. The rampaging Mongols were more successful and did cause much damage. Any importance Bosra managed to retain was mainly because it was on the *haj* route to Mecca.

general decline

The general Ottoman neglect of parts of Syria affected Bosra, and when the *haj* route was moved further westwards the decline accelerated and the number of inhabitants fell. Like other parts of the Hauran Bosra benefitted (population-wise) from the Druze moving there in the mid 19th C. Today the population is mixed, Muslim, Druze and Orthodox Christians.

Site Visit

A visit to Bosra is made up of two parts. The first is a tour of the magnificent Roman theatre and precincts; the second a dusty but thoroughly interesting walk around the ancient city. At least 3 hours will be needed, but better allow for more.

► Bosra theatre

fort or theatre?

Making your way through the modern town of Bosra Ash Sham you arrive at a large archway that is the **western gate**. Go right (S) along the walls until you reach some massive fortifications with square bastions jutting out. This is **the theatre**. You can be forgiven if you mistake this huge structure for a castle rather than a theatre - it was converted into one. Even the great explorer Johann Burckhardt did likewise. His account of his visit in 1810 only mentions it as a castle even after he had examined the interior: *"...just beyond the walls, on the south side [I] came to a castle of Saracen origin, probably of the time of the Crusades: it is one of the best castles in Syria, and is surrounded by a deep ditch. Its walls are very thick, and the interior are alleys, dark vaults, subterraneous passages,..."* ("Travels in Syria and the Holy Land", 1822). He would doubtless have been greatly surprised to learn that it was one of the finest Roman theatres in the east.

Constructed in the latter half of the 2nd C the huge building was initially converted to a fortress in Omayyad times, but more extensively under the Ayyubids. The fortifications completely encircled the original theatre, and a moat was dug with a single bridge for entry.

preserved by centuries of sand

It was only really recognised for what it was at the close of the 19th C. Nearly all the interior had been covered with sand, blown in over the centuries from the desert. Like other places in Syria (eg the synagogue at Doura Europos), the sand had proved the building's saviour by preserving, and preventing looting.

You enter over a bridge that crosses the moat and through a great doorway into a dimly lit vestibule where you pay the small fee. From here turn down the dark passage to your left. Arrows on the wall try to point you to a route, but these are not so easy to follow, and most people end up making their own way up the steep stone stairs (of which there are many).

spectacular amphitheatre

Eventually you'll reach the summit of the building, gazing down on a spectacular amphitheatre which seats up to 9,000 people. Years of restoration work have gone into what can now be seen, and with some minor exceptions (am I being too finicky?) the result is overwhelming. You can almost hear the eloquence of the Greek or Roman players and the roar of the crowds! (There are festivals here from time to time when performances are staged.)

The theatre has 37 tiers, and the width of the semicircle is over 100 metres. The acoustics are exceptional, with a normal voice able to be heard anywhere. An unusual feature of the Bosra theatre is that it is built on level terrain. Most Roman theatres were built on the side of a hill which greatly simplified construction.

The area behind the stage still has some of the original Corinthian columns, and the beauty of these can only prick the imagination as to how it all once appeared. It is here that the modern reconstruction, complete with electric wiring is very evident. To each side of the stage are large *vomitoria*, exit areas for the vast crowds.

▸ The ancient city

After visiting the theatre go back outside and walk around the walls immediately to your left as you exit (alongside the moat), following the thick line on the site plan. Steps will take you down to a once-colonnaded street where the bases of the columns remain. At the end of the street is a **monumental arch** consisting of a high central arch with two lower side arches. You are now on the main east-west decumanus. The best view of the arch is obtained from across the decumanus (north side). (About 500 metre to the west is the arch you saw when you drove towards the theatre.)

palatial baths

Turn right (E) under the arch and after c50 metres on the right are the very large **Roman south baths** which have been recently excavated. Perhaps in the near future the excavation will be followed by restoration, as these were once very palatial, and were the main baths of the Roman city. Dating from the late 2nd C they were built in a T shape with the entrance via an 8-column portico on the north side. There followed an octagonal vestibule with a dome, now collapsed, built of volcanic rock pieces. This led into the cold, warm and hot chambers. There were at least 2 other Roman baths in the city, the **central baths** behind the market, and the **north baths**, north east of the North Gate. Of these very little is left.

beautiful columns

A little further along on the left are four huge columns, 13 metres high. When Burckhardt, no newcomer to fine pieces of architecture from antiquity, saw these he penned, *"...[here] are four Corinthian columns, equalling in beauty of execution the finest of those at Baalbec or Palmyra... they are quite perfect...".* These are remains of a **nymphaeum** (public water fountain) from the 2nd C. They were placed diagonally as they were on a right-angled street junction. On the opposite corner are the remains of an **open shrine**. Further on east are ancient houses converted for modern use by locals.

However do not continue east, but turn left (N) in front of the nymphaeum. A short way along on the left is the rectangular Roman **marketplace**, which at my last visit was undergoing extensive reconstruction and paving.

a very early mosque

About 250 metres from the corner, on the left, is the **Mosque of Umar**. When Burckhardt saw this mosque in 1810 he called it the great mosque of Bosra, indicating that it must have been the most important one. He adds, *"...which is certainly coeval with the first era of Muhammadanism...",* a fact which was later confirmed by archaeologists. Constructed by the Caliph Umar (the third Caliph), it was enlarged by the Ayyubids in the 12th C. In its original form, therefore, it is probably among the oldest surviving Muslim prayer houses.

children at prayer

Along the outer wall of the mosque (the one parallel to the street) you can notice bricked-in Roman arches. This lower part of the wall was only discovered very recently when the road was excavated and lowered to its original depth. The mosque comprises of a courtyard, with arcades on two of the sides and the prayer hall on the south side. The courtyard has been roofed over giving it the appearance of one great hall. Besides being a mosque this establishment serves as a madrasa (religious school) for boys, and at prayer times it is they who in very disciplined manner make up most of the worshippers.

baths on the way to Mecca

Opposite the mosque are the **Hammam Manjak**. These are impressive and should be visited. Usually kept locked, someone in the mosque will know where the guardian, who speaks a passable English, can be found. (He'll most likely find you first as he expects a tip!) Built by the Mamelukes around 1370 to service the needs of those undertaking the *haj* the baths have recently been restored (as Burckhardt did not notice them it can be assumed that at that time they were in a very poor condition), and are quite fascinating. The walls are finished in black and white stone, the black obviously local while the white could have come from the mountains in the south. As you go from chamber to chamber — there are eleven of them — notice the water conduit pipes for hot and cold water run through the walls, à la 20th C. These baths were capable of holding 500 people in one session!

Ponder, if you like, as you explore the rest of old Bosra and its attendant dirt and unkempt children that people here were taking baths regularly when Europeans may have taken one in a lifetime!

Outside the baths turn right towards the **Mosque of Fatima** with its 20 metre minaret. The bath's guardian will be pleased to point you on your way. Named for the Prophet's daughter, this mosque was built in the 11th C. Of the original, three arches still survive. The lofty tower dates from c1300.

baksheesh, baksheesh!

You are warned that around here are children who will pester you for money (or at least a pen or cigarette). Try to ignore them, and do not give them anything or you'll have dozens more swarming on you in seconds!

If you are lucky you may be approached by one of the "local guides". These are boys aged around 10 who speak a smattering of English, French, Italian and almost everything else. Instead of simply demanding baksheesh they offer to direct you. Some of these young people are real entrepreneurs and I like to encourage them. They are polite and helpful, and can save you time in finding what you want to see. Their main advantage is that if you allow one to attach himself to you it keeps the other little ruffians at bay.

a once majestic cathedral

Just east of the Fatima Mosque is the **Cathedral of Bosra**, dedicated in 512. Unfortunately what remains of this church is very damaged but you can gauge its immense size from what still stands. When Burckhardt visited in 1810 it was in a much better state of repair. He described it as *"a square building which within is circular, and has many arches and niches in the wall: on either side of the door within are two larger niches, and opposite to the door on the east side of the circle is the sanctuary, formed of low arches supported by Corinthian pillars, without pedestals. Several beautiful sculptured friezes are inserted in the wall... in front of the door stand four columns..."* .

In the intervening years the walls have all but been destroyed and the masonry has been carted away for use in other building work. As noted by Burckhardt the cathedral was circular, but was contained within a square building. This style was used for quite a number of cathedrals in Syria, and this cathedral seems to have been the earliest example. The cathedral's dome was 24m wide and rested on a clerestory with at least 50 windows which allowed abundant light to enter.

Behind the cathedral are the ruins of an **ecclesiastical residence**.

home of the Christian prophet

Just north of the cathedral is another structure known as Deir Bahira, described as a **basilica**. Dating from the 3rd C, it was only converted for Christian use much later. Burckhardt records, *"The natives have given to this house the name of Dar Bahira, or the house of Bahira"* (see story about Muhammad above).

mosque of the kneeling camel

Some 250 metres further on (if you want to make the detour) in the northeast corner of Bosra is the **Mabrak Mosque**, which is now restored. Of its origins I cannot do better than Burckhardt:

> *"[on the corner] stands the famous mosque al-Mabrak; ... Ibn Affan, who first collected the scattered leaves of the Koran into a book, relates that when Othman, in coming from the Hejaz, approached the neighbourhood of Bosra with his army, he ordered his people to build a mosque on the spot where the camel which bore the Koran should lie down; such was the origin of the mosque al-Mabrak."*

The mosque which stands here today cannot trace its ancestry back quite that far! The earliest portions of this structure date from 1136 and numerous bits have been added throughout the ages. Evidence that the story surrounding its foundation may have a basis in fact is the mosque's very name, which translated means the kneeling mosque (i.e. the spot where the camel kneels).

Some time prior to Burckhardt's visit the building was partly destroyed by the Wahabi (a warlike and fundamentalist tribe from the Arabian Desert whose descendants today people Saudi Arabia).

latter-day squalor among the relics

You must now return the way you came, past the cathedral. Make your way through the lanes keeping east. This is the area where people still dwell and all around are homes fashioned from the ruins. Regrettably, there is a not inconsiderable amount of rubbish strewn about. The Syrian Government has plans to rehouse these people and restore the whole site properly, but this ambitious project is clearly long-term and I suspect we shall enjoy the curious spectacle of Arab villagers inhabiting the Roman ruins for a long time to come.

The next stop is the **Nabatean arch** which in fact lies at the eastern end of the main decumanus you were on previously (past the nymphaeum). Built of black basalt stone this arch may have been an entrance to the Nabatean king's palace or the access to an open sacred area of a pagan Nabatean temple.

pool of the pilgrimage

South of the gateway is a huge *birkat* or **reservoir**. Measuring 150m by 120m it was dug by the Romans. This was Bosra's main water supply and is one of the largest in this part of the world. Supposedly fed by a conduit system, Burckhardt noted a branch of Wadi Zeid that came down from the hills and emptied itself into the reservoir. No doubt the Muslims made great use of it for watering the many thousands of pilgrims who came this way — the local people call it Birkat al-Haj, the pool of the pilgrimage. It is about 8 metres deep and when I was last there bulldozers were clearing out the sludge and mud of centuries and paving was being laid.

At the northeast corner of the birkat is the **Mosque of Abu al-Feda**.

You can return to the car park either by retracing your steps to the Nabatean arch and walking west until you arrive back at the monumental arch at the end of the short colonnaded street close to the theatre (the way you came) or, as the site plan shows, you can take a short cut across open ground directly to the theatre.

AL-JAWLAN (GOLAN HEIGHTS)

The Golan, occupied by Israel since 1967, is an integral part of modern Syria. The "separation of forces" agreement of 1973 returned to Syria some 500 square kilometres of the area, including the main town, Quneitra; it is supervised by the UN and is closed to virtually all outsiders.

The Heights extend from the Sea of Galilee (Lake Tiberius) towards Jabal al-Sheikh (Mt Hermon) which towers over the region from the north west. Consisting of rich volcanic soil the plateau is very fertile, and the climate, cold in winter and hot in summer, is ideally suited to apple growing. The best apples in the region are grown there, especially around the town of Majdal Shams at the foot of the mountain. Nearly all the indigenous population are Druze.

Until a peace is concluded between Syria and Israel that must include, according to the Syrians, return of all of the Golan, you will be unable to visit the area from Syria. When, (and if) this does happen it will be far easier to visit from Damascus (one hour) than from Tel-Aviv (2½-3 hours).

PART III

INFORMATION FOR TRAVELLERS

13. GENERAL INFORMATION

1. TRAVELLING TO AND FROM SYRIA

When to go

While some Middle Eastern countries are suitable to visit in the winter, Syria is not one of them. Although the coastal area is pleasant enough, Damascus, Aleppo and the desert can be very cold indeed.

Mid-summer (July, August, and most of September) are exceptionally hot and would make extensive sightseeing an ordeal. So we are left with spring and autumn. Of these the best is springtime, late March through mid June. At this time the wild flowers are in bloom, as are the orchards, and much of the countryside is verdant. The best part of this season would be April and May, but all the spring months are very agreeable. You may just catch the odd shower until mid-May, but nothing drastic.

The autumn is also a good season for touring and though you will miss the wild flowers and blossoms you will be amply compensated by the abundant fruit — grapes, pomegranates, dates and more. In late October and November there is a chance of rain, but not enough to spoil your visit. The autumn tourist season lasts through to the end of November when the climate should still be temperate.

How to get there

For a country that is not yet on the general tourist map, Syria is surprisingly easy and cheap to get to.

◆ by air

wide choice of airlines

Most travellers will arrive by air. At the time of writing only the national airline, Syrianair, has a direct, non-changing flight from London to Damascus. It flies 2 or 3 times a week, depending on the season and has a brief intermediate stop at Munich, Germany.

However many other European Airlines fly into Damascus from their respective countries, and through ticketing is available. These airlines include Air France, Lufthansa, Olympic, Tarom (Romanian) and Turkish Airlines. The cheapest is Tarom via Bucharest; depending on the season they offer a return flight for around £220. Tarom also have a flight from the US that connects to its Bucharest-Damascus plane. The drawback with Tarom is that their flight arrives in Damascus after midnight.

discounted fares

Syrianair, if booked through a flight discounter (eg Skylord, 2 Denham St, London, tel: 0171 439 3521, fax: 0171 734 0566 and at 22 Deansgate, Manchester, tel: 0161 839 5864), costs around £280 and is the preferred route as there is no changing planes and the flight arrives in the early evening. A well-priced deal is often also on offer from Olympic via Athens.

Transport from the airport into Damascus is either by bus or taxi. A taxi will cost you about US$9.00 while a bumpy ride in an overcrowded ancient bus, US$0.50. The bus terminates at the junction of Kouwatli and al-Azmeh streets, not too far from the centre.

A taxi will take you to the hotel of your choice (see Amenities chapter), wait while you check it out, and if necessary take you to another. This should not add to the fare.

◆ by land

Syria can be entered by land from either Turkey, Jordan, or Lebanon.

From Turkey: There is a bus and train service from Istanbul to Aleppo. The bus trip takes about 24 hours, whilst the train takes at least half as long again. Accurate current details of these can only be obtained in Istanbul.

From Jordan there is a daily bus, and many service (shared) taxis.

From Lebanon likewise: there is a daily bus from Beirut plus service taxis.

Taking your own car

You can bring your own car into Syria, and if you have the time it can be an exhilarating journey. I have driven many times from London to that part of the world.

There are a number of routes to choose from, the commonest being the standard overland route to Istanbul then across Anatolia to the crossing point of your choice, the most convenient being the one east of Antakya. An alternative (and more expensive) route, but with less driving, is to take a ferry from Ancona in Italy to Kusadasi or Izmir on Turkey's Adriatic coast, and then drive across Anatolia.

A rather unusual way and one I have done myself is to first get a ferry from Italy to Greece. Then take a Greek ferry from Piraeus (Athens) to Rhodes. From there a small Turkish boat takes you to Marmaris in south west Turkey (a journey of a couple of hours - the boat takes half a dozen or so cars). From Marmaris there is a spectacular 1000km+ drive along the Mediterranean coast to Iskenderun (Alexandretta).

Most good travel agencies as well as the AA can provide details of car ferries to Greece and Turkey.

At this time there are no car ferries from Europe to Syria, but there is a ferry that may take cars in Cyprus.

documentation required

To take your car you will need a *carnet de passage* obtainable from the AA or RAC. Syrian insurance is compulsory and obtainable at the border.

Roads in Syria are generally good. The main cities are linked by an Autostrada and nearly all the sites mentioned in this book are accessed by asphalted roads.

Organised tours

A do-it-yourself tour may be more challenging and flexible, but there are a number of tour companies who offer well-planned organised and escorted trips to Syria. Two UK specialists of the region are Jasmine Tours, Cookham, Berkshire (tel: 01628 531 121) and Bales of Dorking, Surrey (tel: 01306 741526. They are, however, expensive.

Entry formalities

Visas

A Syrian visa, issued before departure, is required to enter the country. Please note that these are not obtainable at the border and you will not be allowed to board a plane without one.

If you are going on to Jordan or Lebanon and intend to return to Syria you will need a **multiple entry visa**. Visas are readily obtainable from the Syrian Consulate in your country. It is difficult to obtain a visa from the Syrian Consulate if you apply in a country where you are not resident. If you live in a country where Syria does not have diplomatic representation, apply to the nearest one (by post) (eg: residents of the Republic of Ireland should apply to London).

Some consulate addresses are—

UK: 8, Belgrave Square, London SW1 (0171 245 9012)

USA: 2215 Wyoming Avenue NW, Washington DC 2008 (202-232-6313)

820, Second Avenue, New York, NY 10017 (212-661-1553)

In the UK a single entry visa costs £36 and a multiple entry £72 (1995) and allows you to stay for 15 days. If you wish to stay longer an extension is easily obtained whilst there at little or no cost.

other requirements

Your passport must have a further 6 months validity and should have no evidence in it that you have visited Israel or Israeli controlled territory. This may include a border stamp from Israel or an Egyptian or Jordanian stamp showing you crossed over to those countries from one of their borders with Israel. If you have such indication on your passport, obtain a new or second one.

On entry into Syria you complete a landing card in duplicate. One copy is given back to you, duly stamped. This must be presented when leaving the country.

No special inoculations are required by law, but vaccination against tetanus is advisable (ask your doctor).

Leaving Syria

Like everywhere else, you must reconfirm any flights 72 hours beforehand. On arrival at the airport you will have to pay an **airport tax** in Syrian currency. As this is constantly changing find out from the airline what the current rate is. At passport control you will have to present the form you filled in when you arrived.

If you are leaving for Jordan, overland, no tax is payable at the border. A Jordanian visa can be bought at the Jordanian frontier. It is cheaper than buying one in the UK. If you are leaving for Lebanon you must acquire a visa in your own country.

If it is you intention to return to Syria after visiting one of these countries, you will require a **multiple entry visa** (see above).

2. MONEY AND COSTS

Currency

The Syrian currency is the Syrian pound (£S) or lira. This is divided into 100 piasters (qirsh) but these are rarely used.

Until recently the tourist was burdened with two rates of exchange. Now there is only one, and it is this that you will get in the banks. In the summer of 1994 there were £S42 to one US dollar. The US dollar is the currency which the Syrian Pound is quoted against and all other rates stem from this. You will therefore be better taking most of your funds in US currency.

payment in dollars required

Syria is quite a cheap country to visit, and the exchange rate is very favourable to tourists. However in saying this there is one main qualification: hotel prices. All hotel rates, with the exception of the very cheapest, are posted in US dollars and have, by law, to be paid in the same. **Syrian currency, even at the equivalent exchange rate, is not accepted.**

Credit cards

As only 4 or 5 star hotels take credit cards you should assure yourself a supply of US currency before you go. Take $20, $10, and even $5 notes. Car hire also, if you have not pre-paid abroad, has to be paid for in foreign currency. Some agencies will accept a credit card for this.

Changing money

Exchange can only be done (officially) at the Commercial Bank of Syria, the country's sole bank. All main cities and towns listed in this guide have at least one such bank with the exception of Palmyra (Tadmor).

In some towns where there is more than one branch not every branch changes travellers' cheques, but if they do not you will be directed to one that does. All exchange cash. There is commission to pay when changing TCs but not for cash.

You cannot get a cash advance with your credit card, and except in first class hotels or speciality tourist shops they are practically unusable in Syria.

"Change money, mister?"

There is a black market in foreign exchange, but it is illegal. You may get 15-20% more than in the bank, but remember your hotel bill has still to be settled in US$. Everything else can be paid for in local currency. This makes some things particularly cheap.

Budgeting

The costs of hotels, restaurants, car hire, buses etc will be discussed under the various headings.

Budgeting, like everything else, depends on personal tastes and how much you want to spend. The item which will most affect how much you spend is the hotel. A rough guide is as follows.

Based upon a one or two star hotel, a light lunch, dinner in an ordinary Syrian restaurant, cold drinks or bottled water, entrance fees, but *excluding* car hire and petrol or bus fares, an amount of **US$42 a day per couple** should suffice (this is based on hotel costs of between US$25 and US$30 per night). If budget type hotels are used and restaurant prices carefully compared, this could be reduced to around **US$25 per couple**, but hotel accommodation will be very spartan. If you like to stay at more expensive hotels and eat in better restaurants, then adjust the budget accordingly.

At the other end of the scale, 5 star hotels charge upwards of US$200 per room per night.

3. GETTING AROUND

The choice is simple — either by car or by bus.

Driving in Syria

I do not know what kind of driving test there is in Syria, but most Syrians would not pass a UK driving examination — nor any other that I am familiar with! The manner of driving is as near to a free-for-all on the roads as you can get. Driving regulations, if they exist, are ignored, and such niceties as traffic priorities are replaced by whoever gets there first! A taxi driver I once rode with, who was dodging in and out of traffic with nimble agility, told me he had visited England but would never want to drive there. "You have laws," he explained, "I wouldn't know how to drive with laws!"

But having said that, I have never found driving in Syria to be any more dangerous than the UK except when it comes to night driving (see information box below). Obviously you should be an experienced driver, preferably having done some foreign driving.

road conditions

The main cities are linked by Syrian Autostradas. Not of European motorway standards, they are nevertheless perfectly adequate. The desert roads are two-lane affairs, often with long distances of straight driving with only the barren desert on each side. As these roads are quite empty it is tempting to drive very fast. Don't! All sorts of hazards can suddenly confront you including animals, and more especially potholes. Large trucks coming the other way tend to appear abruptly.

NIGHT DRIVING

Try not to drive during the hours of twilight and darkness. The already poor state of Syrian driving is, during these times, compounded by the poor state of many vehicles. I refer mainly to lights, or the lack of them. Many cars and trucks have faulty lights, or less than the required number. The 3-wheeled motorised carts that abound in rural areas do not have lights at all! To make matters worse, on those vehicles that do have lights have they are usually so misaligned that they will dazzle you. One of the most dangerous — but not infrequent — situations is when there is an oncoming vehicle with only its nearside headlamp working!

The worst road I have encountered at night-time is the stretch of the Aleppo-Latakia road which crosses the mountains. Avoid it at night at all costs!

If for some reason you have no choice but to do some driving at night, take it very easy and use your main headlights whenever possible. Better to dazzle an oncoming driver (who is used to it anyway) than collide with a rear-lightless cart!.

tow-away zones

Try not to drive in Damascus and Aleppo. The traffic is so heavy that it is often quicker to walk, and parking space is difficult to find. When you do park be sure that it is not in a tow-away zone. As you might expect, these are indicated by a sign with a car being lifted and towed. However the signs are often rusty and the paint so worn that they are easily missed. If you do get removed you'll spend a lot of time running around to get your car back (see box on next page as to how this is done).

Syrians love to use their horns! They hoot everywhere, at everything, and for every reason. Why? I'm not a psychiatrist!

Keep an eye on your fuel gauge, and before setting out on a long drive other than on the Autostrada make sure you have enough fuel for your journey. Check the spare tyre, and if you do get a flat get it repaired as soon as possible.

WHAT TO DO IF YOUR CAR IS TOWED AWAY

First of all make reasonably sure it has been. Check the street for tow away signs you may have missed. Then ask your hotel for assistance. If this is not forthcoming, here is the procedure:

You must locate the Traffic Police Station, and go there. With the aid of the car's registration number, **and be sure to keep a note of the number separately from the vehicle,** you will be told of the parking lot where it *might* have been taken. You then go there and make sure that the car is indeed there. Remove from the car the papers, and the person in charge of the lot will then give you a note. This note is taken back to the Traffic Police who will, after checking the car papers and your driving permit, inform you of the fine. This is duly paid and a receipt obtained after which you return to the car lot where you pay a towing fee. You are then expected to pay some "baksheesh" to the man there for "looking after" the vehicle. After shaking hands all round you are free to drive away.

You will be treated very courteously at the police station. There will be many handshakes, and over a mandatory cup of tea the officer will, no doubt, apologise for what has happened. You will smile and assure him that in spite of this Syria is a lovely country. Do not get agitated even if it takes time for the officer to locate your car. There will be hundreds of cars to deal with, and no computer assistance.

All the journeying back and forth can be done by taxi with the driver waiting for you, or more than likely, helping you.

The cost? The fine will be between 500 and 600 Syrian Pounds (US$15), cab fares S£100, towing fees S£100, baksheesh S£25. All this is approximate. The greater cost will be in time wasted and nervous agitation!

To save all this, watch out where you park! By and large if you want to park in a downtown street where there are no or only a few other parked cars, beware!

CAR HIRE

The very best way to tour Syria is by rented car. A car will give you the freedom to travel to your own schedule, and enable you to get everywhere without hassle.

The costs compare favourably with many European countries. For example, Budget's 1995 price for a medium-size 1500cc saloon car, booked in the UK, complete with airconditioning (a near essential), insurance and unlimited kilometrage is about US$300 a week if rented for at least 14 days — slightly more if you take it for less. Their prices start at around $250 per week for an economy car without airconditioning.

plenty of choice

Until the last few years car rental in Syria was rare. Now, with the influx of tourists there are many companies, including the big international ones.

If car rental is what you want, I recommend you do it with one of the international firms, booking and paying for it before you leave. This way you save time in locating a rental agency there.

Most of the big internationals have an office at Damascus airport, but you may find it preferable to pick the ordered car up at the agency's Damascus office, especially if you are arriving at night. (The airport is some 25km from the city, traffic whirls around chaotically, one-way zones are unfathomable.) If you are going to visit Damascus at the start of your tour you will in any event not need the car for at least the first day. It therefore makes sense to take delivery on the second day after your arrival. You will then not have to worry about parking, and if you are staying for 15 days a two week hire will fit nicely. After a phone call they may even deliver it to your hotel. You will be asked to leave a blank signed credit card slip as a deposit.

driving licence

An International Driving Permit is required to drive in Syria. These are obtainable, in the UK, from the AA (even if you are not a member). To get one you need your current driving licence, a passport-size photograph and a completed form. They cost £4.00

fuel costs

In October 1994 3 litres of petrol cost about US$1.50

PUBLIC TRANSPORT

Most of Syria is covered by a good and very inexpensive network of bus services.

Interurban buses

Basically there are 3 categories of interurban buses.

Karnak Bus Company

The best, and usually the most convenient, is Karnak, a part-government company. They operate efficient, comfortable and on-schedule buses (recognisable by their orange colour) between most towns from their own centrally located stations. For all services it is advisable to book your ticket the day before you want to travel. To make this booking you will require your passport.

on-board refreshments

Karnak services are point to point and have no intermediate stops except at their own bus stations. This means you cannot flag one down in the middle of a road, even if it is a bus stop. The fares are very low, ranging between US$1 to US$3. There is a steward on every bus who dispenses iced water and sweets throughout the journey. Officially smoking is not allowed on Karnak buses. If someone does light up the steward will soon have it extinguished. There are no standing passengers and everyone has an assigned seat.

on-board entertainment

Another bus service is provided by the privately-owned interurban "pullmans". They are similar to Karnak in comfort etc (some have bothersome Arabic videos) and run mainly on the Damascus-Palmyra-Deir al-Zor route and cost about the same as Karnak. In Damascus they leave from the bus station near the Tekkiye Mosque.

on-board local colour

The third type of bus is what I would call utility, and has lower fares. These are private buses and usually *very* old. They are not renowned for their comfort, but they are much closer to the ordinary Syrian. And both their decoration and passengers are certainly colourful! Sometimes you may have to use them. For example, if you want to get from Tartous to the Krak des Chevaliers, only one of these buses will stop at the turn-off to let you down. They can be full and often there are many standing passengers.

Smoking is allowed and those I have travelled on have always been chokingly smoke-filled! If you travel on one you may notice a quaint old custom we used to have here in Britain. Men stand up to let women, even young ones, sit! Not after a time, but right away. A young man will also rise in deference to an older one, and you, as an honoured guest in the land, will be treated likewise. A male should never sit next to a female! This is considered impolite in Arab custom. If the only seat available is next to a woman, wait a few moments and other passengers will rearrange themselves to enable you to sit.

Minibuses or microbuses ("meecros")

Destinations close to urban centres are served by small buses called locally "meecros". For example they cover the route from Damascus to Ma'aloula and also the service from Aleppo towards St Simeon. These buses are generally quite old and, like the ones above, offer a bumpy ride. In fact all the remarks above apply here as well.

Interurban Taxis

Those readers familiar with the Middle East and Cyprus will know about service or shared taxis. These are either large, 7-seater limousines or, more common today, 9-seater minibuses. Seats are sold on an individual basis and the taxi leaves when full. The Karnak and pullman buses are more comfortable and I have found the "servees" (as they are called) mostly useful only if a bus has been missed. They do have one advantage — they will put you off at any point you request.

Trains

The Syrian rail network reaches most of the main towns. The drawbacks with it are that the stations are, in most cases, outside the towns and the services are sparse. The route from Deir al-Zor to Aleppo could be useful, but you would not be able to stop off on the way. The Damascus-Aleppo and vice-versa service is mainly a night one. If you are using public transport, stick to the buses.

Urban travel

There are bus services in the towns, but for nearly all your purposes it will be better to walk. The city centres are quite compact. For the journeys that may be too far, a taxi is the best bet. They are very cheap — an average journey only costs US$0.20 to US$0.50!

4. WHAT TO TAKE

Clothing etc

When planning your clothing needs (particularly women), remember that you will be travelling in a Muslim country, albeit a not very traditional one. Too much body should not be displayed. Whilst men can wear shorts (see below), they look out of place in the towns, and in any case you will not be allowed into mosques etc wearing them. Women should not wear shorts at all, it is really insensitive to do so. Likewise, miniskirts should be avoided. Completely sleeveless tops should also be avoided — short sleeves are generally OK, but when visiting mosques it's better if the arms are covered, at least to just above the elbow. By following the above guidelines, not only will you feel more relaxed in a conservative environment, but you will keep cooler

— as any Arab knows less clothing does not always mean less hot.

Take the clothing, according to season, that you would take on a visit to, say, Greece or southern Italy. Between April and mid October you should not require a rainjacket.

keeping cool

I can see little use for men's shorts as these would be unsuitable in a Syrian city and you would not be allowed into Muslim buildings wearing them. In any event experience has shown me that very lightweight loose trousers are more comfortable as the sun is kept off your legs. Likewise, if you are the type who sunburns easily think about very lightweight long-sleeved shirts. Take clothes that wash and dry easily and quickly.

sensible shoes

Make sure your shoes are stout and easy on your feet. Trainers are definitely not very good for walking around sandy and stony sites such as Doura Europos and Halebiye, but they may be useful in the cities where you will frequently have to take your shoes off to enter Muslim sites. Take a good pair of sunglasses and a hat (the latter can be purchased locally).

Take with all the bathroom supplies (toothpaste, shampoo etc) you will need. You can of course buy these items in Syria, but you may not find what you are used to and may waste time looking around. Tissues for use as toilet paper etc can be bought in Syria. (Most lower-priced hotels do not supply toilet paper but many put a box of tissues in your room.) For washing your clothes, one of the readily available tubes of specially formulated travel detergent is ideal.

Medical supplies

Stomach upsets

Unfortunately, we who live in a generally sanitised society have lost a lot of natural immunity to even mild stomach infections. The change of diet etc and different ways of preparing food can easily bring on stomach upsets, especially in hot climates. Thankfully these mild (though unpleasant) infections soon pass.

abstinence the best remedy

I have found the best way to deal with them is to abstain from food totally for a day or two. Drink plenty of fizzy sweet drinks. The sugar will sustain you. After the runs have stopped continue for another day or so eating "safe" food such as yoghurt and hard-boiled eggs.

If you have never taken diarrhoea blockers such as Imodium or Lomotil, consult your doctor before buying them. With some people they cause very severe stomach cramps, worse than the infection! You may consider consulting your doctor about taking with an antibiotic for use in case of a severe infection, but if you follow the simple rules outlined in the information box below, it is unlikely you will need them.

A supply of aspirin or paracetamol may be wise to include (also obtainable in any Syrian pharmacy), as would some wound plaster and antiseptic ointment. Don't forget any medications you usually take as well as indigestion remedies if you use them.

Other useful items

I always take a small travel iron, but then perhaps I'm too fussy! I also take an immersion heater for boiling water in a cup plus tea and instant coffee. If you take these don't forget the cup and a teaspoon!

Syrian hotels have 2-pin electrical outlets (220 V) which use the thin pin plug. If you can't find one at home buy it in Syria. A mains testing screwdriver is very useful to make sure an outlet works.

A torch will come in handy for exploring the dark halls and passageways of Crusader castles and crypts.

Don't forget a pocket compass. The guide is written with the use of this in mind!

EATING AND DRINKING PRECAUTIONS

Under no circumstances eat fresh vegetables or salads unless partaken in a good class restaurant. This definitely includes the parsley and mint garnishes often served with grilled meat.

If you do want salad buy the things yourself and make sure they are well washed. If you buy fruit, wash it well or peel it. Don't eat from curbside stalls however tasty they may smell or look unless you are used to such things and generally have a strong stomach.

In ordinary Syrian restaurants the tables are usually formica topped. They are wiped clean with a not very clean cloth. Although your meal comes on a plate, there is no separate plate for the bread. The locals normally put it on the table. Don't! Put it on a paper napkin or tissue. These are always supplied. Tap water is safe to drink, but wash the glass yourself— there is always a sink for washing hands in or adjacent to the main eating area and I use that.

5. THINGS TO KNOW

Time

Syria is two hours ahead of GMT.

Day of rest

Friday is the Muslim day of rest. Unlike many other Arab countries most places are closed all day and do not open after midday prayers. Christian establishments may close on Sunday.

Opening times

Government offices:
8.00am-2.00pm, except on Fridays when they are closed all day.
Banks:
8.30am-12.30pm. In Damascus the bank in the Sheraton Hotel is open all day.
Travel agencies & airline offices:
8.30am-1.30pm and again from 4.30pm-7.30pm.
Shops:
Shops keep non-standard hours. Those in the souks open from early morning through late evening. In the centres hours are from about 8.30am-1.30pm and from 4.30-8.00 or even 9.00pm.

Holidays

There are two types of holiday in Syria, civil days according to a fixed calendar and religious festivals for the different faiths.
The civil holidays are as follows:

1 January	New Year
22 February	Union Day
8 March	Revolution Day
17 April	Evacuation Day (anniversary of French withdrawal)
1 May	Workers Day
6 May	Martyrs Day

The Christian festivals of Easter and Christmas Day are also national holidays.

As the Islamic calendar is lunar and makes no provision for a leap year, the AD date on which the holidays fall moves backwards by about 11 days every year. Since the actual start of

RAMADAN

The fourth pillar of Islam is the fast of the month of Ramadan, the 9th month of the Muslim year. During this time the devout — and the not so devout — abstain from food and drink (and smoking) during the hours from sunrise to sunset. It is not a holiday although activities do slow down somewhat. Government offices keep shorter hours, and often people are in a lethargic mood.

During Ramadan many Syrian eateries are closed during the day but open up in the evening. As a non-Muslim you will not be expected to do without sustenance, but it would be impolite to eat or smoke in an area where everyone else is abstaining. In general look at your surroundings, and if no one is eating then do not eat there. You can always buy some fruit or salad (all the shops are open) and take them back to your hotel room to eat. Large hotels, in any event, carry on as normal.

The fast breaking meal, eaten immediately after sunset and called *iftar*, literally break-fast, is a very celebratory affair. The family table is set with plates of food, while everyone waits for the moment that sunset is proclaimed. Go to a typical Syrian restaurant and see how the tables are laid and the hungry customers wait, just looking at the food spread before them! Syrians will make you very welcome, and if there is no room, room will be made.

For the next few years Ramadan falls in the winter, so it will be unlikely that many visitors will be there: 1995, 1 Feb; 1996, 17 Jan; 1997, 6 Jan; 1998, 27 Dec. As explained above, each year it falls about 11 days earlier and the dates given here may vary by one or two days, depending on the sighting of the new moon.

each feast depends on the sighting of the new moon there is an unpredictable day or two variance as to when they start. There are 2 main holidays as well as the month-long daytime fast of Ramadan (see box above).

Eid al-Fitr:

This is a three day holiday that comes at the end of Ramadan. In 1995 this feast will commence between 2-4 March and in 1996, between 22-24 February.

Eid al-Adha:

Also a three day festival, Eid al-Adha celebrates the willingness of Abraham to sacrifice his son Ishmael (according to the Koran). It commences on the 10th day of the final month in the Muslim lunar year, Zoul-Hijja, the month when the *haj* is undertaken. In 1995 this holiday will fall around 11 May and in 1996 around 1 May.

Post

If you are only going to be in Syria for about two weeks, a letter home will probably be received after your return! That being said postal services are very cheap. Post offices are in the town centres. If you want to receive a letter Poste Restante, it will be at the main post office. The clerk will give you the whole tray of Poste Restante letters for you to look through yourself. This will be without supervision!

Telephones

You can make international phone calls from most post offices. You will use the new card-operated booths, and cards can be purchased at the counter. You cannot make a collect (reverse charge) call from Syria.

Some area dialling codes:

Aleppo	21	Latakia	41
Banias	421	Palmyra	034
Damascus	11	Raqqa	221
Deir al-Zor	51	Safita	321
Hama	331	Tartous	431
Homs	31		

The international code to dial Syria from abroad is 963.

Visa Extensions

Your visa is valid for 15 days. One extra day can be taken, but no more. To extend your visa go to one of the addresses listed in the Amenities chapter. They are open from 8.00am-2.00pm but close on Fridays.

You will need 3 passport size photos (if you know you will need an extension get these before you leave), and you'll have to fill in a form. The extension fee is very nominal, and the procedure is not very time-consuming.

The extension can only be applied for on the 14th or 15th day, so don't go before.

Tourist offices

Most towns have a government tourist office. The staff are not always too knowledgable or helpful, but they do have very good maps to give away, and if you did not get these from the consulate in your country when you received your visa, you can obtain them from the locations listed in the Amenities chapter of this book.

Personal safety

Many people will be surprised (and pleased) to know that Syria is one of the safest countries to visit.

Provided you conduct yourself as a *bona fide* tourist you will not be harassed in any way by the authorities. You can walk everywhere day or night in safety. Women travelling either alone or without male company will experience practically no problems provided they dress in a modest manner, suitable to a Muslim country. I am very happy to say that stealing is a very rare occurrence in Syria. Of course take the usual precautions with your money and valuables. Bags will be safe left in your hotel, and on buses and in cars, and will never be snatched.

trying your patience

In some instances children can badger you, asking for money or more likely a pen (*kalam*, in Arabic) or just wanting you to take a photograph (*sura*) of them. Try not to get too irritated if the harassment continues, it will be of little avail. More importantly, never give in as this only invites swarms of others. If adults notice this pestering they usually put a stop to it.

Newspapers

Foreign newspapers are available from the Sheraton Hotel in Damascus, and from some city centre bookshops. An English language newspaper, the Syrian Times, is published every day. However it is Government controlled. It can possibly provide some news to the totally news starved.

Radio

Although the Syrian Broadcasting Service does provide some news in English, you will be better off tuning into the BBC World Service which relays from Cyprus on 1323 khz. The reception is very good on the coast but still listenable in other areas. It is best heard in your car radio outside the towns and cities.

There is a 10 o'clock evening "news" broadcast in English on Syrian television.

Maps

An essential. The plans in this book are not intended as a substitute. As already mentioned the Syrian Consulates in your country usually provide, free of charge, very good maps area by area, of the whole country.

The Austrian company, Freytag & Berndt publish a large map of Syria with a very detailed map of Damascus on the reverse side. Good maps of Aleppo and Palmyra are also incorporated.

If you have difficulty in obtaining one try Stanford's, 12 Long Acre, London WC2E 9LP, tel: 0171 836 1321 or Daunt Books for Travellers, 83 Marylebone High St, London W1M 3DE, tel: 0171 224 2295.

6. ETIQUETTE

Arabs are a very generous and hospitable people. I have travelled extensively in many Arab countries, and have found the Syrian people especially so.

code of hospitality

The heritage of their desert ancestry, often reflected in the Koran (or even the Bible), prescribes a pattern of behaviour still very much evident today. One only has to recall how guests were treated in biblical narratives to appreciate this. A classic example is the story of Abraham, who, while sitting at his tent door, saw three strangers standing opposite him:

> *"He ran from the tent door to meet them, and bowed himself to the earth, and said, "... Please let a little water be brought and wash your feet and rest yourself...and I will bring a piece of bread that you may refresh yourselves; after that you may go on...""*   Gen.18:2-5

The offer of hospitality by way of food and drink, even to strangers, is part of the Arab way of life. Once, when searching for a particular place in Aleppo I stopped outside a dwelling to ask the owner for directions. His immediate reply was to invite me in for tea. The whole family then had to meet me and tea turned out to be a veritable feast of Arab pastries (baklawa)! This sort of encounter is not unusual, and can greatly enhance your visit.

polite curiosity

It is also the custom for Arabs to ask many questions — especially about a guest's family, profession etc. You should do likewise and show an interest.

You may be invited to a Syrian home for a meal. If so, you will be amazed at the attention lavished upon you.

Shopkeepers also are accustomed to offering refreshments to strangers. To accept does not put you under any pressure to make a purchase — many people tend to think it will from experiences in more tourist-dependent Middle Eastern lands.

handshakes all round

Shaking hands is far more prevalent in Arab society than ours. Almost any meeting between men for any reason will be preceded by handshakes. Arab women do not normally shake hands, but a Syrian will *sometimes* offer his to a non-Arab female guest.

handwashing, too

You may decide to eat on occasion in one of the typical Syrian eateries (not exactly restaurants!) frequented by the locals. Cutlery is not always available — it is usual to do all the eating with your hands or by mopping up with the accompanying flat bread. A wash basin is at hand in a corner, so you can wash before and after eating. The custom is to use the right hand only. At a communal meal where everybody helps themselves from a central dish, make sure to use *only* the right hand.

ladies first

When queuing at a post office, bus ticket office or the like you will notice there is generally a separate line for women which moves faster. In the absence of such an arrangement women just go to the front of the queue. This is part of Arab etiquette. Unlike many western countries today, Syrian men will always offer their seats to a woman on a crowded bus (see above).

If you ask someone the way he may take your arm (if you are a male) and either lead you to the place or to a point where you can be best directed. Do not be offended by this.

Arab men often walk together arm in arm or even holding hands. This is usual heterosexual behaviour in Arab lands. The only contact a visiting couple should make in public is for the woman to link her arm with the man. Anything more would offend some.

Syrian welcome

Take the trouble to learn some simple Arabic greetings and phrases. The exchange of pleasantries is part of everyday life. Almost everywhere you go passers-by, noticing you to be a visitor, will say "welcome to Syria" (or to the town you are in). Just reply *shukran* (thank you). Other suitable replies to greetings can be found in the Arabic language section of this book.

visiting holy places

When visiting mosques and churches there is a need to dress in an appropriate manner as described in section 3 of this chapter, **What to Take**. Shoes have to be removed before entering the prayer hall. In a large, busy mosque like the Omayyad Mosque in Damascus you take your shoes with you. Inside the hall you will see wooden trays for depositing them. In the smaller mosques, just leave them outside. Some churches, too, require you to remove your shoes.

7. ACCOMMODATION

Payment

As explained, hotel accommodation has to be paid for in US$. The exception is for the very low-priced budget-class hotels.

Choice and cost

Hotels in Syria are rated with stars. In practice, however, there may not be a great deal of difference in comfort and standard between 1 star and 3 star hostelries. Some 1 star may be better than some 3 star and vice versa! The always noticeable difference is the price!

check the room first

Before accepting a room always inspect it, especially the bathroom. If it is not satisfactory tell them so and ask if they have a better one. This is normal practice.

Most independent travellers stay at the 1 to 3 star hotels and you can expect to pay between US$20 and US$45 for a double room in these establishments. Some 3 stars may go much higher, especially in Damascus, where all hotels cost more. In nearly every case prices include a good breakfast, though not always in Damascus. Check to make sure. Rooms are difficult to find in Damascus during the Trade Exhibition held in September.

In general, most 1 to 3 star hotels are old, many dating from the French Mandate period. Of course improvements have been done since then, and compared with hotels in Europe they may seem a bit tatty. But most of them are comfortable enough, and as you will only be staying a night or two, manageable. You will find the staff are helpful and courteous to the point of insisting on helping you with your luggage even if it is only one small bag!

Rather than give details of many hotels whose standards often change, I am giving a partial list of hotels in the towns where you will want to stay, together, where possible, with a recommendation. As I nearly always use the 1 to 3 star category, the choices will be mostly in that grade.

The lists, by location alphabetically, are found in the next chapter of this book.

at the lower end

Budget accommodation can be found for as little as US$10-12 for a room. With rare exceptions don't expect much for this. The room may not be too clean and if you do stay at one check that the sheets have been changed! The bathrooms are shared, often with an oriental (squat) toilet. Another factor is that hot water is not always available. When it is, it is usually charged extra. At the prices charged by budget hotels breakfast is not included.

at the upper end

At the other end of the scale, four and five star luxury is available at an appropriate price (upwards of US$200 unless your with a group) via international chains such as Le Meridien and Sheraton and also the Syrian Cham Hotels.

Syria has no youth hostels or self-catering accommodation.

8. FOOD AND DRINK

Diet

Syria, like all the countries that were once part of the Ottoman domains, has a cuisine many people will recognise from visits to Greece or Turkey, but with the addition of a distinct Arab or Middle Eastern character which lends its own flavour.

One important thing you should know at the start. Pork is not served. As in Judaism, Islam proscribes the consumption of the pig. However, there the connection between the dietary constraints of the two faiths part. Milk and meat can be consumed together, and all types of fish and seafood are permitted.

Bread:

The staple bread of Syria is a large thin flat bread that is baked on the inside wall of a very hot oven. It does not rise and is broken in pieces to eat. It is used for "mopping up" the plate as well as a wrap for local sandwiches. Rolls are available in grocery shops and some of the better hotels serve them.

Meat:

Lamb, or mutton, is the standard meat of Arab countries. It does not have quite the same taste as lamb eaten in Europe, but is a fat-tailed sheep which has a far stronger flavour. It is served in a variety of ways:

Shawarma

This comprises of thin layers of meat with alternating layers of fat piled onto a vertical spit and then roasted in front of a gas-heated grill (in the old days this would have been a charcoal grill). As the outer layers become cooked they are sliced off, and the layer underneath gets cooked. Shawarma is usually eaten as a kind of sandwich rolled up in a piece of flat bread garnished with onions and a piquant sauce. In restaurants it is served on a plate garnished with chopped raw onion, parsley and tomatoes (which I suggest you avoid in the average eatery).

Shish-Kabab

Spiced ground meat pressed into oval shapes and threaded on a skewer and grilled. Garnished with raw onion and parsley.

Shashlik

Small pieces of meat threaded on a skewer and grilled. This can sometimes be a bit tough (it is similar to the Greek souvlaki but lamb is used instead of pork).

Kubbeh

This is almost considered the national dish of Lebanon and Syria. Kubbeh is burghul (cracked wheat), ground meat, finely chopped onion and spices pounded and mixed together until the whole becomes a paste. It is then grilled, fried (usually in cigar shapes) or even eaten raw.

There are also a variety of meat and vegetable stews. As already explained, the meat in all of these dishes will most likely be lamb.

tasty chicken

In the local-type eateries chicken is the most popular dish. You will see countless places with huge gas-fired spits outside. The chicken is always freshly grilled and served straight from the spit. The normal plate is half a chicken, and since they are smallish birds and not accompanied by vegetables, most people will not find the portion too much. It is served with the local flat bread, and often a plate of humous (ground chickpea paté). (Sometimes a side dish of fresh salad is included — safest to avoid this!)

(I always enjoy these grilled chickens; whether they are fresher than those we get in European supermarkets or fed on a different diet, they somehow do taste better.)

Arab sweets and pastries:

Baklawa

Anyone who has tasted really delicious baklawa, the stuffed filo pastry cakes that are eaten from the Bosphorus to the Gulf, will already know what a delight they can be. But they must be made from good quality ingredients, and happily most of what you'll find in Syria *are* good, filled with all manner of nuts, particularly pistachios, and drenched in syrup flavoured with rose.

Halawat al-Gibna

These are pastries made of a semolina dough and filled with a cream cheese. These are also drenched in syrup and are sometimes topped with ice-cream.

Knaafa

Knaafa is one of my favourites, usually served in special sit-down shops. It is a sweet made of burghul and a stretchy chewy cheese, served hot with syrup, prepared in a huge round pan, nearly a metre in diameter, and kept warm over a gas burner. Pieces are cut off for each customer. Cafes that serve this often serve nothing else. It's very cheap.

Muhallabiyeh

Another popular desert. A milk pudding made with rice flour and flavoured with orange blossom or the stamen from a type of crocus called *sahlep*. Broken pistachios are sprinkled on top.

I have referred elsewhere to the delicious sugar preserved apricots from the Ghouta orchards around Damascus. Pears, quince, apple and other fruits are also preserved in this manner.

Cheese and dairy:

There are different hard cheeses available. The most popular is *katchkaval* a hard sheep's milk cheese eaten all over the Balkans and Middle East. Yoghurt is much consumed as is a sharp cream cheese made from it called *labaneh*. You may get this for breakfast. It is eaten accompanied by ripe black olives.

Speciality foods:

One of the great eating delights of the Middle East is the Arab *mezze*. These exotic buffets are usually found in the more expensive restaurants, but are still relatively inexpensive. A good mezze could comprise a dozen or so salads, grilled meat, kubbeh, fresh vegetables, and lots of sweet Arab pastries.

In the 4 and 5 star hotels international cuisine is always available. See the Amenities chapter for more details.

Beverages:

Water

There is no reason not to drink tap water in Syria. Many people may still feel more relaxed using the bottled spring water. It comes in 1.5 litre plastic bottles and costs, depending on where you by it, between US$0.20-0.30. You are warned that in a first class hotel the price may be as high as US$2.50! If you do buy from a kiosk or the like, make sure the seal is intact. Some Syrians, especially youths, fill up old bottles from the tap!

Tea and coffee

Tea, *shai*, is the everyday, all day drink. It is served in small glasses and you sweeten it yourself. If you always thought that the British were *the* tea drinking nation you were wrong. The Arabs (and Turks) win hands down! Office workers, shopkeepers and most others drink it constantly. In the souks there are special tea brewers who prepare and deliver glasses of the beverage all day long. Unlike in some Arab countries, tea is drunk in Syria as it is, without herb flavouring.

Coffee is brewed in the manner preferred across the Balkans and Near East: the coffee and sugar are brought to the boil twice and then decanted into small cups, grounds and all. In Syria cardamon pods are usually added and these give the coffee its unique aroma. Generally referred to outside the region as Turkish coffee, every nation which takes its coffee this way claims it as their own: Greek coffee in Greece, Cypriot in Cyprus, and certainly Arab coffee in Syria. However, simply requesting *"ahwa"* ("coffee") is sufficient as it is served in no other way.

a bitter brew

The brew is far stronger and more bitter than we are accustomed to. The beverage served by the Bedouin is stronger and more bitter still, and a portion may be no more than a sip.

When being served with tea or coffee, a glass of cold water always accompanies.

tea gardens

Tea and coffee houses are meeting places, and people may sit there for hours talking and playing the Arab pastime, *shesh-besh,* backgammon. Water pipes, *narghiles*, are also smoked there. You will never see a Syrian woman in a tea house. Women tourists may, but if possible try to sit outside, and never sit alone. In some areas there are "family tea gardens"; these are especially for mixed couples.

Juice

Fresh fruit juice is loved by Syrians, and you will find kiosks selling this almost everywhere. Many are colourfully decorated with strings of fruit hanging outside. Besides the juices you would expect like orange and apple you'll find carrot, pomegranate, melon, strawberry, and many others. Quite often cocktails of various fruits are served.

Alcohol

Islam proscribes the consumption of alcohol. Having made that statement I can continue by saying that alcohol is available in Syria (some 10% of the population is Christian). However you will not find it in everyday restaurants. Syria produces wines and spirits (brandy and arak, the Middle East's Pernod-type drink, and some liqueurs). These can be bought in shops specialising in these beverages. The shops are few and far between. There is a local beer called "al-Chark" which I find very poor quality. However it comes in 680ml bottles and is thirst-quenching when served cold. Imported drinks of any kind are very expensive.

Carbonated soft drinks
The usual array of these is available. The local ones are very cheap while those produced under licence are still cheapish.

For information on where to eat and drink see the Amenities chapter of this book.

9. PHOTOGRAPHY

You are allowed to photograph at will except in the few sensitive spots where there is a sign prohibiting same.

Most people do not mind being photographed, but be careful in the case of women. If they object, leave it. You will get your best shots of people if you use a long lens. For pictures inside the old cities where space is tight, a wide angle lens (35mm, or better still 28mm) is a must. For pictures in the covered souks you will need a flash. As the air can be very dusty make sure you carry a lens dusting brush. Try to keep your films, both exposed and unexposed, as cool as possible. Never leave them or your camera in the car. The temperature in a parked vehicle in the sun can reach well over 45°C!

10. WHAT TO BUY

The first thing that comes to mind when thinking of shopping in Syria is a Damask tablecloth or other damascened textiles, and these are described more fully in the information box on the next page. They are less expensive than you might think!

true or false?
Inlaid woodwork is also a good buy, but prices vary a great deal according to quality. Some cheap items are not real marquetry but just a veneer covering. The veneers are quite effective, but if you examine the imitation and authentic side by

side you can easily spot the difference. Boxed chess and backgammon sets and jewellery or trinket boxes are popular inlay items, the latter making extensive use of mother-of-pearl.

Metalwork is generally of a high standard. Brass and copper trays, platters, coffee pots and even hubble-bubble water pipes are available from craftsmen and shops. Again, quality and method of manufacture determines the price. A copper tray engraved by hand will cost much more than one etched with acid. (A rather battered appearance on the underside denotes the former.)

THE CREATION OF DAMASK

The material we know as Damask came to Syria from China, and has been woven in Damascus since the 11th and 12th centuries. The original Damask was made entirely from silk and woven with very intricate designs. A flat fabric, it is woven on a Jacquard loom. The pattern appears to be raised but this is not the case. The satin pattern is made by allowing the warp to pass over a few wefts or fillings before it again passes underneath. It can pass over 4 threads for a less shiny look and maybe 8 threads for a more shiny appearance.

Today Damask is made from fibres other than silk, but silk is still used in the expensive and beautiful brocades. The very best Damask tablecloths are made from linen, but these are mainly produced in Europe. (The Belgium city of Coutrai is renowned for these.) In Syria the cloths are usually of cotton and rayon, and produced on automatic looms. They are very reasonably priced. A good sized cloth complete with napkins costs around US$20. In an expensive shop you may find ones woven on hand looms, but these will cost far more.

Dress damasks or brocades made of silk are exquisite and these are still woven extensively in Syria. They are produced on ancient hand-operated looms with the patterns being controlled by equally ancient punch-cards. It is fascinating to watch the weavers at work, the shuttle being thrown by hand from selvage to selvage. It takes 11 hours to weave half a metre in this manner!

You can buy the material by the metre or made up: there are fine scarves and blouses for women to choose from, and for men a rather exotic selection of ties and waistcoats. Compared to prices in Europe the cost is very reasonable.

Weavers at work can be seen in the handicrafts market next to the Tekkiye Mosque in Damascus as well as in a few places in the old city.

Persian rugs

Kilim rugs are exceptionally good value although very few are made in Syria. Many are made in Iran and are brought by pilgrims visiting the Shi'ite shrines in Syria to help finance their trip. Others hail from the Muslim states of the former USSR, and from Kurds of different countries — all places noted for their carpet-making prowess. Prices vary a lot and as with the items mentioned above the final price will depend on your bargaining skills!

be prepared to haggle

Remember the merchant expects you to bargain so the initial price is adjusted accordingly. How low to go? Well it's almost impossible to give a figure. My experience has been very varied. On occasion I have cut the price in half. Other times I've only managed to reduce it by 15%. The main thing in the end is that you are satisfied with the price you pay. If you want to avoid traditional Arab bargaining, go to the handicrafts market near the Tekkiye Mosque. There you will find all the items described in this section (and more) at fixed prices.

for the sweet tooth

Some of Syria's delicacies are also good to take home. Fruits preserved with sugar are available attractively packaged. Baklawa is also something to return home with, but try to buy it on your last day so it will be as fresh as possible. These two items are available from many shops situated in and around Midaan Shuhada (Martyrs Square) just west of Damascus's old city.

14. AMENITIES

The listing below is in alphabetical order and represents the towns and cities where you are most likely to stay overnight. It is not exhaustive, and where prices are given they are only meant as a guide. In Syria's burgeoning economy fluctuations must be expected.

ALEPPO

SERVICES

Post Office:
> Corner of Kouwatli and al-Jaala Streets at the north edge of the public gardens.

Bank:
> There are a number of branches in the city. The best one is at the northern end of Baron St, on the right. There is a sign, but it may be difficult to see. It's on the first floor through an arcade. If in doubt, ask.

Visa extensions:
> The immigration office is near the corner of al-Kawakibi St and the road which circles the citadel, on the northern side of the citadel. It's on the second floor.

Tourist Office:
> In the gardens facing the Museum.

Karnak Buses:
> The ticket office is on Baron Street, almost facing the Baron Hotel. The buses leave from a parking area around the corner in al-Maari St.

HOTELS

Aleppo area dialling code: 21

Chahba Cham Palace ***** Luxury hotel situated on the western fringes of the city.

Pullman Hotel **** A first class establishment situated near the university, some way from the city centre. They operate a shuttle bus service into the city. Tel: 249401.

Amir Palace **** A first class hotel right in the heart of Aleppo, not too far from Bab Antakya. Tel: 246510.

Hotel Tourism *** Downtown, facing the public gardens. This hotel has a restaurant that offers an oriental mezze buffet. Tel: 210156

Hotel Baron *** (see box on page 128) Now hardly deserving a three star rating I select this hotel for the pure pleasure of staying in such a place. The rooms are enormous, and the equally huge bathrooms, with antiquated plumbing, have to be seen to be believed. Close your eyes to the decay and enjoy a bit of the past! On Baron St, in the centre. Price around $35 double. Tel: 210156

Hotel Ramsis ** on Baron St. Tel: 216700.

New Omayyad Hotel ** on a street parallel to Baron St, behind the Ramsis.

Ambassadors * on Baron St. Tel: 211833.

These last three hotels are all "adequate", but the Ramsis is a bit pricey (double room around $40) for what it offers.

Budget-priced hotels are located along al-Maari St. The hotels vary in quality, as do the rooms. View first before deciding.

RESTAURANTS

In the district bordered by al-Maari St, Baron St and Bab al-Faraj there are many local-type eateries. A few in the side streets are geared up to attract tourists with door touts dressed in "oriental" outfits. In these you will pay more for a substantially identical menu to others. If you want to eat in this area stick to a place that has many people inside — usually a sign that the food is fresh, and the prices fair.

For better restaurants with (perhaps) more ambience go to al-Shalal St in the al-Azizaiah quarter (take a taxi there). **Restaurant Reef** serves Syrian and European food and wine. **Wanes** is similar. There are two or three more along the same street, all of which serve alcohol. Up the side street by Wanes is **Pizza House**. They serve pizza etc in the American fashion and prices are very reasonable.

You can also eat in the **Baron** but they have a fixed menu which is not too exciting. However a drink in the bar there is enjoyable. As mentioned under hotels, **Hotel Tourism** offers a good *mezze* buffet.

BANIYAS

Most travellers will only pass through this small Mediterranean town. For those, however, who do need to stay there are two small hotels. Don't expect much, but they should be adequate.

Baniyas Hotel 20 rooms
Homs Hotel 10 rooms

BOSRA

If you want to stay here there is only one hotel, the luxury **Bosra Cham Palace.**

DAMASCUS

SERVICES

Post Office:
Not far from the Hejaz Railway Station on al-Jabri St.
Bank:
There are many branches in the city. The best ones for exchange are at Ash Sharm Square and facing the Hejaz Station by the Orient Palace Hotel.
Visa extensions:
Immigration Office, Sharia Falastin (near the Karnak bus station).
Tourist Office:
29 Ayyar St. This is just north of al-Azmeh Square (the square near the Cham Hotel).
Karnak bus station:
About 5 mins walk west of the Hejaz train station.
Transport to Jordan and Lebanon:
Buses for Amman and Beirut leave from the Karnak bus station.

Buy your ticket in advance and it has to be paid for in US$. Service (shared) taxis leave from the plot adjacent to the bus station. For Amman you are better off to go by bus.

Car hire:

I recommend you arrange this from your home country where possible, but some local offices are—

Europcar, Baramkeh St, Tel: 2231737, 2210624-5; Fax: 2237688

Budget, Malki al-Bizm St, Tel: 2239005; Fax: 2232702

Marmou, Tel: 3335959

Consulates:

United Kingdom: 11 Muhammad Kurd St (in the Malki qtr), Tel: 712561.

United States: 2 al-Mansour St (in the Abu Roumaneh qtr), Tel: 3333052

Canada: Tel: 2236851.

Australia: 12 Farabi St (in the al-Mezzeh qtr), Tel: 665317.

Japan: 15 al-Jala'a St, Tel: 3339421.

Republic of Ireland: Refer to the UK consulate.

Cultural Centres:

United States: Behind the Consulate. Tel: 2228527. Newspapers are available for reading here. Bring your passport.

British Council: Abd Makek bin Marwan St (in the Malki qtr) Tel: 3333109.

HOTELS

Damascus area dialling code: 11

In general hotels in Damascus are more expensive than other towns. In fact some charge prices which bear no relation to what they offer, and yet others offer reasonably good value. For sure you'll find no particular bargains. If you are on a tight budget you will have to settle for something less than you might really desire. The "hotel area" is around Shuhada Square. In the square and the surrounding streets are many hotels categorised as 2 and 3 star establishments. The prices vary so much, as do the rooms, not only from hotel to hotel but in them as well. If you arrive late without a booking you are sure to find a room in this area even if you end up paying more than you want. The following day you can find something else — perhaps.

Sheraton ***** The only American hotel in Syria. Situated near al-'Umawiyeen Sq in the west of the city. Tel: 2229300.

Le Meridien Hotel ***** About 15 minutes walk from the centre, on the north side of the Barada river. Tel: 718730.

Cham Palace ***** Right in the centre near al-Azmeh Square. Tel: 2232300.

Fardoos Tower Hotel **** in the city centre (100 rooms) Tel: 2232100.

Le Vendome **** Near al-Azmeh Square (100 rooms) Tel: 2219226.

Hotel Semiramis *** At the corner of Kouwatli St by the flyover (95 rooms) Tel: 2216797. A modern hotel and very comfortable. The prices are high as are most similar ones in Damascus.

Samir Hotel ** Shuhada (Martyrs) Sq (70 rooms) Tel: 2219502.

Ramsis Hotel ** Shuhada Sq (37 rooms) Tel: 2216702.

Venezia Hotel ** In the centre on Bahsa St (100 rooms) Tel: 2229991.

Orient Palace Hotel ** Facing the Hejaz railway station. Oldish but adequate establishment. There is a car park outside (66 rooms) Tel: 2220501.

Sultan Hotel * Just west of the Hejaz station on al-Baroudi Street. Fair value at around $28 double. Tel: 2225768.

Hotel Candels * A few minutes walk west of the Hejaz railway station. Take the first street on the right along al-Baroudi St. The hotel is on the right. This is an old hotel but I find it good value and satisfactory (unless, of course you want something in the upmarket category). Breakfast is not included, but there is a snack bar. (Double room around $20.) Tel: 2211318.

Remember, in most hotels the rooms vary, so if the first one they show you does not suit, ask to see something else.

There are a number of budget priced hotels but some are dreadful. The worst of Syria's budget hotels are in Damascus. Any hotel with any sort of comfort is placed in the "star" range.

RESTAURANTS

Around Shuhada Square are many restaurants serving Arab food. They vary in price, the ones who try to pull you in being usually the more expensive. The food in all of these places will be good, but the menu limited. North of al-Azmeh Square on 29th Ayyar St are more of the same. These may be more comfortable but the food will be similar.

If you tire of Oriental fare try the **Cham Hotel**. Although more expensive than a local food restaurant the prices are still surprisingly low compared to a luxury hotel in Europe. They have an Italian and a Chinese restaurant. If you want to splash out, the **Sheraton** has a splendid array of eateries, all expensive by Syrian standards but reasonable compared to elsewhere. I once went to their seafood buffet where you could eat all you liked for US$20. I ate enough lobster to last a lifetime!

For a night out, the **Omayyad Palace** restaurant, near the Omayyad Mosque in the old city is ideal. Beautifully decorated, you sit Middle East style at low tables. It is a help-yourself buffet and the Arab salads and starters are outstanding, among the best I have eaten. On some days there are a couple of Whirling Dervishes for entertainment. It's all a bit unreal but enjoyable.

DEIR AL-ZOR

SERVICES

Post Office:
Hassan Taha Street (the main north/south street).
Bank:
Shari'a 'am Street (the main east/west street).
Karnak Bus station:
This is not too easy to find, of course if you arrived there.... It's in the centre of town near the Euphrates diversion channel.
Microbuses:
Going south: at the south end of Hassan Taha Street.
Trains:
The station is on the north bank of the river about 3 kms north of the town. There are 2 trains a day for Aleppo, one in the morning, and one just past midnight. Check actual current times.

HOTELS

Deir al-Zor area dialling code: 51

Except for the luxury **al-Furat Cham Palace** on the outskirts of town there are really only two (not counting the budget ones). **Al-Waha (Oasis) Hotel ***** is near the railway station so also out of the town. Tel: 25418.

The Raghdan Hotel * near the centre facing the river channel is therefore my choice. It's conveniently situated, and although from a bygone era (French Mandate?) is comfortable with polite staff. Some rooms even have (noisy) airconditioning! They charge a bit more than its worth (around $28 double), but there again so do most Syrian hotels. Breakfast is included, and there is a decent and reasonably-priced rooftop restaurant. Tel: 22053.

Budget hotels: The best is probably the **Hotel Damas** on Hassan Taha Street, around the corner from the Raghdan Hotel (tel: 21481). Others are the **Amal** and the **Ghassan** but they are quite atrocious.

RESTAURANTS

On Hassan Taha Street are many of the usual popular Syrian eateries, but they tend to close in the early evening. Along the Euphrates by the suspension bridge are two or three open-air places that purport to be "tourist restaurants". Although the riverside setting sounds nice it's so dark that you cannot see anything. They are far from clean with hard earth floors into which all manner of bits and pieces have been trodden. They do not display prices and tourists are definitely charged more. If you are around in daylight hours they are pleasant enough to sit in for a cold beer or arak. The best place to eat is the rooftop restaurant at the **Raghdan Hotel.** Prices are fair, the food is quite good and they also serve alcohol.

HAMA

SERVICES

Post Office:

On the corner of Kouwatli and Abdul Nasser streets.

Bank:

Next to the post office.

Visa extension:

Hama is not an ideal place to do this, but if you have to the passport office is in the centre of town. Ask your hotel for precise directions.

Tourist Office:

In the gardens between the centre and the Cham Hotel

Karnak Buses:

In the cafe Aphamia facing the gardens and water wheel. The buses stop outside.

HOTELS

Hama area dialling code: 331

The Aphamia Cham Palace ***** Tel: 27712.

Basman Hotel *** on Kouwatli Street just past the post office. This hotel has three stars but does not deserve them. The entrance may look slightly upmarket but the rooms are just about adequate and nothing more.

There are two hotels in the non-star range which are certainly no worse than the Basman and a lot lower in price:

The Cairo Hotel (tel: 22280) on Kouwatli St before you get to the post office is fairly comfortable by Syrian standards. Two doors away is the **Riad Hotel** which has recently been refurbished. The rooms here are very satisfactory. At both establishments you can pay in local currency. A double room will cost the equivalent of US$16-18. At the time of writing these are the only hotels in Hama worth talking about.

RESTAURANTS

In town, along Kouwatli street, there are a few standard places. The best, and a place I enjoy eating at, is down a side street almost facing the Cairo Hotel. It's on the right just before you reach the road by the river. They only serve chicken, but it's very fresh, tasty and clean, and comes with a plate of humous.

There is a new cafe-restaurant by the Orontes in the park in the centre. It is between two channels of the river and makes a congenial spot to have a cold drink or ice cream during the day (no alcohol served). For meals, although the grills are passable avoid the "pizza". Any resemblance to the Italian dish is purely coincidental.

In the south of the city by the river is a restaurant called the **Four Norias**. It's right by the group of four water-wheels. The restaurant is attractively situated, and you eat on a large veranda which overlooks the river. The food will be no better than a standard Syrian eatery, but the setting and service is. You will pay for these luxuries.

There is of course a restaurant in the five star **Cham Palace Hotel.**

Back on Kouwatli St there are a number of places serving Arab sweets. They are all good, and will make a delicious and inexpensive dessert.

HOMS

If you are travelling by car you should have no need to stay here. Bus travellers, though, might need to.

SERVICES

Post Office:
At the western end of Kouwatli Street, on the north side.
Bank:
North of Kouwatli Street, just off Ibn Khaldoun Street. This is the

second street on the right going west on Kouwatli.

Tourist Office:
In the small garden at the end of Kouwatli Street, on the south side.

Karnak Buses:
Homs has a modern Karnak station. Its about 2 kms north of Kouwatli St. on the Hama road, just before a major road intersection.

HOTELS

Homs area dialling code: 31

Safir Hotel ***** Tel.28120.

Hotel Homs **** Tel.82600.

Basman al-Jadid (Grand Basman) * The best choice for the average traveller, on Esh-Sharm St. It's small but comfortable.

Semiramis Hotel * On Kouwatli St and similar to the foregoing. Tel: 21847.

Budget hotels can be found off Kouwatli St near the tourist office. Expect what you pay for, but not too bad is the **al-Nasr al-Jadeed Hotel**.

RESTAURANTS

There are plenty of ordinary Syrian eateries around Kouwatli St. The **Amir** and the **Toledo** are both quite good.

KASSAB

In case you want to rest in this airy mountain village north of Latakia there are a few small places to stay:

El-Rawda, 27 rooms, **Ramsis**, 20 rooms, **Semiramis**, 30 rooms.

LATAKIA

SERVICES

Post Office:
Off Baghdad Street, going towards the port.

Bank:

On Baghdad Street just before the roundabout, on the east side.

Visa extensions:

The immigration office is in the police station off 14th Ramadan St (near the statue of Assad).

Tourist Office:

Near the roundabout at the junction of 14th Ramadan St and al-Maghreb al-Arabi St (facing the Riviera Hotel).

Karnak Buses:

At the southern end of Baghdad St.

HOTELS

Latakia area dialling code: 41

Le Meridien ***** If you want luxury you will find it 10 kms north of the city, on the sea front. Tel: 29000.

Cote d'Azur Cham ***** not quite so far out as the Meridien. Tel: 26329.

Along the sea road in town are a number of mid priced hotels such as the **al-Gandoul Hotel** ** Andalos St. They charge about US$26 for a double room without breakfast. There is airconditioning and a small fridge in most rooms. Good value. Tel: 237680.

In town is the **Riviera** by the roundabout at the junction of 14th Ramadan St and al-Maghreb al-Arabi St, a comfortable hotel but around US$60. I like the **al-Noor Hotel** on the left down 14th Ramadan St. The elderly owner speaks no English, but excellent French, and is helpful and polite if you can communicate. The rooms are clean and comfortable and breakfast is included for a double room price of around US$22. Tel: 423980.

Budget accommodation is to be found further down 14th Ramadan St near the statue of Assad. Close to the mosque is the **Afamia Hotel,** and in the street to the left is the **al-Nahhas.** Both of these hostelries accept local money. Whatever price you are quoted, you may have to pay a little more for a hot shower!

RESTAURANTS

In town you are not going to find much more than standard fare. The **Riviera Hotel** does have a restaurant which serves this standard food in more congenial surroundings at a price to suit.

Along the sea there are some sea food restaurants, but I find their charges inflated for what you get.

If you want a good dinner at a fair price, go to one of the big hotels.

PALMYRA

SERVICES

Post Office:
You'll find this in a new building at the entrance to the town.

Bank:
At the time of writing there is no bank in Palmyra, but in an emergency your hotel will help.

Tourist Office:
Along the road to the site before you come to the Zenobia Hotel.

Karnak Buses:
The office is at the entrance to the town next to a garden restaurant.

Pullman Buses:
Some of these leave from a cafe along the town's main street (ask) and some leave from the Karnak office. If you are waiting outside the office don't buy your ticket until the bus comes. That way you can take whatever comes first.

HOTELS

Palmyra area dialling code: 034

Cham Palace **** Along the main road from Damascus before you reach Tadmor. Tel: 37000.

Hotel Zenobia *** Situated on the edge of the site, near the Temple of Baal-Shamin. Built during the early part of the century it was once the only hotel in Palmyra. It must have seemed like heaven for travellers who had undertaken the arduous journey from Damascus. Recently taken over by new owners, the Zenobia has undergone a facelift and been extensively modernised. It is also airconditioned. It still retains a little of it's old world charm. A very good hotel at around US$60 for a double room. Unlike most Syrian Hotels, the Zenobia accepts major credit cards. Tel: 107000

Along Tadmor's main street are a number of adequate hotels such as the **Palmyra Hotel** *.

My preference is the **al-Nakhil Hotel** just off the main street. (Anyone will direct you.) Built and owned by a Bedouin family, it offers all the hospitality that Bedouin culture dictates in a brand new building. The rooms and bathrooms are of European standard. Breakfast is included. Groups often stay here so try to call in advance. US$25-30 for a double room. Definitely recommended. Tel: 220744.

RESTAURANTS

You can eat in the restaurants of the **Cham Palace** or the **Zenobia Hotel**. Otherwise all you will find are along the main street. As tourism is the mainstay of Tadmor expect to pay a little more for the same fare. There is a garden restaurant at the entrance to the town facing the museum. It's a relaxing place to sit, but has inflated prices. Other eateries that can be considered are near the tourist office on the way to the Zenobia Hotel. They are outdoors, and you may be bothered by flies.

RAQQA

Only if you are travelling by public transport will you need to consider an overnight stay here. Please don't expect very much.

Tourism Hotel Between the clock tower and the Baghdad Gate. Near the clock tower is the **Ammar Hotel** which I have been told is quite acceptable. There are a few more places in the same vicinity. All the hotels in al-Raqqa are budget class and payment can be made in Syrian pounds.

SAFITA

This is a hilltop resort town, and consequently sports quite a few lodging places:

Safita Cham Palace **** less expensive than other Chams, but still over US$120. There are hotels in the two and three star range not far from the Cham.
Budget accommodation will be found near the bus station as will the **Burj Safita Hotel** * which has passable rooms around US$25.

TARTOUS

SERVICES

Post Office:
On the corner of Tishrin and Abdul Nasr streets.

Bank:

At the top of Almenshya St, just down from Khalid ibn Walid St.

Tourist Office:

On Khalid ibn Walid St.

Karnak Buses:

The office is on al-Thawra St about 200 metres north of Abdul Nasr St, on the left. Buses stop outside.

HOTELS

Tartous area dialling code: 431

For a town its size Tartous does not have too many hotels.

Tartous al-Kabir (The Grand) is the supposed best. Situated on the sea front corniche about half a km south of the centre. Expect to pay US$40-50, Tel: 25475.

The Shahine Hotel, a new affair, is in a side road just off the corniche about 250 metres south of the centre. Prices here are more than the al-Kabir. In the same area is the **Cleopatra Hotel**, Tel: 20915 and the **Al-Azrak**, Tel: 20650 with prices from US$25.

Al-Baher Hotel: also along the sea front corniche south of the centre is a comfortable place and costs around US$20. Sometimes what looks a bit shabby turns out to be the best deal.

The Daniel Hotel: Although classed as a budget hotel this has always been good enough for me. Situated on the right almost at the end of the street that runs down to the small fishing harbour, you'll find the hotel on the first floor. Once clearly a high class establishment now, alas, it is quite run down. However the rooms are spotlessly clean, as is the linen. The bathrooms, while badly in need of a plumbing overhaul, serve their purpose. The son of the owner who runs the place speaks good English and French, and I often wonder why he seems content to spend his life at the hotel desk. Most prices include a good breakfast prepared by the son's wife and mother and are quite modest. You should not have to pay more than the equivalent of US$16-17 in Syrian pounds.

There are other budget hotels in the same area, but they are not comparable.

RESTAURANTS

You will not be eating the best meal of your visit to Syria in Tartous!

Along the seafront corniche are a few fish restaurants, but they are expensive for what they serve. The one at the end of the street where the Daniel Hotel is located — on the right facing the sea — is about the best. There are a few of the usual grills back in the town.

If you can eat early you might find one of the fish restaurants on the quayside at Arwad an agreeable place for a meal. You will be caught with the price, but it will still be affordable and the situation is better than anything on the Tartous mainland.

In the evening it's enjoyable to sit in one of the tea and coffee houses along the corniche.

15. LANGUAGE

ABOUT ARABIC

To most westerners Arabic appears a daunting language. This is
mainly because it is written in a different script, which to the
unaccustomed eye may appear more like scribble than identifiable
letters, and also because it is written from right to left. While it
is true that to master Arabic can take years, the colloquial, or
conversational, language is surprisingly simple to learn.
Transliteration into the Latin alphabet helps speed the process!

three versions

It can be said that there are three forms of the Arabic
language: the Arabic of the Koran, Modern Standard Arabic,
often called MSA, and colloquial Arabic.

The first, Koranic or literary Arabic, is the most difficult.
Fortunately this is no longer in everyday use. Modern Standard
Arabic is the language that unites Arabs from the Gulf to the
Atlantic. With MSA a newspaper published in Oman can be
readily understood in Morocco. A news broadcast from Syria will
be understood in Algiers.

Colloquial Arabic, on the other hand, differs from region to
region. It is difficult for example, for Arabs from the Maghreb to
comprehend Yemenis or Saudis or for Egyptians to understand
Kuwaitis.

diverse dialects

Spoken Arabic has no written form, and any written material
will revert to MSA. The version spoken in Syria is similar to that
spoken in Jordan, but different to that of Cairo. However it is
close enough so that if you have any knowledge of the Egyptian,
you will be understood in Syria.

ahlan wa-sahlan!

Besides being polite to be able to speak a few words of your host's language, Syrians will be very pleased if you know the familiar greetings in their language. Arabic is full of pleasantries and they are used in profusion, even to people you meet casually.

There are many ways to greet somebody, but whatever the greeting it is always accompanied by handshaking, or in the case of friends hugging and kissing. Each person kisses the other on each cheek. Never ask a question of anyone without first greeting them. Even if you ask in English, try to express the greeting in Arabic.

Getting by in Arabic

A good idea is to copy on a small piece of card some of the most common words you may need, keeping this in your shirt pocket. It will always be handy for quick reference. A useful addition to this is a list of the numbers used in Arabic for figuring out shop prices, bus numbers etc. (I hesitate to call them Arabic numerals because the ones we use are titled just that — though most likely they are derived from elsewhere and were simply introduced to the west by Arab scholars.)

pronunciation

A word on pronunciation. Some sounds may be difficult to produce as we do not have them in English. In the vocabulary they are given as follows.

gh this is like the French "r".

kh similar to ch in Scottish "loch"

'   a glottal stop similar to how butter may be pronounced by those who drop the t's, bu'er, but farther back in the throat.

H this is a very aspirated 'h'. When making it you should feel a slight grating in your throat.

h is almost identical to the English and always sounded with the normal "h" exhaling breath sound.

VOCABULARY

Greetings

An initial greeting and one that is frequently used is *salaam alaikum* meaning "peace be to you" the reply is made by reversing the order of words, *alaikum salaam* "to you [also] be peace".

Other common greetings are:

hello!	*marhaba* or *ahlan wa sahlan* or just *ahlan*
hello as reply	*marhabtein* or *ahlan beek* (*beeki* f)
how are you?	*kayf haalak* (*kayf haalik* f)
fine	*kwayyis* (*kwayyisa* f). (A useful word which covers fine, nice or even beautiful, eg *"Suriya kwayyisa"* — "Syria is fine/nice/beautiful?")
thanks be to God	*ilHamdu lillaah* is often the reply to "how are you?"
God willing	*inshallah*, an answer to everything!
goodbye	*ma'a salaama*
good morning	*sabah ilkheer*
good morning (reply)	*sabah innur* (meaning "morning of light")
good evening	*masa ilkheer*

Common words and phrases

yes	*na'am* or *aiwa*
no	*la*
thank you	*shukran*
for nothing *or* you are welcome	*afwan*
please (request)	*min fadlak* (*fadlik* f)
I'm sorry	*ana 'assif* (*'aaifa* f)
what is your name?	*shu ismak* (*ismik* f)
my name is...	*ismi...*
where are you from?	*min wain inta?* (*inti* f)
I am from...	*ana min...*
do you speak English?	*bititkalim* (*bititkalimi* f) *ingliisi?*
I speak...	*ana bititkalim*
how much (does it cost?)	*bikaam* or *adaish*
expensive	*ghaali*
cheap	*rakhees*
very	*'awi*
something	*Haaga*
something cheaper	*Haaga 'arkhas*
may I?, is it possible?	*mumkin*
impossible, you can't	*mish mumkin*

how many?	*kam?*
how many kms?	*kam kilometer?*
is there (any)?	*fi...?*
there is not (any)	*ma fish...*
open	*maftuuh*
closed	*musakkar*
what is this?	*shu hadha?*
big	*kabeer*
small	*sagheer*

Getting around

aeroplane	*al-tayara*
airport	*al-mataar*
bank	*bank*
bus station	*mahattat al-bas*
bus	*bas*
car	*sayyara*
church	*kaneesa*
gate	*bab*
hospital	*mustashfa*
left (direction)	*shimaal*
mosque	*jami*
petrol (gas)	*benzeen*
pharmacy	*saydaliyya*
police	*shurta*
post office	*maktab bareed*
railway station	*mahattat al-qitaar*
right	*yameen*
ruins (historical)	*khirbet*
site (historical)	*ataar*
square	*midaan* (*midaan shouhada* - Martyrs Square)
straight on	*duughri*
street (add name)	*shari'a* (where is Kouwatli St. *wain shari'a Kouwatli?*)
tourist office	*maktab al-siyaha*
train	*qitaar*

At the hotel

breakfast	*fitar*
clean	*nardif*
dirty	*wishikh*
full	*malyaan*

hot water	*mayya sukhna*
hotel	*otel, funduq*
night	*leela*
room	*ghurfa*
shower	*doosh*
soap	*sabun*
the bill	*al-hissab*
towel	*futa, manshafa*

Food and drink

apple	*tuffaaH*
apricots	*mishmish*
bananas	*mooz*
bread	*khubz, aish*
butter	*zibda*
carrot	*gazar*
cheese	*gibneh*
coffee	*'ahwa*
egg	*beid*
fish	*samak*
fruit	*fawakeh*
juice	*'asir*
meat	*lahma*
milk	*halab*
mineral water	*mayya ma'daniyeh*
orange juice	*'asir burtu'aan*
orange	*burtu'aan*
restaurant	*mat'am*
tea	*shay*
vegetables	*khudra*
water	*mayya*
yogurt	*laban*

Time

day	*yom*
hour	*sa'a*
today	*al-yom*
tomorrow	*bukra*
week	*usbu'a*
year	*sana*
What time is it?	*assa'a kam?*
It is 3 o'clock	*assa'a talata*

In Arabic the days from Sunday through Thursday are simply called "the first" through to "the fifth". Saturday is called the sabbath even though Friday is the Muslim day of rest:

Sunday, *ilhadd;* Monday, *iltneen;* Tuesday, *ittalaat;*
Wednesday, *ilarba';* Thursday, *ilkhamees;* Friday, *ilgum'a;*
Saturday, *isabat.*

Numerals

The number always comes after the noun except in the case of "one" e.g. one night, *wahad leela;* three nights, *leela talata.*

Numbers 1-10: *wahad, itneen, talata, arba'a, khamsa, sitta, saba'a, tamanya, tisa'a, ashara.*

Numbers 11-20: *hidashar, itnaashar, talattaashar, arba'taashar, khamastaashar, sitaashar, sab'ataashar, tamantaashar, tisa'taashar, ishreen.*

half *nuss;* quarter *ruba;* threequarters *talata ruba.*

Gesticulations are an important part of person to person communication. Two of the most common:

"No" is quite often indicated by the slight throwing back of the head and lifting of the eyebrows. Such a "no" can be taken as final!

"What do you want?" is queried by an outstretched hand and a flick of the wrist. Taxi drivers often do this in the expectation that you may want to hire them, as do shopkeepers standing by their shop fronts if they think you are out shopping.

The Arabic numerals are as follows:

١ = 1	٦ = 6
٢ = 2	٧ = 7
٣ = 3	٨ = 8
٤ = 4	٩ = 9
٥ = 5	١٠ = 10

GLOSSARY

The glossary explains the following—

♦ Architectural terms used.
♦ The various nations, dynasties, and groups of people referred to.
♦ Non-English words normally rendered in the original.

Abbreviations: **L** Latin; **Fr** Medieval French; **Gr** Greek
I Italian; **A** Arabic; **R** Russian

Abbasids (A)	Caliphate dynasty (750-968) centred on Baghdad which succeeded the Omayyads.
Achaemenian Persians	Ancient Persian dynasty which lasted from 559-330 BC. Their empire stretched at one time as far west as Macedonia and Libya. Rulers included Cyrus II and Xerxes. It came to an end in 330 BC when Darius III was defeated by Alexander at Issus.
acropolis (Gr)	Elevated part of a Greek city.
agora (Gr)	Market and public meeting place.
aisle	The part of a basilica that lies either side of the nave.
Alawis (A)	Islamic sect (see box on page 29).
apse (L)	Curved and vaulted end of the nave in a church.
aqueduct (L)	Elevated bridge-like structure for carrying water.
Assassins (A)	An Ismaili sect (itself a sect of Shi'ites) which originated in Persia. They were a ruthless people who used hashish to bolster their boldness. (Assassins=Hashasheen)
Ayyubids (A)	The dynasty (1176-1260) founded by Salah al-Din or his father.

bab (A)	Gate
Bacchus (legend of)	Bacchus, god of wine in Roman and Greek mythology. Also called Dionysos.
basalt (L)	Hard, black volcanic rock.
basilica (L,Gr)	Building, usually a church with a central nave and an aisle each side.
bastion (Fr)	Strongpoint usually, but not necessarily, in a castle.
Ba'ath (Political) Party	Ba'ath, Arabic for resurrection, is a socialist, nationalist political party with opposing wings in power in Syria and Iraq
Bedouin (A)	Desert-dwelling Arab. In the past they were all nomadic. Now many are settled.
Byzantine (L)	That part of the Roman Empire which was ruled from Byzantium (Constantinople).
caliph (A)	Head of Islam after Muhammad. From the Arabic word *Khalifa,* meaning successor. Caliphs eventually became dynastic with no relationship to religious knowledge, and the first four were not accepted by all Muslims.
capitals (on columns)	The head of a column often decorated.
cardo maximus (L)	Main street of Roman city, usually running from north to south.
cella (L)	Sacred chamber of a temple.
citadel (It)	Fortified part of a city, often elevated.
colonnade (L)	Area flanked by columns and roofed.
Corinthian (capital) (Gr)	Column capital decorated with ananthus leaves.
cuneiform (L)	wedge shaped letters.
cupola (L)	Dome.
decumanus (L)	Major east/west street in a Roman city.
diwan (T)	Arched relaxing/reception area at one end of the courtyard in an Ottoman house.
donjon (Fr)	The keep or fortified part of a castle.

Eastern Orthodox	That part of the Byzantine rite which has as its head the Byzantine Patriach of Antioch. Often called Greek Orthodox, they use Arabic as their prayer language.
exedra (L)	Semi-circular area with seats, usually by a nymphaeum.
Fatimids (A)	A Shi'ite dynasty (970-1055) of caliphs centered on Cairo.
Franks	Name often used for the Crusaders.
frieze (Fr)	Horizontal band of decoration around a building, door or gate.
glacis (Fr)	Sloping surface in front of a castle wall or tower (or even city wall) that makes it difficult to scale.
Greek Orthodox	General term for followers of the Byzantine rite of Christianity, but correctly only applies to the Orthodox Church of Greece.
hammam (T)	Turkish or Arab bath.
haremlek (T)	Family area in Ottoman house
Hospitallers, Knights of St. John	Order of (Christian) Knights who once had resposibility for taking care of pilgrims in Jerusalem. In Crusader times they became a military order.
iwan (T)	See **diwan**.
jabal	Mountain or mountain range
khan (T,A)	Inn where travellers and merchants could stay and trade in a city. Also called caravansersai but the latter term is more correctly used for inns outside cities.
Kufic (A)	Stylish Arabic script used in the early Muslim era.
lintel (Fr)	Horizontal beam (of stone) above a door.
madrasa (A)	Islamic theological school.
Mamelukes	Slave soldiers of Turkic origin who took power in 1250 in Cairo and controlled most of the region from 1260 to 1516.

mihrab (A)	Niche in wall of a mosque's prayer hall to orient worshippers towards Mecca.
minbar (A)	Pulpit in a mosque.
Mongols	Central Asian warrior people.
muhaafaza (A)	Governorate or province.
Muslim Brotherhood	A Sunni Muslim fundamentalist group.
Nabateans	People from Arabia who established themselves in what is today Jordan. As they lived on the caravan routes from the east and the Red Sea they were prosperous. With the decline of the Seleucids they took control of much of southern Syria, including Bosra and Damascus. Eventually incorporated into Roman Empire. Their capital was the rock city of Petra (in southern Jordan).
narthex (Gr)	Entrance hall in an (early) church.
Nestorian	Christian who follows the teachings of Nestorius. Once Patriarch of Constantinople, after the Council of Chaldecon was branded as a heretic because of his doctrine on the nature of Christ. The Church is sometimes called the Church of the East and is based mainly in Iran and Iraq.
noria (A)	Wooden water-wheel used to lift water from a river.
nymphaeum (L)	Public water fountain, dedicated to nymphs.
Omayyads (A)	Caliphate dynasty (661-750) founded by Mu'awiya, centered on Damascus.
Ottomans	Turkish tribe centered on Anatolia. Took Constaninople in 1453 and in early 16th C all the Middle East and parts of Europe. The Ottoman Empire lasted until 1918.
pasha (T)	Title given to an Ottoman governor.
portcullis (Fr,L)	Grille that can be lowered across a castle gateway to prevent entry.
portico (L,It)	Porch, or area confined within columns.
qala'a (qala'at) (A)	Fort or Castle

redoubt (Fr)	Heavily fortified refuge in a castle.
Sasanian Persians	Persian dynasty from 224-650 AD founded by Ardashir 1. They constantly harassed the power of Rome and Byzantium. Destroyed by the Arabs in 650.
Sea People or People of the Sea.	People from Aegean islands and coasts who invaded the Levant with disastrous results c1200BC. Little is known about them.
Shi'ite (A)	Muslims who supported the right of Ali, Muhammad's son-in-law, to succeed him. From the word *shia* which means faction, i.e. faction of Ali.
souk (A)	Market street or area.
steppe (R)	Vast treeless plain with sparse vegetation.
Stylite (Gr)	Type of Christian hermit monk who lives atop a pillar. (From Greek *stylos*)
Sunni (A)	Orthodox Muslim, i.e. not a Shi'ite.
Syrian Orthodox	The Syrian Church which separated from the Byzantine rite after the Council of Chalcedon, re-organised by Jacob Baradeus.
talus (L)	see **glacis**
tekke (T)	Dervish monastery.
tell (Aramaic)	Hill, usually an artificial one, made up of layers of succeeding civilisations.
Templars, Knights	Crusader military order.
tetrapylon (Gr)	Pattern of columns marking a major street junction in a Roman/Greek city.
trifora (L)	Gallery on top of an arch.
turba (T)	Tomb.
Turkomans, Turkomen	Name applied to various Turkic tribes.
via sacra (L)	Sacred way for pilgrims to a shrine.
vomitorium (L)	Exit and entranceway to a Roman theatre.
wadi (A)	Seasonable water course.

BIBLIOGRAPHY

The most comprehensive history of Syria is *History of Syria, including Lebanon and Palestine* by Philip K. Hitti. London 1951.

For a good history of the Arabs read *A History of the Arab Peoples* by Albert Hourani, London 1991.

Although published in 1946, Robin Fedden's *Syria - An Historical Appreciation* seems to have material he collected earlier. It makes for interesting reading.

For a sixties look at Damascus coupled with historical material, fact and fable, *Mirror on Damascus* by Colin Thurbron. London 1967.

Informative accounts of the making of modern Syria are *The Struggle for Syria* and *Assad: The Struggle for the Middle East* both by Patrick Seale.

For German speakers, Johannes Odenthal's *Syrie*, Koln 1982, has a wealth of information.

If you are interested in Ugarit get *Ugarit: Ras Shamra* by Adrian Curtis. Cambridge 1985.

Nineteenth century exploration is interestingly chronicled by Johannes L. Burckhardt in *Travels in Syria and the Holy Land*. Originally published in 1822, it was recently republished by Darf Publishers.

The Travels of Ibn Jubayr pp 260-312 gives a fascinating account of Aleppo and Damascus (and some places in between) in the late 12th C. Translated by R.J.C. Broadhurst it was published by Jonathan Cape in 1951

If the Assassins interest you then *The Assassins - A Radical Sect in Islam* by Bernard Lewis will satisfy your curiosity. London 1985.

The Druze are written about in Philip Hitti's book *The origins of the Druze People and Religion* 1928, and also in *The Druze* by R. Betts 1988.

Crusader history in Syria is covered by *The Crusaders in Syria and the Holy Land* by R.C. Smail, London 1973. The same author also wrote *Crusading Warfare (1097-1193)*, Cambridge 1956.

For those who read French and want to know more about Palmyra *Palmrye - Metropole du desert* by Gerard Degeorge, Paris 1987 or *Palmyre - guide archeologique* by Jean Starcky, Paris 1952 might suit.

Other books which may be of interest are:

The Land of The Bible - A Historical Geography by Yohanan Aharoni. London 1974.

Dar ul Islam by Mark Sykes. First published in 1904 it was republished in 1988 by Darf Publishing.

An introduction to Shi'ite Islam by M. Momen 1985.

INDEX

Abbreviations used: **Ch** church or chapel **Fr** French

Cath cathedral **Gr** Greek

A Arabic **OT** Old Testament

L Latin **NT** New Testament

Names in **bold type** refer to places and sites visited in the full tour

A

Abbasids 10, 49, 104, 113

Abraham 7, 46, 112, 48

Abu Kemal 95

Acre 11

    pasha of 12, 51

Adil Saif al-Din 55

Afrin valley and river 131, 132

Ahmad Jazzar, Pasha 12

Ain Dara, Temple of 132

Ain Dywar 108

Ain Jalud, battle of 114

Akkadians 7, 100, 135, 87

Al-Ashraf Khalil, Sultan 120

Al-Bara 136

    Kapropera (Gr) 136

Al-Jawlan (see Golan Heights)

Al-Mahdi, Caliph 179

Al-Mansour, Caliph 104

Al-Mansurah 104

Al-Mayadin 94

Al-Qanawat 189

    Canatha (L, Gr) 190

    Decapolis city 190

    Kenath (OT ref) 190

    Seraya (palace) 190

    Temple to Helios 190

    Temple to Zeus 191

Al-Riha 136

Al-Tibne 102

Al-Zaher Ghazi 114

Alawis 11, 14, 16, 19, 25, 29

ALEPPO 11, 19, 27, 43, 51,
        81, 101, **110-129**

    Aleppo Museum 129

Bab al-Maqam 122

Bab Antakya 117

Bab Qinnesrin 119

Baron Hotel 128

Beit Ajiqbash 125

Beit al-Dalal 125

Beit Balit 125

Beit Basil 125

Beit Ghazale 125

Beit Wakil 125

called Halab 112

Cath. of St Helena 121

Citadel 120

Great (Omayyad) Mosque
    121

Hammam al-Nahasin 119

Hammam al-Nasri 123

Jdeide Quarter 124

Khan al-Gumruk (Customs
    Khan) 118

Khan al-Nahasin 118

Khan al-Sabon 122, 126

Khan al-Saffihye 119

Khan al-Wazir 122

Mosque of al-Adeliye 119

Mosq.of al-Bahramiye 117

Mosque of Abraham 121

Mosque of al-Tuteh 117

Madrasa Faradis 123

Madrasa Moqaddamiye 117

Madrasa Sultaniye 123

Madrasa Zahirye 123

Maristan Arghun Kamili 119

Museum of Traditions 125

named Beroia 112

Old City 115

B

Q

R

S